*Yoshitsune and the Thousand Cherry Trees*
A MASTERPIECE OF THE
EIGHTEENTH-CENTURY
JAPANESE PUPPET THEATER

TRANSLATIONS FROM THE ASIAN CLASSICS

New York  COLUMBIA UNIVERSITY PRESS

A MASTERPIECE

# *Yoshitsune and the Thousand Cherry Trees*

OF THE

EIGHTEENTH-

CENTURY

JAPANESE

PUPPET

THEATER

*Translated,*

*annotated,*

*and with an*

*introduction by*

STANLEIGH H. JONES, JR.

Copyright © 1993 Columbia University Press
Paperback edition, 2016
All rights reserved

Library of Congress Cataloging-in-Publication Data

Takeda, Izumo, 1691–1756.
[Yoshitsune senbonzakura. English]
Yoshitsune and the thousand cherry trees : a masterpiece of
the eighteenth-century Japanese puppet theater / translated,
annotated, and with an introduction by Stanleigh H. Jones.
p. cm.
"Translations from the Asian classics"—half t.p.
Includes bibliographical references
ISBN 978-0-231-08052-1 (cloth : alk. paper)—
ISBN 978-0-231-08053-8 (pbk. : alk. paper)—
ISBN 978-0-231-51502-3 (ebook)
I. Jones, Stanleigh H. II. Title.
PL794.6.Y3E5   1993
895.6'232—dc20                                    92-46481
                                                      CIP

Casebound editions of
Columbia University Press books
are printed on permanent and
durable acid-free paper.

Cover Image: Woodcut by Sugie Midori

TRANSLATIONS FROM THE ASIAN CLASSICS

Editorial Board

Wm. Theodore de Bary, Chair

Paul Anderer

Donald Keene

George A. Saliba

Haruo Shirane

Burton Watson

Wei Shang

DEDICATED WITH MUCH AFFECTION
TO MY WIFE
JOSETTE

FRONTISPIECE
AND TITLE PAGE
ILLUSTRATIONS

The frontispiece is a papercut created by Sugie Midori of Osaka, a leading Japanese artist in the medium. The subject is the choreographed *michiyuki* travel scene of act 4, scene 1, "The Journey with the Drum." Tadanobu is at the top, Lady Shizuka is at the bottom playing the drum, the magical fox between them, all against the background of a giant cherry tree.

On the title page, the Japanese script reads *Daimotsu funayagura, Yoshino hanayagura: Yoshitsune senbon zakura (The Shipboard Watchtowers of Daimotsu Bay, The Cherry Tree Towers of Yoshino: Yoshitsune and the Thousand Cherry Trees)*—the full title of the play along with its subtitle. The calligraphy is in the form known as the *Kantei-ryū*, or Kantei style, used particularly in the Bunraku and Kabuki theaters in advertising posters, playbills, and texts. It was kindly written for me by Mr. Ikoma Takami of the National Bunraku Theater in Osaka.

The two crests are those of the Takemoto Theater (three clusters of three bamboo leaves each within a hexagon of bamboo stalks) and the Toyotake Theater (the phonetic character *to* and *yo* joined inside a circlet of bamboo stalks). The two crests are used by the Bunraku puppet theater today.

CONTENTS

| | |
|---|---|
| *Acknowledgments* | *xiii* |
| *Introduction* | *1* |
| *Yoshitsune and the Thousand Cherry Trees* | *35* |
| *Dramatis Personae* | *37* |
| *Prologue* | *41* |

*Act One*

SCENE 1.
THE IMPERIAL PALACE 43

SCENE 2.
THE HERMITAGE AT
NORTH SAGA VILLAGE 53

SCENE 3.
THE HORIKAWA MANSION 64

SCENE 4.
KAWAGOE TARŌ COMES AS ENVOY 72

## Act Two

SCENE 1.
BEFORE THE FUSHIMI INARI SHRINE    89

SCENE 2.
THE TOKAIYA    102

## Act Three

SCENE 1.
THE PASANIA TREE    135

SCENE 2.
THE DEATH OF KOKINGO    150

SCENE 3.
THE SUSHI SHOP    159

## Act Four

SCENE 1.
MICHIYUKI: THE JOURNEY
WITH THE DRUM    197

SCENE 2.
THE ZAŌ HALL    209

SCENE 3.
THE CONFERENCE AT
THE ZAŌ HALL    212

SCENE 4.
THE MANSION OF
KAWATSURA HŌGEN    222

SCENE 5.
THE FOX    234

## Act Five

SCENE 1.
IN THE MOUNTAINS OF YOSHINO    263

*Bibliography*    273

ACKNOWLEDGMENTS

For encouragement, assistance, and warm hospitality in ways too varied to enumerate while I was in Japan, I would like to thank the following persons: Ikoma Takami, Gotō Shizuo, Yoshida Minosuke, and Kiritake Monju of the Bunraku Kyōkai in Osaka; Professors Torigoe Bunzō, Uchiyama Mikiko, and Fukui Shigemasa of Waseda University in Tokyo; Professor Yoshinaga Takao of Hanazono Gakuen in Osaka; and Nakamura Tetsurō in Tokyo. My thanks to Fujito Yoshiko and Miyata Shigeyuki for much appreciated help with difficult passages in the translation. Jay and Sumi Gluck were exceptionally tolerant hosts to my comings and goings while I stayed with them in Ashiya; and Sugie Midori of Osaka has very graciously given me permission to use her lovely papercut of a scene from the play. I am also indebted to the Tsubouchi Memorial Theatre Museum of Waseda University in Tokyo for permission to use from its collection several photographs of a production of the play. These appear on pp. 133, 182, 204, and 238. All others were taken by the author. Donald Keene of Columbia University has been a mentor and inspiration to many students of Japanese literature and theater; however far removed from him in time and place, I count myself fortunate to be among them. I would also like to thank Leonard Pronko of Pomona College, who kindly read the translation and offered useful commentary.

There is one other person who deserves my gratitude, whom I wish I could name. As is customary among publishers, a manuscript is sent out to readers for evaluation. One of those who read this manuscript was exceptionally conscientious and helpful in catching errors and suggesting improvements, virtually all of which have been incorporated in the present work. Though I appreciate the rule of anonymity in these matters, I wish I could express my thanks more personally than is possible here.

I am especially indebted to the Translation Program of the Division of Research Programs of the National Endowment for the Humanities, an independent federal agency, for a grant that enabled me to go to Japan for the purpose of research on the puppet theater in 1980–81. Very warm thanks also go to Ms. Susan A. Mango of the Translation Program; her encouragement and assistance in matters pertaining to that grant were invaluable. I am also grateful to the Department of Modern Languages of Pomona College for a summer travel grant in 1987 to work on the play in Japan. All of the foregoing have been generous in their support, but none bear responsibility for any sins of commission or omission that might still be found here; those creatures are camped on my doorstep.

That my wife Josette's name comes at the end of this list in no way diminishes my thanks to her for much support during the process of this work, and it is to her that this volume is very affectionately dedicated.

*Yoshitsune and the Thousand Cherry Trees*
A MASTERPIECE OF THE
EIGHTEENTH-CENTURY
JAPANESE PUPPET THEATER

INTRODUCTION

At the end of World War II, much of Tokyo was wreckage and rubble, including most of its theaters: near the Ginza, both the famous Kabuki-za and the Shinbashi Enbujō stood as shells gutted by fire. One theater that survived the bombings was the Shōchiku Company's Tokyo Gekijō, known as the Tōgeki, in the Tsukiji district of the city. The Occupation of Japan was scarcely three months old when, at the Tōgeki, traditional Japanese theater—in this case kabuki—encountered its first crisis under the new order.

In November 1945 the combined kabuki troupes of Matsumoto Kōshirō VII and Nakamura Kichiemon I staged the first postwar production of kabuki at the Tōgeki, an event that led to both specific and then broad censorship of Japan's traditional popular theater. The late

Kawatake Shigetoshi has left us an interesting account of the circumstances.[1] On the morning program the selections included the *michiyuki*, a dance travel scene ("The Journey With the Drum" in the present translation), of the play *Yoshitsune and the Thousand Cherry Trees*; and on the evening bill appeared, "The Village School" ("Terakoya"), the most celebrated scene from the play *Sugawara and the Secrets of Calligraphy*.[2] Opening day was November 4.

According to Kawatake, a Japanese citizen wrote to Occupation headquarters protesting that at a time when emphasis was on the democratization of Japan it was outrageous for a theater to be staging "Terakoya," from one of the most famous plays to extol the extremes of feudal loyalty (in the play a father sacrifices his own son in order to save the son of his former master). Inspired by this letter, Occupation censors arrived at the Tōgeki on November 14 to view the production. An order came the next day advising the theater management "to exercise self restraint" and drop "Terakoya" from the program. It was off the bill within a few days.

In subsequent meetings between the Shōchiku management and Occupation authorities, a list of banned works was drawn up, the list growing longer as time moved on. In the case of *Yoshitsune and the Thousand Cherry Trees*, nearly the entire play was proscribed as being undemocratic and promoting ideas of feudalistic loyalty and sacrifice. Only the above noted *michiyuki* dance scene and the one that usually follows, "The Mansion of Kawatsura Hōgen," escaped censorship. Fortunately for kabuki and the theater of puppets known as Bunraku, the ban was comparatively short lived. Within a couple of years of the Terakoya Incident plays on the Occupation's black list were back on the stage, and before the end of the Occupation in 1952 even "Terakoya" was being performed.[3]

1. The following is drawn from Kawatake Shigetoshi, *Nihon engeki zenshi*, 960–65.
2. See my translation, *Sugawara and the Secrets of Calligraphy*, 221–54.
3. Edward G. Seidensticker, *Tokyo Rising: The City Since the Great Earthquake*, 174.

When *Yoshitsune and the Thousand Cherry Trees* underwent its American proscription in 1945, it was within two years and a month of being two centuries old, having had its premiere December 17, 1747[4] at the playhouse in Osaka known as the Takemoto-za, the Takemoto Theater.[5]

*Yoshitsune and the Thousand Cherry Trees* (*Yoshitsune senbon zakura*) is one of three plays generally regarded as representing the pinnacle of the puppet theater's golden age. The previous year, 1746, had seen the premiere of *Sugawara and the Secrets of Calligraphy* (*Sugawara denju tenarai kagami*); in the following year, 1748, what was to become the most popular puppet play of all time, *Kanadehon Chūshingura* (*The Treasury of Royal Retainers*), came to the boards.[6] All three dramatic masterworks were written by the playwriting team of Takeda Izumo, Miyoshi Shōraku, and Namiki Senryū. These plays remain so popular that they are among the very few performed today more or less in their entirety, and hardly a year goes by that some part of each does not grace the puppet or kabuki stage.

*Yoshitsune and the Thousand Cherry Trees* is a play of the type known as *jidaimono*, or "period piece," set in the near or remote past and peopled with civil or military aristocrats pursuing their dramatic fates in fine mansions and in or about the palace of the emperor. The earliest puppet plays were essentially *jidaimono*. In the early eighteenth century another type of play came into being, the *sewamono*, or "domestic drama," in which the characters are commoners in their own lowly settings, beset with the anguish of love and jealousy and the economic problems brought on by a

4. By the lunar calendar in use at the time of the play's premiere, this was the equivalent of the sixteenth day of the Eleventh Month, 1747. Unless otherwise indicated, all dates noted hereafter are based on the lunar calendar; by Western reckoning they would generally fall approximately a month later.

5. Interestingly, the first visit of the Shōwa Emperor (the formal posthumous name of Emperor Hirohito) to a Bunraku performance in Osaka occurred in June 1947, a few months before the two hundredth anniversary of the premiere of *Yoshitsune and the Thousand Cherry Trees*. The *michiyuki* from the play was part of that June 1947 bill. Yoshida Minosuke, *Zukin kabutte gojūnen*, 70–72.

6. See Donald Keene's translation, *Chūshingura: The Treasury of Loyal Retainers*. The play is usually known by the shorter title of *Chūshingura*.

developing monetary economy, all elements easily appreciated by their plebeian audiences. From the mid-1720s it becomes increasingly common to find a *sewamono* scene or two incorporated into the long *jidaimono*, giving a view of life that highlights or contrasts with the grand settings and noble personages of the rest of the play. *Yoshitsune and the Thousand Cherry Trees* illustrates this amalgam: the first part of "The Tokaiya" scene in act 2 and all of "The Sushi Shop" in act 3 are *sewamono* slices of down-to-earth plebeian life of the eighteenth century into which more lofty characters find their way in the course of the drama's story.

The subtitle of the play—"The Shipboard Battletowers of Daimotsu Bay, The Cherry Tree Watchtowers of Yoshino"—refers to the sea battle that takes place in act 2 ("The Tokaiya") and to the last scene of act 4 ("The Fox"), set in the mountains of Yoshino, an area south of Kyoto famous for its cherry blossoms in the spring.

Several important historical characters figure in the plot of *Yoshitsune and the Thousand Cherry Trees*. The drama takes place immediately following the wars of 1180–1185 between the rival military clans of the Minamoto and Taira, also known by their respective Sino-Japanese names of Genji and Heike. Central to the play's story is Minamoto no Yoshitsune (1159–1189), younger brother of Minamoto no Yoritomo (1147–1199), the founder of Japan's first military government in Kamakura (near modern Tokyo). These years of strife ended in the utter defeat of the Heike clan, due in no small measure to Yoshitsune's bold and imaginative military tactics in the field against the Heike. He is known, historically and in the play translated here, by another name: Genkurō. *Gen* is the Sino-Japanese reading of the Chinese character read Minamoto in Japanese; *kurō* indicates that Yoshitsune was his father's ninth son (Yoritomo was the third).

Historically, Yoshitsune's principal fame lay in his brilliance during the Genji-Heike wars. His early life is largely a blank; his military career is documented, notably in the thirteenth-century martial chronicle, *The Tale of the Heike* (*Heike monogatari*). Not long after the Genji victory over the Heike, there was a falling-out between Yoshitsune and Yoritomo, and Yoritomo sent out numerous search parties to kill or capture his younger brother. Yoshitsune fled from Kyoto and embarked on an evasive journey (known to us today more through legend than fact). He is picked up by history again in 1187 in the far north at the town of Hiraizumi (in modern Iwate Prefecture), where he sought refuge with Fujiwara no Hidehira, a powerful regional warrior who had befriended him earlier. Less than a year after Yoshitsune's arrival there, however, Hidehira died; his sons possessed less loyalty to Yoshitsune and less backbone than their father to stand up to Yoritomo. Under threat of assault by Yoritomo, Hidehira's heir attacked Yoshitsune in 1189. Rather than be taken by his attackers, Yoshitsune died by his own hand. Thus ended what had been for a brief five or six years a remarkable military career.[7]

It may seem curious to Western readers that Yoshitsune, known for his aggressive behavior on the battlefield, is so passive a figure in *Yoshitsune and the Thousand Cherry Trees*. He is usually depicted on stage as an almost effetely noble personage, his role regularly taken by a child actor in the Nō theater. Partly, this is theatrical convention. But, as Helen McCullough has pointed out,[8] it is also strongly rooted in the traditional Japanese esteem for the gentility—the literary and scholarly skills, the sense of etiquette and decorum—associated with the civilized ways of the aristocratic class, a class perhaps most perfectly portrayed in the great eleventh-century novel *The Tale of Genji*. Indeed, one of the several reasons that Japanese still have such sympathy for the defeated Heike is that so many of them, particularly those described in *The Tale of the Heike*, had very successfully emulated their social arbiters, the members of the noble Fujiwara clan.

Satō Tadanobu (1161–1186) is prominent in the Yoshitsune saga as a paragon of loyalty to his master. With his older brother Tsuginobu, he was a retainer to Yoshitsune's benefactor Fujiwara

---

7. For a more detailed account of Yoshitsune, see Helen Craig McCullough, tr., *Yoshitsune: A Fifteenth-Century Chronicle*, 3–30.

8. Ibid., 53–54, 65–66.

no Hidehira. In 1180, as Yoshitsune left northern Japan to join Yoritomo in the uprising against the Heike, Hidehira dispatched the Satō brothers into his service.[9] Tsuginobu was killed in the battle at Yashima in 1185 shielding his master from an enemy arrow. Tadanobu accompanied Yoshitsune in his flight from Yoritomo's men, eventually committing suicide after safeguarding his lord's escape. He figures in such plays of the aristocratic Nō theater as *Tadanobu* and *Yoshino Shizuka*.

Three generals of the Heike clan are also central to the plot of *Yoshitsune and the Thousand Cherry Trees:* Taira no Tomomori (1151–1185), Taira no Koremori (1157–1184), and Taira no Noritsune (1160–1185). Tomomori is often referred to by his title of New Middle Councilor; Noritsune, as Lord of Noto. All three fought in various battles in the Genji-Heike wars. Noritsune's arrow slew Satō Tsuginobu—and both he and Tomomori died dramatically in the Third Month of 1185 at the great battle of Dannoura, which signaled the end of the Heike clan. (Koremori drowned himself about a year before Dannoura.) Though the title of the play would suggest that Yoshitsune is the most important character, the more compelling roles belong to the three fugitive Heike generals.

Many of the heroes of Japan's martial past were well known to all levels of Japanese society, particularly the more commanding figures of the Heike and Genji clans whose epic conflict left an indelible mark on much of later Japanese culture. Although stories of the dashing warriors from the old military narratives and romances were not prominent in the plebeian schools of the day—the temple schools (*terakoya*), where the fare tended more toward dry Confucian works used both to inculcate basic literacy and to encourage a set of proper moral values—they were part of a widely known cultural legacy, and one would certainly find them included in printed popularizations of the classics and as subjects of the well attended dramatic lectures known as *kōshaku* that were ubiquitous in the larger urban centers.[10] The humorous

---

9. Ibid., 14.
10. See R. P. Dore, *Education in Tokugawa Japan*, 131–32, 271–90; and Ogi Shinzō et al., eds., *Edo Tōkyō gaku jiten*, 620.

burlesques of classical literature that formed a part of the popular literature of the day indicate that the literary monuments of past centuries were well known among the eighteenth-century Japanese populace.[11]

*Chūshingura* was inspired by the famous vendetta of the forty-odd loyal samurai conducted on a winter's night in early 1703 on behalf of their master, who they believed had been unjustly condemned to ritual suicide roughly two years earlier. A playwright hardly needed much encouragement to bring this historical event to the stage. It was in itself the stuff of high drama. And many writers had indeed tried their hands, for plays on the theme appeared almost annually following the historical event up to the 1748 premiere of *Chūshingura*.[12] Several stories describe what prompted the authors of *Sugawara and the Secrets of Calligraphy* to write that play,[13] but, to the best of my knowledge, there are no such collateral tales to embellish the background of the creation of *Yoshitsune and the Thousand Cherry Trees*.

It is said that the popularity of *Chūshingura* is such that it generally has guaranteed a good house to any theater experiencing a lull at the box office. Judged by the plethora of literature centering on the life and legend of Yoshitsune, this figure of romance possessed a similar perennial appeal, and this doubtless served as some inspiration for the writing of the play. Whatever the process, once the decision had been taken to use Yoshitsune as the centerpiece of a play, it remained for the playwrights to find ways of presenting their drama in a manner that would make it unique. Their decision was to make *Yoshitsune and the Thousand Cherry Trees* a play of deception and surprise revelations.

Virtually anyone who attends a performance today knows,

---

11. Popular literary fare of the seventeenth and early eighteenth centuries included parodies of such classics as the tenth-century *Tales of Ise (Ise monogatari)*, the eleventh-century *Tale of Genji (Genji monogatari)*, and the thirteenth-century *The Tale of the Heike*. See Howard Hibbett, *The Floating World in Japanese Fiction*, 42–43, 90–94. Implicit in such parodies, of course, is the fact that the works themselves were well known to a great many readers in eighteenth-century Japan.
12. See Keene, *Chūshingura*, 6–7.
13. Jones, *Sugawara and the Secrets of Calligraphy*, 12–13.

or is informed in the printed program, the story of the play. Imagine, however, the first audiences at the play's premiere. The title character was the best-known figure of the Genji-Heike struggle, Yoshitsune. Undoubtedly the audience was familiar with many of the stories about the Heike clan's destruction from reading *The Tale of the Heike*. *Yoshitsune and the Thousand Cherry Trees* presents an imaginative sequel to *The Tale of the Heike*, its freely drawn portrayals of the Heike generals part of the literary license commonly taken by playwrights.

In act 1 Yoshitsune is visited at his Horikawa mansion by Kawagoe Tarō, an emissary from his brother Yoritomo, who questions Yoshitsune about the severed heads of three Heike generals (Tomomori, Noritsune, and Koremori), sent to Yoritomo to verify their deaths. Confronted by Kawagoe with the assertion that the heads are false, Yoshitsune defends his actions: If the three men are thought to be alive they could become rallying points for scattered Heike survivors who escaped the destruction of their clan. If they are believed dead, however, the country may be spared further strife. And in the meantime, says Yoshitsune, his warriors are secretly hunting down the fugitives.

Spectators accustomed to the stories they had long known about these Heike generals were suddenly presented with the premise that they had not died after all. The story of the fugitives unfolds in acts 2, 3, and 4, with the audience kept in the dark until the moment when the truth—the play's truth at least—is dramatically disclosed. In act 2, the doughty commoner Ginpei is revealed to be Tomomori; his "daughter" Oyasu is in fact the young emperor Antoku, and his "wife" is the emperor's wet nurse, both of whom according to history also perished at the battle of Dannoura. Act 3 concludes with "The Sushi Shop," in which the mask of Yasuke, the shop's apprentice, is drawn away to reveal him as Koremori. And in the dramatic final scene of act 4, the true identity of the imposing Zen priest Yokawa no Kakuhan is divulged: he is Noritsune, Lord of Noto.

Another surprise is the striking change in character of Gonta, the ne'er-do-well son of Yazaemon, the proprietor of the sushi shop in act 3. Presented initially as a shiftless ruffian and greedy swindler, Gonta rises at the end of the scene to an unsuspected nobility of character as he sacrifices all, himself and his family, to save his father and Koremori.

But more surprises were to come. In the first scene of act 2 ("Before the Fushimi Inari Shrine"), Yoshitsune's mistress Shizuka is rescued from peril by the timely arrival of Satō Tadanobu. In appreciation for Tadanobu's valor, Yoshitsune bestows upon him a suit of his own armor and the privilege of using his name of Genkurō. At the opening of act 4, in the *michiyuki* scene ("The Journey With the Drum"), Tadanobu escorts Shizuka through the colorful Yoshino mountains as they search for Yoshitsune, but in the closing scene of act 4 this "Tadanobu" is transformed on stage to his real identity, that of a magical fox who had assumed Tadanobu's form. From the name Yoshitsune gave him, he gains the sobriquet Genkurō Kitsune, "Genkurō the Fox"; from his impersonation of Tadanobu, he is known as Kitsune Tadanobu.

Perhaps the most theatrical bit of staging occurs in connection with the magical fox. Tadanobu's entrance in the *michiyuki* at the opening of act 4 is preceded by that of a white fox which romps along the forestage and then vanishes behind a mound, a piece of flat scenery. Within seconds the flat folds down revealing Tadanobu; the principal manipulator of the puppet has also undergone a swift change of costume. In the final scene of the act when it becomes clear that the "Tadanobu" seen thus far is in fact the fox, the audience is treated to several surprising appearances and disappearances of the fox, now played by the Tadanobu puppet dressed in a white furry garment suggesting his feral nature. He speaks in a jerky falsetto, is equipped with hands bent sharply downward at the wrist and fingers curled inward to suggest paws, and his actions have the quick nervous quality of an untamed animal.

## Sources

The authors of *Yoshitsune and the Thousand Cherry Trees* had a rich trove of material to draw upon, the first being works dealing with Yoshitsune himself. Where a factual history of Yoshitsune left off, imagination and romantic invention were soon busy creating colorfully embellished stories of his personal life and tribulations, making him a favorite in the gallery of Japanese heroes who struggle heroically against overwhelming odds only to lose all in the end. In fact, his career gave the Japanese language a word denoting sympathy for the mythic ideal that he represents: *hōgan-biiki*. Yoshitsune's position as a lieutenant in the imperial police accorded him the title Hōgan, a frequently used sobriquet by which he is known to history. *Hōgan-biiki*, literally "sympathy for the lieutenant," has come to describe traditional Japanese sympathy with any similar exemplar of the noble-minded underdog. Works written specifically about his career are known generically as *Hōgan-mono*, or works about the Hōgan.[14]

*The Tale of the Heike* was a major source for the playwrights in creating *Yoshitsune and the Thousand Cherry Trees*. Another work from the same time and covering much the same ground is the less literary *Genpei seisuiki* (*A Chronicle of the Fortunes of the Genji and Heike*). The *Gikeiki* (*Chronicle of Yoshitsune*),[15] an anonymous work of the fifteenth century, is the earliest collection of tales about Yoshitsune's youth and his trials as a fugitive. It does not have the caché of accuracy as a work of history but is rather a compendium of the beginnings of the romantic legend of Yoshitsune. It was well known to Japanese in the eighteenth century, and many of the subsequent literary treatments of Yoshitsune drew upon it as well as the other works noted here for episodes in the hero's life.

Plays from the Nō theater, dramatic dances known as *kōwakamai*, various short stories, and a number of other plays for the puppet theater have taken Yoshitsune's life and the legends surrounding it as story material.[16] My purpose here is not to provide

14. For details of the Yoshitsune legend, see McCullough, *Yoshitsune*, 30–66; and Ivan Morris, *The Nobility of Failure: Tragic Heroes in the History of Japan*, 67–105.

15. Translated by McCullough as *Yoshitsune*.

16. The dance drama known as *kōwaka*, which barely survives on the island of Kyushu today, was a common form of entertainment among samurai from about

a comprehensive discussion of this body of literature (for it is vast in scope) but to note certain earlier works that directly contributed to the creation of the puppet masterpiece *Yoshitsune and the Thousand Cherry Trees,* the most famous of all of the literary *hōgan-mono.*

From the fourteenth-century Nō theater at least four plays were influential. *Funa Benkei* (*Benkei in the Boat*) and *Ikari-kazuki* (*Drowning with an Anchor*) both provided plot and staging details for the "Tokaiya" scene that concludes act 2. From *Funa Benkei* came Tomomori's plan to make himself appear to be an apparition and to kill Yoshitsune and his party in the waters off Amagasaki as well as some lines that were incorporated into the puppet play's text. Tomomori's white, ghostlike costume was suggested by the one he wears in *Funa Benkei*. In *Ikari-kazuki* the ghost of Tomomori tells of his fight at Dannoura and how he then determined to end his life in the sea.

> He dons two suits of armor,
> Two helmets on his head.
> To make himself more weighty,
> He pulls with a mighty heave
> Upon a great rope
> Set into waters deep
> And draws an anchor forth.
> Above his helmets
> He lifts the anchor aloft,
> Hoists the anchor high,
> Then leaps into the ocean's depths.[17]

---

the middle of the sixteenth century. Episodes from the Genji-Heike wars form a major subject area in *kōwaka,* and several of these deal with the Yoshitsune legend. See James Araki, *The Ballad Drama of Medieval Japan,* 125–33, which includes summaries of twenty *kōwaka* dramas dealing with Yoshitsune; none of these, however, had any discernable influence on the play at hand. The earliest puppet play, *Jūnidan zōshi* (The Storybook in Twelve Sections), known at least as far back as 1485, is about Yoshitsune's imagined early life; it is summarized in C. J. Dunn, *Early Japanese Puppet Drama,* 31–34. It does not bear on *Yoshitsune and the Thousand Cherry Trees* but is part of the larger body of Yoshitsune legend.

17. Tsukamoto Tetsuzō, ed., *Yōkyoku shū,* 2:392.

Clearly this inspired the much more dramatic staging at the end of the "Tokaiya" scene where the mortally wounded Tomomori ascends a great rocky outcrop at the ocean's edge, ties a huge anchor to his waist, and lets it drag him to a watery death after failing in his attack on Yoshitsune.

The Nō play *Yoshino Shizuka* (*Shizuka in Yoshino*) may have suggested the *michiyuki* scene, "The Journey with the Drum," at the beginning of act 4. In the Nō play, as Shizuka and Tadanobu travel through Yoshino in disguise, Shizuka performs a dance invoking the gods' protection of Yoshitsune. The *michiyuki* in *Yoshitsune and the Thousand Cherry Trees* is much the same: Shizuka and Tadanobu are traveling through Yoshino in disguise, and Shizuka performs a dance out of longing for Yoshitsune. The puppet playwrights also drew upon the Nō play *Kagekiyo* at the end of the *michiyuki* as Tadanobu recalls and mimes the action at the battle of Yashima where his brother Tsuginobu was killed.[18]

The playwrights also seem to have appropriated material from several earlier puppet plays. Written in 1701, Chikamatsu Monzaemon's play *Tenko* (*The Heavenly Hand Drum*) revolves about the attempted theft of an heirloom drum which is protected by two thousand-year-old foxes, a father named Yazaemon-gitsune (Yazaemon the Fox) and his son Yasuke-gitsune.[19] There can be little doubt that the authors of *Yoshitsune and the Thousand Cherry Trees* adopted the magical fox from Chikamatsu's work and transformed him into the fox who, having exercised his legerdemain to masquerade as Yoshitsune's retainer Tadanobu earlier in the play, becomes the dominant dramatic presence in the concluding scene of act 4, "The Fox." And from the same play came the names for Yazaemon, the owner of the

---

18. *Funa Benkei* is translated in Nippon Gakujutsu Shinkōkai, ed., *Japanese Noh Drama*, 167–82. Arthur Waley has translated *Kagekiyo* in *The Nō Plays of Japan*, 123–33. For *Ikari-kazuki* and *Yoshino Shizuka*, see Tsukamoto, *Yōkyoku-shū*, 2:387–92 and 368–71, respectively. Other possible sources from the Nō theater are *Settai*, for its account of the death of Tsuginobu, and *Shōzon*, which deals with Tosabō Shōzon's plot against Yoshitsune and how Benkei foiled it.

19. See Waseda Daigaku Engeki Hakubutsukan, ed., *Engeki hyakka daijiten*, 4:96–97 and 5:517; Iwanami Shoten, ed., *Nihon koten bungaku daijiten*, 4:371–72.

act 3 sushi shop, and his young apprentice Yasuke, the disguise under which the Heike general Koremori is hiding. Noritsune, another of the Heike generals in *Yoshitsune and the Thousand Cherry Trees,* has adopted the disguise of a Zen priest, taking the name Yokawa no Kakuhan. He is finally unmasked at the end of act 4, and is killed by Tadanobu in act 5 following a spirited fight scene, one that appears to have been taken in broad outline from another of Chikamatsu's plays, *Yoshino Tadanobu (Tadanobu in Yoshino),* which premiered in 1697.[20]

In 1727 Namiki Senryū (then using the name Sōsuke), along with Yasuda Abun, wrote a play dealing with Yoshitsune and several other characters who appear in *Yoshitsune and the Thousand Cherry Trees,*[21] and this no doubt gave Senryū important early experience in working with the Yoshitsune story. Takeda Izumo's father had written a play in 1734, *Ashiya Dōman ōuchi kagami,* which involved the workings of a magical fox, a possible additional source of inspiration for the fox in the Yoshitsune play.[22]

Rewriting or appropriating elements from earlier works was commonplace in eighteenth-century Japan; virtually every playwright and popular author engaged in the practice, untroubled by notions of plagiarism. For a work to have appeared in public made it fair game, and both the original creators and the borrowers seem to have been comfortable with the practice. What mattered was the success of the play during its opening run. The result has been that the best plays have survived on stage and the poorer ones have not; what we see today represents the cream of the tradition. While *Yoshitsune and the Thousand Cherry Trees* is unarguably indebted to earlier works, it was the creative genius of its writers that made it the best of the numerous plays treating Yoshitsune's adventures, and that has assured its continued vitality on the stage.

20. *Nihon koten bungaku daijiten,* 6:162; *Engeki hyakka daijiten,* 5:518–19, where the date for the play is given as 1707.
21. The play is *Seiwa Genji jūgodan.* See *Engeki hyakka daijiten,* 3 359.
22. Ibid., 1:38–39.

The very successful six-month run of *Sugawara and the Secrets of Calligraphy* starting in the Eighth Month of the previous year, 1746, may have led the playwrights of *Yoshitsune and the Thousand Cherry Trees* to copy several structural elements of the plot of that earlier work for use in the new play. Their thinking may have been, in effect, that if a formula had worked so well before, why not try it again, with modifications. One is led to this line of thought because of certain similarities between the two plays, bearing in mind too that both were written by the same team of playwrights.

In the Sugawara play the authors had built an important part of the drama around three particular characters (the triplet brothers Matsuōmaru, Umeōmaru, and Sakuramaru) and three instances of the separation in death of a parent and a child. The unifying thread of the play was the fortunes of the statesman Sugawara no Michizane (845–903), the hero of the title, with whom the three parent-child tragedies were directly linked. In act 2 a parent kills the murderer of her child; in act 3 a child kills himself for reasons of honor; and finally in the fourth act a parent sacrifices a child, motivated by loyalty to a former master. Also in act 4, one of the triplets, Matsuōmaru, undergoes a startling metamorphosis of character that redeems his earlier evil nature in the famous scene already noted, "The Village School."

A similar structure is found in *Yoshitsune and the Thousand Cherry Trees*. In place of the triplet brothers are the three Heike generals thought to be dead but actually still at large. Tomomori kills himself essentially for reasons of honor in act 2. Gonta is killed by his father Yazaemon in act 3, after his earlier villainous nature has been transformed to one of nobility; and he sacrifices his own wife and child for reasons of loyalty not unlike those that had earlier moved Matsuōmaru. Gonta thus incorporates in one character more than one aspect of the Sugawara play. Yoshitsune and his fortunes constitute the unifying theme of the play; and just as Sugawara appears in the earlier work in all of the important acts but act 3, so Yoshitsune is present in all acts of *Yoshitsune and the Thousand Cherry Trees* except act 3.

There are certain resemblances also in the *michiyuki* dance scenes of the two plays (the beginning of act 2 in the Sugawara play, the opening of act 4 in the present translation). In both, characters travel in disguise through unfamiliar territory; the travelers hear (or have heard) of the place where the titular hero of the play has gone, and they set out to find him there; and in both *michiyuki* the lines include snatches of bucolic folk songs as the journey progresses. In the Sugawara play two of the three figures in the *michiyuki* are lovers; while Tadanobu and Shizuka in *Yoshitsune and the Thousand Cherry Trees* are not lovers, more than one commentator on the play has noted a certain amorous quality between them as they travel through the lovely cherry blossoms of Yoshino. Perhaps one should not press such a comparison too far, but given the circumstances—the close proximity in time of the two dramas and the common authorship—there is no reason to be surprised at congruous elements in the two plays.

## *Collaborative Authorship*

Joint authorship of dramatic works is not unknown in the West,[23] but it is more usual to think of single plays written by individual authors. By way of contrast, most Japanese puppet plays still on the boards today were created through the practice known as *gassaku,* or collaborative authorship. Multiple authorship occurred in the puppet theater as far back as the 1720s and from the mid-1740s onward hardly any plays were the product of a single playwright. The playwrights might number two or three, sometimes four writers, but as time went on and plots became increasingly complex and diverse—becoming almost a series of shorter plays consolidated into a single work—the playwriting team might be considerably expanded.

From the 1730s onward, the typical puppet play was com-

23. For instance, the plays of Beaumont and Fletcher in the early seventeenth century, the Quintero brothers of Spain in the first two decades of the twentieth century, and such American collaborators as George Kaufman and Marc Connelley.

prised of an overall story line into which were set several subplots detailing the adventures of various characters connected with the main plot. The first act set up the story and conflict for the entire play. Acts 2, 3, and 4 developed the specific subplots, and in the final act usually some sort of resolution was achieved that tied up all the threads of the play.

We do not know precisely why the practice of *gassaku* arose, but there are several possible reasons. The demand for new productions in the rivalry between Osaka's chief playhouses, the Takemoto-za and the Toyotake-za, might have required more than one man's efforts in creating a play. In 1723 the popular double suicide plays had been banned by the Tokugawa government, leaving available only the longer history plays, the *jidaimono*. The great length of these dramas would thus have been another factor, for they were generally all-day performances, many plays lasting ten hours or more in a full production. Some playwrights also had other duties that limited their time for writing without collaboration: Takeda Izumo II, one of the authors of *Yoshitsune and the Thousand Cherry Trees,* was manager of the Takemoto-za and this doubtless placed upon him time-consuming responsibilities. Finally, in much the same way that playwrights sought to appeal to audiences by including dramatic and emotional variety within a play, it may well have been thought desirable to achieve this in part through the varying predilections and talents of several authors.[24]

Joint authorship of plays could, of course, lead to inconsistencies and uneven quality. Most puppet and kabuki plays presently exist on stage as certain scenes or acts from originally much longer works. As a rule, only the better written or more ingeniously plotted parts of many plays have continued to appeal to audiences. *Yoshitsune and the Thousand Cherry Trees* has not escaped this flaw:[25] there are two short scenes ("Zaō Hall" and

---

24. See Eduard Klopfenstein, "Gassaku: Co-Authorship in Classical Jōruri of the Eighteenth Century," 283–89.

25. Some inconsistencies and questionable passages in *Yoshitsune and the Thousand Cherry Trees* are pointed out in the notes to this translation.

"The Conference at Zaō Hall" in act 4) that bear the earmarks of undistinguished hackwork written merely to set up the more important scene that follows. Neither of these scenes is ever performed today. Act 5 is also rarely staged, since it is little more than a summation or ultimate outcome of the more engaging action that has gone before. In productions of almost all *jidaimono* plays the omission of act 5 has long been commonplace in both the puppet and kabuki theaters.

## The Authors

Biographical information about playwrights in Japan's traditional plebeian theater is sketchy at best, the case of the authors of *Yoshitsune and the Thousand Cherry Trees* being no exception.[26] Takeda Izumo II (1691–1756), who had until the premiere of *Yoshitsune and the Thousand Cherry Trees* signed himself Koizumo, was the son of Takeda Izumo I, himself a playwright and the director of the Takemoto-za. Koizumo's name appears on some twenty-six plays (some say twenty-eight) that appeared between 1739 and his death, all of them *gassaku* efforts and some written under the name Takeda Geki. In nearly all of these, Miyoshi Shōraku was among the other playwrights. At his father's death in 1747, Koizumo inherited the Izumo name (becoming Izumo II, though he signed himself only Takeda Izumo) and became both chief playwright and manager of the Takemoto Theater.

Equally sketchy is our information about Miyoshi Shōraku. Unlike Izumo, who was a native of Osaka, the home of the puppet theater, Miyoshi Shōraku came originally from the westernmost province of the island of Shikoku. He was listed among the writers of a 1771 play, where he was said to be seventy-six years old. His dates may thus be 1696–1771, or thereabout. He is variously described as having previously been a physician, the

---

26. What follows repeats in some degree what may be found in my translation of *Sugawara and the Secrets of Calligraphy*, 9–12, and Donald Keene's translation of *Chūshingura*, 7–11.

proprietor of an Osaka tea house, or a Buddhist priest of the Shingon sect who returned to the laity after some indiscretion. Shōraku's name first appears among the authors of a play that premiered at the Takemoto-za in 1736; all of the more than fifty plays with which he was associated were *gassaku* works. It is difficult to know what characterized Shōraku's style, but the weight of opinion is that he was very much a secondary writer, perhaps even that he was little more than a kind of assistant.[27] But he had sufficient stature as a dramatist that his name appeared on a great number of plays, many of which have become classics of both the puppet theater and kabuki.

The last of the three authors of *Yoshitsune and the Thousand Cherry Trees*, Namiki Senryū (1695?–1751), was in his early years a priest in a Zen temple in southwestern Japan. He left the temple, came to Osaka, and became a disciple of the playwright Nishizawa Ippū (1665–1731) at the Toyotake-za around 1725, the same year that Chikamatsu Monzaemon died. At this time he used the name Namiki Sōsuke. Along with Ippū and Yasuda Abun (dates unknown) his name first appears on the play *Hōjō Jirai ki (The Chronicle of Hōjō Tokiyori)* in 1726, and its success clearly marked his swift rise, for he became in the very next year the chief playwright, or *tatesakusha*, at the Toyotake-za. He continued in that position until 1740, writing fourteen plays in collaboration with Yasuda Abun. From 1740 to 1742 he withdrew from the position of *tatesakusha* and stayed on assisting other playwrights at the Toyotake-za. He left the Toyotake-za and joined a kabuki troupe from 1742 to 1744, still using the name Sōsuke. The following year he was back writing for the puppets, though this time with the rival Takemoto-za and with a change of name to Namiki Senryū.[28] He stayed at the Takemoto Theater until 1750

---

27. Ōnishi Shigetaka and Yoshinaga Takao, eds., *Bunraku*, 45–46; Tsurumi Makoto, ed., *Takeda Izumo shū*, 22–25; *Nihon koten bungaku daijiten*, 5:648; Donald Keene, *World Within Walls: Japanese Literature of the Pre-Modern Era, 1600–1867*, 282–85; Keene, *Chūshingura*, 8–10.

28. Sōsuke may have adopted the name Senryū from that of Tanaka Senryū (dates unknown), who was at the Toyotake-za when Sōsuke began his playwriting career there, and who may have been his formal master. *Nihon koten bungaku daijiten*, 4:552, 175–76.

collaborating with other writers on eleven plays, including *Yoshitsune and the Thousand Cherry Trees* and the other two plays that make up the triumvirate of puppet masterworks.

Senryū may have become restless as the years progressed; after seventeen years at the Toyotake Theater he never continued in one place for more than half a dozen years. It may be that his talents were in such demand that he could be enticed away to different theatrical positions. Or, there may have been other circumstances that persuaded him to move about. Whatever the case, in 1751 he returned both to the Toyotake-za and to his earlier name of Sōsuke. He had completed act 3 of *Ichinotani futaba gunki* (*The Martial Chronicle of the Battle of Ichinotani*) when he died in 1751. The play was finished by others and staged later that year; its most famous scene, "Kumagai jinya" ("Kumagai's Camp") from act 2, is thought to be Senryū's creation and remains today a staple of the puppet and kabuki repertoire.[29] Altogether, he wrote over forty plays, usually in association with other writers but sometimes as the principal playwright.[30]

In a five-act *jidaimono* play such as *Yoshitsune and the Thousand Cherry Trees*, the three most important scenes are the final scene, known as the *kiri*, of act 3, then the *kiri* of act 4, with the *kiri* of act 2 last in the hierarchy. In the list of authors' names at the end of a play the first name was usually that of the most important playwright (the *tatesakusha*) and the last was the writer of next importance.[31] Any names in between would be those of lesser playwrights. According to this scheme, Izumo, as principal playwright, would have been the author of the *kiri* scene of act 3 ("The Sushi Shop"); Senryū would have written the act 4 *kiri* (the latter part of the scene called "The Fox"); and the act 2 *kiri* (the latter portion of "The Tokaiya") would have been the creation of Shōraku. Complicating the issue, however, is the differing

---

29. There is a translation of the kabuki adaptation of this scene in James R. Brandon, tr., *Kabuki: Five Classic Plays*, 186–211.

30. Biographical information on Senryū is drawn from Tsurumi, *Takeda Izumo shū*, 25–28, and from the entry by Uchiyama Mikiko in *Nihon koten bungaku daijiten*, 4:552–53.

31. Mori Shū, "Ningyō jōruri no tenkai to taisei," 49–50; Keene, *Chūshingura*, 7–8.

order of the playwrights' names at the end of the text of the play and in the contemporary *banzuke*, or printed announcement of the play indicating the authors and performers. In the text Izumo's name is first, but Senryū's comes first on the *banzuke*. The order of names apparently is not necessarily an accurate indicator of who was the *tatesakusha* of a given play.[32]

There is also scholarly disagreement on the division of labor in *Yoshitsune and the Thousand Cherry Trees*. Mori Shū believes that the *kiri* scenes of acts 2 and 4 are by Senryū and the act 3 *kiri* is by Izumo, the implication being that other significant parts of the play were written by Shōraku. Uchiyama Mikiko, arguing that Senryū's standing and experience as a playwright was superior to that of Izumo (Senryū was, after all, for some fifteen years the *tatesakusha* of the Toyotake Theater), believes that Senryū was probably the principal playwright even if he did not hold the title of *tatesakusha*. Noting the dark and pessimistic mood of many of Senryū's plays and a similar tone in the *kiri* scenes of acts 2 and 3, Uchiyama feels that these acts were most likely the work of Senryū, whom she regards as Japan's finest playwright since Chikamatsu. Izumo's fondness for the theme of love and devotion between parent and child is evident in the act 4 *kiri*, which Uchiyama feels should be assigned to him.[33]

Who wrote the other parts of the play? My own guess is that, apart from the more important scenes of acts 2, 3, and 4, the other portions of the play were most likely the work of playwrights-in-training on the theater's staff who were under general guidance from and whose work was subject to emendation by the higher ranking authors. Interesting as such studies and speculations are, in the end we may never know with any certainty

---

32. *Nihon koten bungaku daijiten*, 4:553.
33. Ibid.; Uchiyama Mikiko, "Jōruri no gikyoku sakuhō," 216–17; Kuroki Kanzō, *Chikamatsu igo*, 12–13. Uchiyama argues that Izumo's participation in the playwriting effort was probably largely concerned with aspects of the play that would make it a winning vehicle on the stage. In her opinion, Senryū wrote the bulk of the play through act 3 (with the exception of the opening scene of act 2, "Before the Fushimi Inari Shrine"), and Shōraku wrote acts 4 and 5. See Uchiyama, "Bunraku no sakusha-tachi: Chikamatsu, Izumo, Sōsuke," 54.

just who wrote which parts of *Yoshitsune and the Thousand Cherry Trees*.

A word should be said about the nature of a Japanese puppet play and its text. Studies of the Bunraku puppet theater emphasize the fact that it is *katarimono*, or spoken and sung narrative, a form growing out of a centuries old tradition of oral storytelling in which the narrator accompanies himself on, or is accompanied by, a musical instrument. In Bunraku this instrument is typically the three-stringed samisen (or shamisen), and Bunraku stands as perhaps the most highly refined form of *katarimono*.

Central to the *katarimono* tradition in Bunraku is the narrator, or *tayū*, who appears in full view of the audience and is a marvelously dramatic presence in his own right, giving voice to all of the characters on stage and speaking the narrative lines in a remarkable range of subtle and histrionic delivery. Indeed, one of the great pleasures of Bunraku is to watch this enormously expressive narrator seated to the audience's right, near the stage, vigorously giving vocal life to the puppets, while on stage the puppet manipulators bring to their charges a kinetic vitality that is difficult to dismiss as unlifelike. The narrator has essentially two functions: to render the dialogue of the mute puppets and to move the drama along smoothly by telling some of the story or by describing the inner landscapes of the characters as they confront their dilemmas. Though the narrator is the voice for all of the play's characters, he does not portray them strictly through mimicry; his task is rather to characterize their personas vocally and convey to the audience a sense or impression of who a character is, much as the variety of puppet heads gives to the spectator visual clues about a character's nature. The *tayū*'s narrative lines punctuate the progress of the play, sometimes introducing or characterizing a figure on stage, sometimes underscoring or explaining what we see before us, at other times merely identifying a speaker or bridging the lines of one character and those of another.

Dialogue in puppet plays, particularly that spoken by characters of ordinary social station, is close to the colloquial language of the day. That spoken by more exalted figures becomes more formal, graced by the flourishes one might expect of well educated and high ranking personages. Such persons often refer to others (and similarly may themselves be referred to by the narrator) by their titles or by offices they hold (a practice I have not usually followed, aiming instead at keeping the names of characters consistent and thus more easily recognizable). The text of a play is governed by the rules and vocabulary of classical Japanese, adhered to most strictly in the lines of the narrator in his role as the teller of the tale and in the dialogue of the more elevated characters.

Unlike the usual Western play, where the text is divided into the various lines uttered by the characters, the text that rests on a stand in front of the Bunraku narrator is a continuous series of lines, unbroken by any punctuation and in which the narrative lines—that is, the storytelling lines—are not set off in any significant way from the characters' dialogue. So integrated, in fact, is the dialogue with the rest of the text that it is often difficult to distinguish narrative from dialogue, or in the case of dialogue, to determine who is speaking. Even the poetic composition of many of the *tayū*'s narrative lines—usually characterized by a certain poetic elevation of language and the presence of alternating groups of seven and five syllables, the traditional meter of classical Japanese poetry—is not indicated by any arrangement of lines in the style of poetry.

We in the West expect a play to progress principally on the basis of what the characters in the play say and do, not through a recitation of the story by someone external to the play. There are, of course, exceptions—Thornton Wilder's *Our Town* and Dylan Thomas' *Under Milkwood* come to mind—but they are rare. Imagine, for example, the opening scene of Shakespeare's *Macbeth* written in the following fashion, with the narrator setting and then closing the eerie scene, delivering the witches' lines, and depicting the atmosphere as he goes. Though, as noted, the lines would not be cast in the contours of poetry, I have done so here to suggest their lyric quality.

> To this place of lonely desolation,
> Fog drifting in the dark and murky night,
> Sky rent by thunder, shot by bolts of light,
> There come three witches garbed in black.
> One speaks: When shall we three meet again,
> In thunder, lightning, or in rain? she says.
> When the hurlyburly's done, when the battle's
> Lost or won, the Second Witch replies,
> Peering through the churning gloom.
> That will be ere the set of sun, says Three.
> Where the place? the First Witch asks. Upon the heath,
> Witch Two responds. There to meet with Macbeth,
> Speaks Three, and beckons to her sisters.
> I come, Graymalkin, speaks Witch One.
> Paddock calls, says Two; Anon, cries Three.
> Drawing midnight robes to withered breasts,
> Through the swirling mists they go, exclaiming:
> Fair is foul, and foul is fair;
> Hover through the fog and filthy air.[34]

The puppet theater was lifted from rudimentary and unsophisticated origins by perhaps the most important of Japan's playwrights for the popular theater, Chikamatsu Monzaemon, who created great plays and new forms of plays. He pointed the way to a theater which was to become in the hands of later authors the flower of the Tokugawa period's literary and dramatic accomplishments. Chikamatsu wrote for a theater of smaller and less expressive dolls operated by one man, where much of the literary burden, and a fair amount of the plot, was carried by

---

34. This rendition of the opening scene of *Macbeth* and some of the immediately preceding material originally appeared in my essay "The Richness of *The Love Suicides of Sonezaki*," in Patricia Pringle, ed., *An Interpretive Guide to Bunraku*, 20–21. It is used here with permission and with my thanks.

the narrative recitativo of the tayū. As the puppet theater changed rapidly in the years following Chikamatsu's death in 1725, his plays became less suited to the new technical virtuosity of which the theater became capable. Shifts in the audience's tastes, changes in the physical theater, and competition with kabuki were met by playwrights of a different stamp. In their plays, plots ripened into complex configurations; sets and costumes grew increasingly lavish; and the story was carried more by the action and dialogue of puppets capable of subtle and lifelike movement and less by the storytelling narrative, as rival playhouses and their playwrights sought new ways to draw paying spectators through the gates. There was no going back to the earlier order of theatrical reality represented by Chikamatsu's plays, and for the most part his works ceased to be staged from shortly after his death until revivals of some of them in relatively recent times, the 1950s. And these revivals were inspired at least as much by the urgency of attracting audiences being lured away by competing entertainment forms as they were a genuflection to Chikamatsu and the magic of his name.

It is some measure of Chikamatsu's greatness that later playwrights often turned back to his works for inspiration, sometimes incorporating elements from his dramas into new plays, sometimes simply rewriting them and presenting them as new renditions of the older works. But for all that, the theater that in the nineteenth century came to be known as Bunraku offered playgoers a different dramatic appeal from that of Chikamatsu's day. Most of the plays still on the boards today, works hailed as classics of the puppet and kabuki theaters, flowed from the brushes of play crafters who came after Chikamatsu and ushered in the theater's golden age.

## *Adaptation to Kabuki*

Kabuki has always had the advantage of the charisma and potential for expression of live actors in its appeal to audiences, and its larger stage equipped with elaborate machinery has for centuries been more sophisticated than that of the puppet theater. What it traditionally lacked, in comparison to the puppet playhouses, were great playwrights and a growing repertoire of fine plays.

It was during the heyday of the puppet theater in Osaka and Kyoto, roughly from the years immediately following Chikamatsu's death in 1725 into the 1760s, that there occurred the remarkable phenomenon of a theater of inanimate puppets becoming overwhelmingly more popular than kabuki. By 1734, the puppets had developed from primitive and relatively unexpressive dolls operated by one person to much larger figures (reaching about two-thirds life size), each manipulated by a coordinated team of three handlers who, as the phrase has put it, learned "to breathe together" as they presented the dolls ever more realistically. Facial features on the puppets took on movement (eyes and eyebrows, mouths, even noses and ears in some cases), enhancing the puppets' range of expression. This nearly four-decade-long golden age of the puppet theater also was enriched by the talents of great narrators such as Takemoto Masatayū, Takemoto Konotayū, and Takemoto Shimatayū.[35] Leading the cast of puppet manipulators was Yoshida Bunzaburō, the greatest name among puppet handlers in the history of the theater. In addition to performing the roles of Ginpei, Tomomori, Yazaemon, Tadanobu and the fox in *Yoshitsune and the Thousand Cherry Trees,* Bunzaburō also devised the costume for Tadanobu as he appears in the *michiyuki,* one that remains a standard feature of the play today. Adapting the narrator Masatayū's family crest, the *Genji-guruma* or "Genji Wheel," he made the pattern of the upper garment a large carriage wheel, the axle centered at Tadanobu's neck and the spokes radiating out toward the waist and sleeve ends. The movable ears of the fox puppet were another of Bunzaburō's innovations.[36] This assemblage of talent prompted one observer of the theatrical scene to declare grandly the year before the appearance of *Yoshit-*

---

35. For a full listing of the narrators at the premiere of *Yoshitsune and the Thousand Cherry Trees,* see Tsurumi, *Takeda Izumo shū,* 43.

36. *Jōruri-fu,* in Kawatake Shigetoshi, ed., *Jōruri kenkyū bunken shūsei,* 358; *Engeki hyakka daijiten,* 5:514; Tsurumi, *Takeda Izumo shū,* 44–45.

*sune and the Thousand Cherry Trees* that "the puppet theater has grown so much in popularity that kabuki seems hardly even to exist."[37]

The competition between the two puppet playhouses, the Takemoto-za and the Toyotake-za, was mirrored in the rivalry between the puppets and kabuki. Always ready to capitalize on any puppet play success, kabuki was quick to appropriate the work for its own stage. This was done with such zeal and frequency, in fact, that probably fully half of the current kabuki repertoire consists of plays originally written for the puppets. Thus, kabuki's interest in *Yoshitsune and the Thousand Cherry Trees* was neither surprising nor exceptional. In the First Month of 1748, within two months of its triumph at the Takemoto-za, the play was being performed at the Osaka kabuki theater known as Ise no Shibai. Four months later it was mounted in Edo (modern Tokyo) at the Nakamura-za, with such stars as Nakamura Denkurō II in the role of Ginpei and Ichikawa Ebizō as Yazaemon and Kakuhan.[38] A month after that it was staged at the Morita-za in Edo with the famous *onnagata* (female impersonator) Yoshizawa Ayame performing the roles of Tadanobu and the fox. Then back home again to Osaka's kabuki stage at the Naka no Shibai, where it went on the boards in the Eight Month of 1748, a little over nine months after the puppet premiere.[39]

Adaptations to kabuki understandably involve changes to make the play work at its best in a theater of live actors.[40] To fill the much larger kabuki stage and to provide a smooth transition into the main story of a scene, minor characters may be added,

---

37. *Jōruri-fu*, 352.

38. For the new production, the narrator Takemoto Sengatayū and the samisen player Tsurusawa Tomokichi of the Takemoto-za, along with two other samisen performers and six puppet handlers, including Kiritake Monjūrō, were brought from Osaka to the Nakamura-za to guide the rehearsals. See Ihara Toshirō, comp., *Kabuki nenpyō*, 3:10.

39. Tsurumi, *Takeda Izumo shū*, 45–46, where additional actors are noted for the various productions.

40. For other discussions of kabuki adaptation see Jones, *Sugawara and the Secrets of Calligraphy*, 15–21, and Stanleigh H. Jones, Jr., "Miracle at Yaguchi Ferry: A Japanese Puppet Play and Its Metamorphosis to Kabuki," 180–89.

along with dialogue appropriate to the scene but not necessarily important to the progress of the plot. Such small alterations occur in several places in the kabuki version of *Yoshitsune and the Thousand Cherry Trees*.[41] Another change might be to augment a character's lines for some special, often comic, effect. The technique known as *tsukushi* (or *monozukushi*), a literary catalogue of things, may be found even in pre-Tokugawa period Japanese literature and drama, but an example occurs in Chikamatsu Monzaemon's puppet play *The Battles of Coxinga* (*Kokusenya kassen*) of 1715. In the opening scene of act 2, the narrator describes a husband and his wife gathering shells along a beach, the narration punning on the names of a variety of shells (*kai* in Japanese), producing both a virtuoso catalogue of shells (*kai-tsukushi*) and simultaneously describing the affection between the couple. The effect is a kind of literary tour de force on a particular theme or subject that must have appealed to audiences by its ingenuity.[42] The kabuki rendition of *Yoshitsune and the Thousand Cherry Trees* includes two such *tsukushi* not found in the original play. In the opening scene of act 2, "Before the Fushimi Inari Shrine" when Tōta and his men fight with Tadanobu, the kabuki Tōta delivers a long-winded castigation of Tadanobu, the lines cast in the form of a *kuruma-tsukushi*, a catalogue of wheeled vehicles (*kuruma*).[43] In the "Tokaiya" scene that concludes act 2, when the arrogant Sagami Gorō is driven off by Ginpei, Gorō, clowning with a confederate from a safe distance and in the style of the classical *kyōgen* farces of the fourteenth-century Nō theater, berates Ginpei in a speech appropriate for a man of the sea, a *sakana-tsukushi*, or catalogue of assorted fish.[44]

41. Toita Yasuji, ed., *Meisaku Kabuki zenshū*, 2:244–45, 255, 264, 282, 317.

42. See Donald Keene, *The Battles of Coxinga*, 114–15. Some sense of the technique might be gained by a look at the lyrics of Cole Porter's title song for the 1953 American musical *Can Can*.

43. Toita, *Meisaku Kabuki zenshū*, 2:261. The choice of *kuruma* for this *tsukushi* doubtless related to the carriage wheel design that adorned Tadanobu's costume. It is evident in the frontispiece illustration of this book.

44. The kabuki actor Danjūrō VII (1791–1859) was the innovator who added the *sakana-tsukushi* to the play. Ibid , 237, 267.

Kabuki has a penchant for incorporating comedy into its plays, and this is evident in the kabuki adaptation of *Yoshitsune and the Thousand Cherry Trees*. In the first scene of act 2 in the kabuki version, Tōta (a stock comic character in kabuki) and his six men enter along the *hanamichi*, the runway leading through the audience from the back of the theater to the stage. Near the stage they stop and Tōta addresses his minions. His speech is delivered in a sharply rhythmical manner and in the classical metric pattern of alternating groups of five and seven syllables; the scene is typical kabuki comedy.[45]

TŌTA: Listen to me men,
   Listen to me now.
   In the battle tactics
   Of every engagement,
   Don't think the foe is weak
   And hold him in contempt;
   Don't see a mighty force
   As something to be feared.
   If they appear courageous,
   Be the first one to retreat.
   If they look to be quite weak,
   Grab them and tie them up.
   Take credit for your bravery:
   That's the most important thing.
   Be sure you don't forget this.
   You got that, men?
SOLDIERS: Yessir, we've got that, boss.
TŌTA: Then let's be quick about it.
SOLDIERS: Right. *(All move a bit closer to the stage.)*
TŌTA: Wait a minute, men!
   Wait, wait, wait!
   When you head for battle,
   There's no need to be first.
   Count on all those men

---

45. The text that follows is from ibid., 259–60.

Who bring up the rear.
The most important thing: provisions.
If your stomach's empty,
You cannot do your work.
Since over there's a tea house,
Go and cook your meal.
You got that, men?

SOLDIERS: We've got that, boss.

TŌTA: Then, let's be quick about it.

SOLDIERS: Right.

*(The group rhythmically troops about on the hanamichi runway through the audience until the soldiers are in the lead, Tōta in the rear.)*

TŌTA: Men, what's going on here?

SOLDIER #1: Sir, you keep telling us
 To be quick about it . . .

SOLDIER #2: . . . but if we go ahead
 And then fall back . . .

SOLDIER #3: . . . we're not going to get
 Anywhere at all.

SOLDIER #4: From here on we'll go first,

SOLDIER #5: . . . and you accompany us.

SOLDIER #6: So come along and follow,

SOLDIERS: And let's be quick about it.

TŌTA: I've got that, boss.

SOLDIERS: If you've got that,
 Come on, let's go.

*(Tōta bringing up the rear, they approach the stage, where they see Shizuka.)*

SOLDIERS *(astonished)*: Hey, look!

SOLDIER #1: Sir, there's one helluva person up there.

TŌTA: What? There's a helluva guy up there? Quick, let's get out of here!

*(Tōta tries to flee, but his men stop him.)*

SOLDIER #2: Sir, it's a woman.

TŌTA: What's that? A woman?
 Now that's what I like.

Quickly capture her, and
We'll get credit for the catch.

SOLDIER #3: Uh . . . sir, we don't have to capture her. She's already tied up.

TŌTA: What? She's tied up? Now that's a stroke of luck. And if she's just a woman . . . *(Tōta looks at Shizuka carefully.)* Hey, hey! Look! Don't you guys know who she is? That woman there is Yoshitsune's lower, Lady Boisterous!

SOLDIER #4: Uh . . . sir, it's Yoshitsune's *lover* . . .

SOLDIER #5: . . . Lady Shizuka . . .

SOLDIER #6: . . . *the quiet one*, sir.

*(In his excitement, Tōta gets mixed up and calls Shizuka "Lady Boisterous" [her name means "quiet"].)*

TŌTA: Well done. You men are . . . uh, well informed. Anyway, she's all tied up with a rope, that's great. And this drum here, it's Yoshitsune's treasure called . . . called . . . what's it called?

SOLDIER #1: It's called the Hatsune Drum, sir.

TŌTA: Oh, yeah, so it is. If Shizuka and the drum are both here, then there's no question that Yoshitsune's hiding somewhere along this road. Now, first take Shizuka into custody.

At this point the narration from the puppet version continues, and in a moment Tadanobu enters and begins to fight with Tōta and his men. The kabuki fight scene choreography is a good deal more elaborate than that found in the puppet theater.

Perhaps nothing is more characteristic of kabuki than its flamboyant, "rough-house," or *aragoto,* style of acting. Typically, *aragoto* actors employ exaggerated costumes and props, declaim with bravura and engage in extravagant poses as they portray their larger-than-life roles. Since its inception as an innovation of the great actor Ichikawa Danjūrō I nearly seventy-five years before the premiere of *Yoshitsune and the Thousand Cherry Trees,* the *aragoto* acting style became a standard feature of kabuki, particularly in plays performed in Edo. It is not surprising that the kabuki adaptation of *Yoshitsune and the Thousand Cherry Trees* introduced an *aragoto* scene not found in the original puppet play. At the end of the last scene of act 2, "Kawagoe Tarō Comes as Envoy," Benkei battles the men who have come to kill Yoshitsune, lopping off several heads and tossing them into a giant rain barrel. He then climbs atop the barrel, tears a plank from a nearby roof and uses it to stir the heads in a scene known as "Benkei Washes the Potatoes" ("Imo-arai no Benkei"). This was borrowed from a scene devised by Ichikawa Danjūrō IV for the 1773 play *Gohiiki kanjinchō*.[46]

The puppet theater has also borrowed innovative performance practices from kabuki to enhance its own productions. One of the best-known examples is the scene "Tearing the Carriage Apart" ("Kurumabiki") in the 1746 play *Sugawara and the Secrets of Calligraphy*. On a smaller scale, a similar infusion from kabuki is found in modern puppet productions of *Yoshitsune and the Thousand Cherry Trees*. A number of kabuki plays employ harnesses to attach actors to overhead machinery in order to lift them into the air and move them across the stage as though they are endowed with the magical ability to fly. In the last scene of act 4, the wizardry of the fox is demonstrated in kabuki by having the actor "fly" through the air and into the rear balcony of the theater. It is a specialty of the athletic and popular actor Ichikawa Ennosuke III, who more than any other actor has popularized this dramatic scene among kabuki audiences. Though not new to kabuki,[47] Ennosuke's application of the technique to the fox scene in *Yoshitsune and the Thousand Cherry Trees* has been so striking that audiences have come to expect nothing less. The puppet theater has in recent years adapted the practice to its own performances, with the manipulator hoisted above the stage, still working the puppet for Genkurō the Fox as he is drawn off into the stage right wings. The spectacle works superbly in kabuki

46. Ibid., 237, 255.
47. *Chūnori* or *chūzuri*, as the technique is called, may go back as far as 1700 when Ichikawa Danjūrō I is said to have used it in a kabuki play based on the story of the Soga brothers. It was frequently employed in other plays of the Tokugawa period and later became a specialty of several actors, among them Ichikawa Ennosuke I, grandfather of Ennosuke III. *Engeki hyakka daijiten*, 3:591.

where it is greeted by enthusiastic applause, but it is far less effective in the puppet theater.[48]

I was in Japan during 1980–81 on a grant from the Translations Program of the National Endowment for the Humanities, and it was in May 1981 that Bunraku play schedules were in my favor and I had the good luck for several days running—and literally all day long—to see repeatedly an almost full production of *Yoshitsune and the Thousand Cherry Trees* at the National Theater in Tokyo. Seeing the play on stage, it was impossible not to be impressed with its scope, variety, and ingenuity, let alone the talent of the performers; given these factors and the play's status in the repertoire, it begged to be translated. With Donald Keene's translation of *Chūshingura* and my own of *Sugawara and the Secrets of Calligraphy,* all three of the acknowledged best and most popular plays of Bunraku are now available in English. A German translation of *Yoshitsune and the Thousand Cherry Trees* was published in 1982 by Eduard Klopfenstein; I am aware of no other translation of the play into English.

The staffs of the National Theater (Kokuritsu Gekijō) and of the Bunraku Association (Bunraku Kyōkai) generously permitted me to attend dress rehearsals and to photograph the play under almost ideal circumstances. Some of the photographs that accompany this translation come from that experience. Viewing the play a number of times and recording it on audiotape has made it possible to include stage notes that are never mentioned in the usual text of the play. I have also benefited greatly from Yūda Yoshio's production notes to those frequently performed por-

---

48. The rivalry between kabuki and the puppet theater continues today: recent puppet productions of the *michiyuki* scene of *Yoshitsune and the Thousand Cherry Trees* include the surprise appearance of the fox puppet prior to its transformation into Tadanobu. In a device (called *kendai-nuke*) installed in the new National Bunraku Theater in Osaka (inaugurated in 1984), the stand (*kendai*) holding the play text in front of one of the narrators splits in two, and through a trap door beneath the stand the puppeteer manipulating the fox puppet quickly emerges and moves onto the stage.

tions of the play contained in *Bunraku jōruri shū*. I have also consulted *Kessaku jōruri shū*, edited by Higuchi Yoshichiyo, for those parts of the play contained therein. *Takeda Izumo shū*, edited by Tsurumi Makoto, contains the most complete text of the play, including very helpful notes, but even that text has had to be supplemented as noted in the footnotes for the *michiyuki* scene that begins act 4.

In general, where action on stage is clear from the narrator's lines I have added no notes of my own. Where I have felt that some idea of stage activity would enhance a reader's appreciation of the play, I have added staging notation based either on Yūda's notes in *Bunraku jōruri shū* or on my own experience with the play in the theater. Throughout these notes are certain terms that should be explained here. SL and SR mean, respectively, Stage Left and Stage Right, from the perspective of the performer, not the audience. Shōji, sliding doors that are characteristic of traditional Japanese architecture, are simple plain wood frames with a wooden latticework covered on one side by translucent white paper.

For those interested in well-illustrated works on Bunraku, I warmly recommend Donald Keene's *Bunraku: The Art of the Japanese Puppet Theater* (the large format 1965 edition) and Barbara Adachi's two books, *The Voices and Hands of Bunraku* and *Backstage at Bunraku*. For an excellent presentation of the puppets of Bunraku, with many illustrations in color, the best book to appear so far is *Bunraku no ningyō*, edited by the Bunraku Kyōkai and published in 1976. A short illustrated essay on the structure of the puppets may be found at the end of *Sugawara and the Secrets of Calligraphy*.

There has long been scant material available in English about the important element of music in the puppet theater.[49] Yet,

---

49. William Malm has until recently been almost alone in producing studies of the music of the kabuki and puppet theaters. See his "A Musical Approach to the Study of Japanese Jōruri," in James R. Brandon, ed., *Chūshingura: Studies in*

throughout the performance of any Bunraku play there is the continuous presence of music, provided by the narrator, who sings a great many of the lines, and his accompanist on the samisen. Remove them and the theater is mute of dialogue, of many instrumental passages that set the tone and atmosphere for a scene, and of singing that gives a richness to the perception of the character's inner self. So close is the artistic relationship between the narrator and the samisen player that Japanese often refer to the latter as the *nyōbō-yaku,* one who performs the "wife role" to the narrator. I do not have the musical training necessary to deal with the subject; accordingly, there is little mention of the role of music in the accompanying translation. Now, however, an important part of this gap has been filled by C. Andrew Gerstle, Kiyoshi Inobe and William P. Malm in their book *Theater As Music: The Bunraku Play "Mt. Imo and Mt. Se: An Exemplary Tale of Womanly Virtue."*

The line drawings that appear at the beginning of most scenes in the present translation of *Yoshitsune and the Thousand Cherry Trees* come from *Gidayū nenpyō (Meiji-hen)*, pp. 226–27 and 460–61. They were created for the March 1892 production by Nakagawa Shinkichi, the scenic artist of the Bunraku Theater. Some of these drawings appear in Yūda, *Bunraku joruri-shū,* pp. 147–228. They represent traditional set designs for the play, and many continue to be used essentially as Nakagawa conceived them. However, set configurations, as well as stage movement, evolve over time; current productions include both new or modified movement and sets. This was certainly true of the 1980–81 production, on which I have based most of the details of sets and staging in this translation. These drawings are included here for their visual value, even though differences may occur between my descriptions and Nakagawa's drawings.

---

*Kabuki and the Puppet Theater,* 59–110. He also deals with the music of the puppet theater to a lesser extent in his "Music in the Kabuki Theater," in James R. Brandon, William P. Malm, and Donald H. Shively, *Studies in Kabuki: Its Acting, Music, and Historical Context,* 133–75.

*Yoshitsune and the Thousand Cherry Trees*

# *Dramatis Personae*

*Yoshitsune and the Thousand Cherry Trees* is a long play that normally occupies a full day at the theater. It is a complex play with a large cast, over thirty characters of importance, plus a number of lesser figures such as maids, soldiers, farmers, boatmen, priests, and underlings. Those not significantly involved in the progress of the plot are omitted here. The list is in alphabetical order according to the name of the character used most commonly in the play. The more complete name appears in parentheses in the normal Japanese order with family name first. Though Yoshitsune's older brother Yoritomo (sometimes referred to in the play as the Lord of Kamakura), never appears in the play, his presence is strongly felt throughout as the man whose jealous machinations make Yoshitsune a fugitive and drive him to some of the adventures in the play.

ANTOKU (Emperor Antoku), child emperor supposedly drowned during the great sea battle at Dannoura, when the Taira were decisively defeated; now posing as Oyasu.

ASUKA, wife of Kawatsura Hōgen.

BENKEI (Musashibō Benkei), burly retainer of Yoshitsune.

FOX, a magical fox who adopts the appearance of TADANOBU.

GINPEI (Tokaiya Ginpei), shipping agent at the Tokaiya ship chandlery and inn in Daimotsu Bay (see TOMOMORI).

GONTA (Igami no Gonta), ne'er-do-well son of Yazaemon.

GORŌ (Sagami Gorō), retainer of Hōjō Tokimasa in Kamakura; in reality, a retainer of Tomomori.

HAYAMI NO TŌTA, retainer of Tosabō.

INOKUMA (Inokuma Dainoshin), underling of Tomokata.

KAJIWARA (Kajiwara Kagetoki), retainer of Yoritomo.

KAKUHAN (Yokawa no Kakuhan), Zen master on Mount Yoshino (see NORITSUNE).

KAMEI (Kamei no Rokurō), retainer of Yoshitsune.

KAWAGOE (Kawagoe Tarō Shigeyori), councilor to Yoritomo and father of Kyō no Kimi.

KAWATSURA (Kawatsura Hōgen), chief priest of all the Mount Yoshino temples.

KOKINGO (Kokingo Takesato), retainer of Koremori.

KOREMORI (Taira no Koremori), Heike general thought to have died during the wars between the Heike and the Genji; now in disguise posing as Yazaemon's apprentice Yasuke in the sushi shop.

KOSEN, wife of Gonta.

KYŌ NO KIMI, formal wife of Yoshitsune.

MOTHER (unnamed in the play), wife of Yazaemon and mother of Osato and Gonta.

NAISHI (Wakaba no Naishi), wife of Heike general Koremori and mother of Rokudai.

NORITSUNE (Taira no Noritsune, Lord of Noto), Heike general who supposedly died at Dannoura, now masquerading as Kakuhan.

ORYŪ, Ginpei's wife (see TSUBONE).

*Dramitis Personae*

OSATO, Yazaemon's daughter.
OYASU, daughter of Ginpei and Oryū (see ANTOKU).
ROKUDAI, young son of Naishi and Koremori.
SHIZUKA, Yoshitsune's mistress.
SURUGA (Suruga no Jirō), retainer of Yoshitsune.
TADANOBU (Satō Shirōbei Tadanobu), retainer of Yoshitsune.
TOMOKATA (Fujiwara no Tomokata), Minister of the Left and General of the Left Guards in the imperial court.
TOMOMORI (Taira no Tomomori), Heike general who supposedly drowned at Dannoura, now posing as Ginpei.
TOSABŌ (Tosabō Shōzon), underling of Yoritomo.
TSUBONE, wet nurse to the young Emperor Antoku; supposedly drowned at Dannoura, now posing as Ginpei's wife Oryū.
YASUKE, apprentice to Yazaemon in the Tsurube sushi shop; in reality, Koremori.
YAZAEMON, master of the Tsurube sushi shop and father of Gonta and Osato.
YOSHITSUNE (Minamoto no Yoshitsune, also referred to as Lord Hōgan), victorious general in the wars against the Heike clan; younger brother of Yoritomo.
ZENTA, young son of Kosen and Gonta.

# *Prologue*

•  •

*(As the prologue begins, the stage is concealed by the standard curtain, consisting of alternating broad vertical stripes of green, rust, and black.)*

NARRATOR: Loyal! Ah, such a one is Tadanobu.
    Faithful! Ah, that is Tadanobu too.[1]
    Long ago in China, Fan Li
    Discharged the wishes of his master,
    Kou Chien, the King of Yueh.
    Having served his lord with merit,
    Gaining honor for his name,
    Fan Li forsook the public world
    And drifted like a leaf
    Upon a pillow of waves,

    1. These lines play upon the Chinese characters read in Sino-Japanese as *chū* (loyalty) and *shin* (fidelity). In their native Japanese pronunciations of *tada* and *nobu,* they form the name Tadanobu, a loyal and faithful retainer to Yoshitsune who figures prominently in the play.

At ease among the lakes that number five.[2]
He it was who served as escort
To the lovely lady Hsi Shih.[3]
That is a story from China,
But we too in Japan have tales
Of love and loyal service.[4]
Peaceful, vast in their expanse,
Spread the four seas, but brief
The reigning years of Emperor Antoku,
An era inaptly named Juei—
Long and everlasting life.[5] And even this,
By another sovereign's writ,
Became the shorter-lived Genryaku.[6]
In the fence with gate unlatched
The rape bloom prospers in its season,
Like the snow white banners of the Genji
In the flush of martial fame.

   2. The five large and scenic lakes near the city of Hangchou in China's Chekiang province.

   3. Fan Li (also known as T'ao Shu Kung) was a wise minister to Kou Chien, who in 496 B.C. became king of the state of Yueh along China's eastern coast. Kou Chien ignored Fan Li's advice not to make war on the northern state of Wu, and he was soundly defeated there by the Wu forces under the command of Fu Ch'ai (died 473 B.C.). Kou Chien sent Hsi Shih, a famous beauty, under Fan Li's care to Fu Ch'ai, who was so smitten with Hsi Shih that he neglected his duties and was easily defeated by Kou Chien. Later Fan Li, declaring that he had given much of his life to public service, resigned his office and enjoyed a sybaritic life of retirement. See Herbert A. Giles, *A Chinese Biographical Dictionary*, 217, 271, 373.

   4. This tale of Fan Li is introduced as a Chinese equivalent of Tadanobu escorting Shizuka in search of Yoshitsune in the *michiyuki* scene of act 4.

   5. Emperor Antoku's reign (1182–85) lasted only thirty-eight months.

   6. Historically unrecognized, this was the brief era designated by the retired priestly Emperor Goshirakawa. It lasted sixteen months during 1184–85.

# Act One

## SCENE I

## THE IMPERIAL PALACE

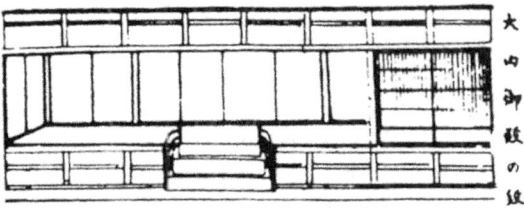

*(The curtain opens to reveal a large room extending the width of the stage and raised some two feet above the ground. Downstage a low balustrade extends across the front, interrupted in the middle by a stairway of three steps flanked by its own balustrade. All of this is painted a light tan, with black for its iron fittings. Upstage at SL and SR are large tan panels with stylized horizontal cloud patterns in gold; at center is a wide arched opening framed in black lacquer, the opening itself covered by a black bamboo blind with vertical bands of black; on either side of the archway, the wall is decorated with stylized moundlike islands in dark blue and green seeming to float in a golden sea. Minister of the Left Fujiwara no Tomokata, dressed in black robes edged in red and wearing a tall coronet of state, is seated*

*at center in front of the archway. On his left and right are two Court Attendants dressed in gold lamé robes.)*

NARRATOR: The Emperor Antoku,
    Eighty-first in his imperial line,
    Having slipped beneath the waves at Yashima,[1]
    The reins of state have been assumed
    By the Emperor Goshirakawa,
    Retired and priestly sovereign.[2]
    Close to him as counselor
    Is Minister of the Left,
    And General of the Left Guards,
    Fujiwara no Tomokata.
    Thus favored by the Emperor,
    He has given to his sycophants
    Advancements in both rank and post,
    Flaunting bias to his favorites.
    To question this would be
    Offensive to the imperial will,
    Think other members of the court,
    So each has held his tongue.
    The Grand Recorder takes in hand
    His brush, bound in colored threads,
    And draws his ink stone to him.
    Now led in through the palace gate
    Comes the great Genji general,
    Genkurō Hōgan Yoshitsune,[3]

---

1. This is in error. Though there was a major battle between the Genji and the Heike at Yashima on the island of Shikoku, Antoku was drowned about a week later, much further to the southwest in the narrow strait of Dannoura between Japan's main island of Honshu and the smaller Kyushu.

2. Goshirakawa reigned from 1155 to 1158, when he abdicated and withdrew to a Buddhist monastery, becoming a retired emperor in priestly orders (*Hōō*) but continuing to be the power behind the throne in the political jockeying between the court and the rising military clans of the Genji and Heike.

3. The *Gen* in Yoshitsune's name is the Sino-Japanese reading of *Minamoto*, the name of Yoshitsune's clan. *Kurō* indicates that he is the ninth child of his father Yoshitomo. *Hōgan* was an honorary title for the rank of lieutenant in the office of imperial police (the *Kebiishi-chō*). Yoshitsune held that rank, and he is

## Scene 1: The Imperial Palace

Radiant in his splendid robes,
Ornamented sword at his side.
Joining him, his famed retainer,
Musashibō Benkei of the Western Tower,
Now wearing a tall court hat
And robe bedecked with crests.
Eschewing his more normal priestly garb,[4]
He cuts a splendid figure.
*(Recorder, Yoshitsune, and Benkei enter from SR.)*
The Grand Recorder announces them.

RECORDER: The Genji warriors present themselves.

TOMOKATA: Well now, Yoshitsune, the priestly Emperor has yet to hear the details of the battle of Yashima. Tell us, then, about the drowning of Emperor Antoku and the destruction of the Heike clan, so that it may be entered in the court record.

NARRATOR: Yoshitsune acknowledges the command.

YOSHITSUNE *(throughout his narrative, Yoshitsune mimes the action of the events)*: I will do as you ask.[5] In this battle, the Heike appeared to have some one thousand mounted troops, and they had set up their camp along the Yashima beach. I had but slightly more than four hundred horse, and I did not think we would carry the day. But when we surprised them

---

known through much of the literature about him as *Hōgan-dono*, or Lord Hōgan. See Yūda, *Bunraku jōruri shū*, 152, n. 2.

4. Priests of low rank, such as Benkei, were not allowed in the imperial palace. Here he appears as one of Yoshitsune's warriors, dressed in robes appropriate to the surroundings. There is about as much legend attached to Benkei as to Yoshitsune. The addition of "Western Tower" to his name appears to come from the time he was a monk in the western compound of the great Enryakuji Temple on Mount Hiei near Kyoto. For stories about Benkei, see McCullough, *Yoshitsune*, III and *passim*.

5. Yoshitsune's description that follows is actually a conflation of events that historically took place at Yashima, on the northeast coast of Shikoku, and those that occurred about a week later at Dannoura, near Kyushu. For the *Heike monogatari* account, see Helen Craig McCullough, tr., *The Tale of the Heike*, 360–70, 375–80 (hereafter, all references to *The Tale of the Heike* are to McCullough's translation).

and rode in shouting our war cries, the Heike were flung into confusion. Taking the Emperor Antoku with them, they rushed to board their ships and move offshore. We then set fire to their fortress and in the brilliance of the flames they seemed to come to their senses. Noritsune, Lord of Noto, switched to a smaller vessel. Famed as a formidable archer, he swiftly let fly a volley of arrows aimed at me. But just as he did so, Satō Tsuginobu drew his horse up to shield me from them, taking an arrow in his ribs and falling down from his own horse. When Noritsune's man Kikuōmaru left the boat to come to the beach and take the dead man's head, Tsuginobu's younger brother Satō Tadanobu brought him down with an arrow. At that point, both sides withdrew and held memorial services for their fallen comrades. Thus ended the fighting that day. When the next day broke, the enemy put forth a fan and dared us to shoot at it. Our own Yoichi Munetaka shot it down. Then when Miyonoya from our side lost his helmet to the Heike general Kagekiyo, the enemy were much moved, and we too shouted praise. The battle was finally won by the Genji. On the Heike side, with their forces beaten back, Noritsune, Lord of Noto, clasped Aki no Tarō and his younger brother Jirō on either side of him and leaped into the sea. Taira Norimori and his brother Tsunemori took this occasion for their passage to the land of shades. After them, Sukemori, Arimori, and Yukimori all followed and threw themselves into the sea. Then Taira Tomomori, the new middle councilor, splashed into the water to be with the Emperor's ship. The nun, Lady Nii, wondering what was to become of the Emperor, and seizing an unguarded moment, took him in her arms and leaped with him into the sea. This I have heard, but we have not yet been able to recover their bodies. The only one rescued was the Empress Kenreimon'in. As for those who were captured, I have noted them in a list presented earlier. Since His Majesty may peruse this for himself, I need not go through them now.

NARRATOR: As he relates the matter in detail,

*Scene 1: The Imperial Palace*

His words are taken down, just so,
And placed into the record.
Then speaks Tomokata,
A sour look upon his face.

TOMOKATA: Such have been your exploits, Yoshitsune. Now, tell us of the offense for which you were sent away from Koshigoe without seeing Yoritomo.[6]

NARRATOR: Hearing this, Benkei steps forth.

BENKEI: Lord Noriyori may be my master's older brother, but he is untalented. Unsuccessful himself on the battlefield, he complained about Lord Yoshitsune. In trying to make Yoshitsune's achievements seem his own, Noriyori has had all his flunkies say malicious things about Yoshitsune.[7] Now, if the Lord of Kamakura was unaware of this, it's because he carried out no investigation.

NARRATOR: The words are hardly spoken
Than Yoshitsune rebukes him.

YOSHITSUNE: Hold your tongue, Benkei! Whatever may be the work of those who would malign me, I was unable to vindicate myself in the eyes of my brother Yoritomo. I returned downhearted from Koshigoe because Yoritomo made me an object lesson for others to see: that even his own brother would be dealt with harshly if necessary. What you have said, Benkei, is thoughtless calumny that makes no distinction between right and wrong. You are impudent in the extreme!

TOMOKATA: Ah, admirable Yoshitsune. You have reported to the throne the particulars of the battle, and the Emperor will take that as he will.

NARRATOR: He speaks flatteringly on the surface,

6. On his way to see his brother Yoritomo following the rift between them, Yoshitsune was kept out of Kamakura in the nearby town of Koshigoe, from which he sent Yoritomo several letters justifying himself and pleading for an audience. It was never granted, and it was from this point that Yoshitsune was forced to embark on a long and meandering flight from Yoritomo's men.

7. Benkei's criticism doubtless reflects the rivalry and antagonism between Yoshitsune and Noriyori. Yoshitsune was clearly the more astute and accomplished general on the battlefield, but Yoritomo chose to reward Noriyori. For other examples of incidents that point up this bad blood, see McCullough, *Yoshitsune*, 15, 18–19, 135.

But within his heart there lies
Some unfathomed stratagem,
As though to seize a bird
Asleep upon a roost.
Taking with him the Grand Recorder,
Tomokata withdraws
To the inner precincts of the palace.
From the shadows of a shuttered window,
In comes one from Tomokata's staff,
A villain no less evil than his master
And with a brutish name: Inokuma Dainoshin—
"Wild boar and savage bear."

INOKUMA: See here, Lord Yoshitsune, you have been negligent. You say you have put down the Heike, but you have left at large Wakaba no Naishi, the wife of Taira Koremori. Why was she not accounted for?

YOSHITSUNE: What is so terrible about that? She's a mere woman with a child! Among the many tens of thousands of people in the country, they can hardly be a danger to the state. We can leave her as she is.

INOKUMA: Mmmm, leave her as she is, you say. If you are going to leave her to the chances of fate, then you should leave her to us. My master, Lord Tomokata, has taken a fancy to Wakaba no Naishi.

NARRATOR: Before he can finish, Benkei interrupts.

BENKEI: No, there'll be none of that! The Lord of Kamakura has directed that, apart from other forms of alliance, taking for oneself the wife of a member of the Heike clan is the same as becoming a Heike ally. It is forbidden.

NARRATOR: Benkei's words are scathing.

INOKUMA: Don't be impertinent with me! Isn't Yoshitsune the son-in-law of Taira Tokitada?[8] I know without your saying

---

8. Tokitada (1127–86) was a high ranking Heike noble, brother-in-law to Taira Kiyomori, the leader of the Heike clan at its peak of power. At the battle of Dannoura he was captured by Yoshitsune. In an effort to save himself and restore his fortunes, he proposed a marriage alliance between his daughter and Yoshi-

anything. And I suppose Yoshitsune has been chirping like a love bird with Wakaba no Naishi too.[9]

BENKEI: Chirping like a love bird, huh. Are you making my lord out to be a sparrow? Well, if we're like little birds, you're like a fly, so stop buzzing your mouth around, and just get out!

NARRATOR: Benkei grabs him, throws him,
And down he goes with a thud.

INOKUMA: Oh! Ow! Ouch!

YOSHITSUNE: Musashibō! I'll have no brawling here. Leave us! Go!

NARRATOR: As he restrains the rowdy priest,
The blind before the room next door rolls up,
Revealing General of the Left Tomokata,
In his hands a curious box,
Anger in his countenance.

TOMOKATA: See here, Yoshitsune, show some respect and hear what I have to say. I have here the drum named "Hatsune," which has been kept within the imperial palace since the time long ago when Emperor Kammu used it to pray for rain.[10] The Emperor, hearing that for some time you have desired it, now gives it to you as a reward, and with it he sends a message. Here, examine it.

*(He hands Yoshitsune a black lacquered box tied with a thick red cord.)*

---

tsune. This drew a strenuous objection from Yoritomo, at whose command Yoshitsune had already married Kawagoe Shigeyori's daughter, Kyō no Kimi. Tokitada was exiled to the remote island of Noto in the Sea of Japan. See McCullough, *Yoshitsune*, 22; Satō Hirosuke and Hirata Kōji, eds., *Sekai jimmei jiten: Nihon hen*, 388. In the play, however, the marital connection between Yoshitsune and Kawagoe has not yet been revealed.

9. Tsurumi (p. 176, n. 85) notes that the verb used here (*chie chu kuu*), which sounds onomatopoetically like the chirping of a bird, also means to have illicit sexual relations.

10. Emperor Kammu, who established Japan's capital at the city known today as Kyoto, reigned from 781 to 806. He is said to have prayed successfully for rain in 788 after a long period of drought. The event is recorded in the *Shoku Nihongi* (comp. 797). See Yūda, *Bunraku jōruri shū*, 386, n. 60; Tsurumi, *Takeda Izumo shū*, 182, n. 89.

NARRATOR: Yoshitsune takes it, bowing low.
YOSHITSUNE: For one so insignificant as myself, this is more than I deserve. I am most grateful to receive for my successes in battle this rain-summoning drum.
NARRATOR: Reverently, he lifts the box to his head.
YOSHITSUNE: What is the imperial command that comes as a message, I wonder. Let me see. *(He opens the box and looks inside.)*
NARRATOR: He removes the lid from the box,
But inside is the drum alone.
TOMOKATA: Ah, as you see, Yoshitsune, that is all. In other words, the drum itself is the Emperor's message. All things have in them the two forces of Yin and Yang.[11] The leather skins on each end of this drum symbolize elder and young brother. His Majesty likens this drum to brothers who suckled at the same breast—the back drum head stands for Yoshitsune and the front one stands for Yoritomo. His message is that you strike the drum.
NARRATOR: Yoshitsune responds promptly.
YOSHITSUNE: I see. If this drum is the Emperor's message, then is it his command that Yoritomo and Yoshitsune should be on good terms and work together harmoniously as protectors of the imperial palace?
TOMOKATA: No, that is not his meaning. His Majesty the retired Emperor believes that Yoshitsune is outstanding in his imperial devotion, and he feels that Yoritomo, who is hounding Yoshitsune like a criminal, is hostile to His Majesty. The message is that you are to strike at your brother Yoritomo and chastise him.
NARRATOR: Such is the scheme that bends all reason
And seeks to pit brothers against each other.
Yoshitsune faces a dilemma, eyes downcast.

11. Yin and Yang, a Chinese philosophical system of great antiquity, posits that all things partake of a balanced and complementary duality. Yin is characterized by such elements as the female sex, earth, moon, and water, while Yang includes such elements as the male sex, sun, and fire.

## Scene 1: The Imperial Palace

YOSHITSUNE: This is unlike His Majesty. I haven't the least intention of attacking my brother, even if it means going against the Emperor's wishes. If Yoritomo is guilty of any offense, I too should be punished. That is how a younger brother should act. If I do not accept this Hatsune drum, I need not accede to the imperial wish.

NARRATOR: He hands back the drum,
But Tomokata's face
Wears a look of triumph.

TOMOKATA: The Emperor's words are absolute; they cannot be withdrawn. Go against this command, Yoshitsune, and you become an enemy of the court. Do you understand?

NARRATOR: Though recognizing this intrigue
As one that twists together
Injustice and brutality,
Yoshitsune is fearful how to respond
To such a royal bidding,
And can only answer briefly, "Yes."
Impatient, Musashibō speaks up.

BENKEI: Look here, Lord General of the Left, or whoever you are, a ruler is the mirror of his country. If he's made to say things that are unjust, then all within his realm will do the same. Understand? If there's injustice, why, as one of the nobles of the court, don't you advise the Emperor of this injustice? You think you can overcome with words a general who wouldn't flinch before a menacing army. I've had enough! Now, take back what you said. Apologize!

NARRATOR: He is defiant in his anger.
Yoshitsune glares at him.

YOSHITSUNE: Shut up, Benkei! I have already told you that it is abominable insolence to level such abuse at a ranking officer of the court. Get out of here! You are not to come into my presence any more!

NARRATOR: Yoshitsune is outraged,
But there is nothing Benkei can do.
Helpless, he bows in apology. *(Benkei exits SR.)*

> The disagreeable Inokuma
> Chuckles to himself in glee,
> But Yoshitsune ignores him
> And turns to Tomokata.

YOSHITSUNE: This drum—once the object of my desire, but now my enemy—if I refuse it, I am in opposition to His Majesty. If I accept it, I become my brother's foe. *(Pauses in thought.)* Ah, I have an idea whereby I may offend neither party. The Emperor wishes me to strike the drum. If I accept the drum but never strike it, I will not be in the wrong. I shall accept it.[12]

NARRATOR: He takes the drum by its cords,
> And knowing all too well
> Tomokata's evil stratagem, he leaves.
> Here is a man who will be honored
> By generations yet to come
> As a worthy general indeed—
> Steadfast in his loyalty
> And stately in his stature.
> In the long imperial reign,
> His presence will be like
> A thousand cherry trees
> Bursting all together into bloom.[13]

---

12. Such is the text at this point, despite the muddiness of Yoshitsune's logic.
13. This line is the source for the play's main title.

SCENE 2

THE HERMITAGE AT
NORTH SAGA VILLAGE

*(A simple thatch-roofed cottage extends from SL
approximately two-thirds of the way across the stage
raised about two feet off the ground on supports. At
SR is an entryway, outside which stands a rustic
latticed gate. One room of the cottage is open toward
the audience. At far SL is another smaller room
enclosed in shōji panels. The back of the open room
consists of a set of four sliding doors decorated with
an ink painting of lotus leaves and blossoms rising
from a pond. Next to these panels is a Buddhist
altar set into the wall and situated above a cupboard with sliding doors of brown wood. The exposed
post and lintel construction is light brown; the interior of the room is colored a dull gray. In the yard
at SR, just outside the lattice gate, stands a low
plum tree bearing white blossoms. At far SR is a
tall pine. The near background shows dun colored
rice paddies with pathways on the dikes between*

them. *At the foot of a brownish mountain rising in the distant background are groves of evergreen trees. As the curtain is drawn open, young Rokudai is seated at SL in the open room.*)

NARRATOR: Once there was a time
   When amid the damask hangings
   In the regal chambers of the Empress
   She blossomed like a flower,
   Waited on by others.[1]
   But since the Heike fled the Capital,
   Koremori's wife, Wakaba no Naishi,
   And her son, the young Lord Rokudai,
   Have both dwelled in secret
   At a simple hermitage
   Concealed in North Saga,
   In the deep recesses of Mount Arashi.[2]
   Religious disciplines for the Buddha
   And bringing water from the valley stream—
   These are unaccustomed tasks for Naishi.
   Now she and the nun in charge
   Return to the rustic cottage,
   Bearing a pail of water
   On a pole they carry on their shoulders.

   1. An allusion to a poem by the Chinese poet Po Chu-i (772–846), possibly written when Po was living in a cottage in the vicinity of the Lu Shan mountains. The lines contain the term *Lan sheng,* which has two meanings: a kind of secretariat office in the government, and the chambers of an empress. While the latter meaning seems intended in the play, Po more likely was referring to the governmental office. The original lines are:

   When flowers bloomed around the secretariat,
   I dwelled beneath the damask hangings.
   Now I am in a hut of grass
   On a rainy night in the Lu Shan peaks.

See Arthur Waley, *The Life and Times of Po Chu-i,* 120; Tsurumi, *Takeda Izumo shū,* 183–84, n. 1.

   2. A continued allusion to the poem by Po Chu-i noted above. The text says *Lu Shan,* used as a metaphor for the remote North Saga village located in the hilly northwestern outskirts of Kyoto in the vicinity of Mount Arashi. See Tsurumi, *Takeda Izumo shū,* 184, n. 3.

## Scene 2: The Hermitage at North Saga Village

*(Naishi and the nun enter from SR, each carrying on her shoulder one end of a bamboo pole, from the middle of which hangs a wooden water pail, flowers on its lid. They enter the cottage.)*

NUN: Oh, madam, I worry about you and feel so sorry for you helping me every day carrying water on this pole. There, there, your shoulder must be sore. Surely you never dreamed you'd be performing the tasks of the common folk. How pitiful the times are for you. Oh look, young Rokudai has heard us and is smiling. How nicely he's watched over the house while we've been gone.

NARRATOR: How warmly she treats her guests,
But Naishi is low in spirits.

NAISHI: As you know, my husband Koremori and all the Heike clan escorted Emperor Antoku when he fled the Capital. Since then you've taken care of both of us for such a long time in this hermitage. That's because we've known each other since long ago when you served in our household. I've heard so many rumors—that Koremori drowned in the battles of the western seas, that he's still alive somewhere. I've taken the day he left the Capital as the day to observe his passing. Since today is the one to commemorate especially the death of my father-in-law Shigemori,[3] I've burned some incense and picked some flowers, and I've scooped up water with my own hands to offer with my prayers. And this is the very month that his soul will return to us. If we were to conduct a memorial service as we did in the past, there would at least be a mass said to the Buddha.

NARRATOR: Narrow now the confines of her life,
Slender as the bolts of Kefu cloth.[4]
She sheds her humble short-sleeved cloak—
White as the rape flower's bloom—
Its collar double folded.

---

3. Koremori's father was Taira Shigemori (1138–79), the oldest son of Taira clan leader Kiyomori.

4. Bolts of cloth made in the village of Kefu in the northernmost province of Mutsu (now largely Aomori prefecture) were narrower than most.

And now she attires herself
In the courtly robes that once she wore:
Dyed pale pink like the plum, and—
As though numbered by the tribulations
Now she's come to know—
A full twelve layers deep.
Back flow the memories, as over these
She dons a crimson trouser-skirt.
See there: there once again is she,
Dressed in stately service at the court,
Garbed so gaily in her silks.
From a little lacquered box,
Dusted over in flakes of gold,
She takes a portrait of Shigemori,
Father of her husband,
And in the altar's alcove
Gracefully she puts it,
Joins her hands in prayer
And intones the dead one's Buddha name.

*(During the narration, Naishi changes from her nondescript gown to the bright brocaded robes she wore at court. Rokudai too has changed to similarly colorful attire. Both kneel and bow before the Buddhist altar.)*

NAISHI: Komatsu no Daifu Jōren Daikoji,[5] may you attain the bliss of Buddhahood. See, Rokudai, *(showing him the portrait)* it is your grandfather Shigemori. You are still young, but you are a direct descendant of the leader of the Heike clan. Bring your hands together and pray. This portrait here, why it looks just like your father Koremori. Ah, truly if Shigemori were still alive, the Heike would surely not have been swept away. *(Speaking to the portrait:)* Oh, it is good that you are not here to see the misery your grandson Rokudai must endure.

NARRATOR: Looking at the portrait, she speaks
As though Shigemori were there indeed,

---

5. The formal posthumous religious name given to Taira Shigemori.

## Scene 2: The Hermitage at North Saga Village

And to him she pours out her tale of woe,
Then crumples to the floor in tears.
Just then, footsteps sound out front.
Quickly appraising the situation,
The nun brings out a folding screen
And sets it up to hide her guests.
A moment later the door is pulled open,
And straightaway a man comes in.

(*A man enters at SR, pauses at the gate, then goes to the entry of the house.*)

MAN: See here, you've got to come and bring your official seal to the village headman.

NUN: I don't understand what you mean. I'm just a nun. I haven't needed my seal till now except for the religious inspections once a year. What's more, you're not the runner who comes to collect the taxes each month. What is going on? Speak up.

MAN: Well, it's probably got nothing to do with you, but there are people in Saga who pretend to be worshipping the Buddha but who have with them pretty women with long hair to lure in passersby. Once they served in the palace, or in some nunnery. Now they're plying their trade as prostitutes, going by such names as Taikai and Shōkai,[6] and selling their favors by the hour behind a screen. They burn incense before the Buddha, but they practice their professions in secret. Women of doubtful background, y'know—like those dancers Giō, Ginyo, and Hotoke[7]—who become nuns and are around here in Saga. The headman says that they're making the place positively indecent, so we're checking up on everyone. There aren't any of those slatterns here, are there?

---

6. *Great Sea* (*Taikai*) and *Little Sea* (*Shōkai*), names reminiscent of those used by courtesans in the pleasure quarters of eighteenth century Japan.

7. Giō and her younger sister Ginyo were famous dancers. Giō became a beloved concubine of the Taira leader Kiyomori, only to be abruptly replaced in his affections by a dancer named Hotoke; and Hotoke herself was eventually abandoned by Kiyomori. All three later became nuns. Their melancholy story is told in the *Heike monogatari*. See *The Tale of the Heike*, 30–39.

*(As he speaks, he looks furtively about the room.)*
NUN: Oh, *that's* what you're after, is it? Nothing can be hidden from the Lord Buddha. How could there be people like that here? Go away. I'm being defiled just listening to you.
MAN: All right, I'm going. Quickly now, bring in your seal.
NARRATOR: He looks around the house, then leaves.
Feeling ill at ease, the mistress nun
Pushes the folding screen aside.
NUN *(to Naishi)*: Did you hear what just went on? I didn't have any idea what he was talking about. And he certainly did give me a creepy feeling, the way he looked about the house so carefully. Uh-oh, that awful man has gone and taken one of your sandals. He was just a common sneak thief! Just took it when I wasn't looking!
NARRATOR: Naishi's eyes swim with tears.
NAISHI: Hiding from the world like this, I can't help worrying about everything. What a wretched pair we are, a mother and her child.
NARRATOR: Within the house, a cloud of despair,
But from outside there comes
The cheery springlike voice
Of a seller of broad hats of sedge.
His load swinging on his shoulder,
He peeps in from the gate.
*(A hat seller comes in from SR. He carries a balance pole with large baskets on each end. Inside, the two women start in fright.)*
HAT SELLER: Would you care for a sedge hat?
NUN: Not in the least. Why would the house of a nun need a sedge hat? You look a bit suspicious to me.
NARRATOR: To her scolding he responds.
HAT SELLER: You don't have to worry. See, it's me.
NARRATOR: He removes his hat and enters,
And they see he's Kokingo Takesato.[8]

---

8. Kokingo is apparently modeled on a warrior named Takesato, a minor figure in *The Tale of the Heike*. He was a retainer to Taira Koremori, accompanied him to Mount Kōya where Koremori took the tonsure, and later witnessed

## Scene 2: The Hermitage at North Saga Village

Lady Naishi leaps up.

NAISHI: Oh, I had heard nothing from you, and just the other day I was worrying what had become of you. Now, you're here!

NARRATOR: Kokingo bows low.

KOKINGO: First of all, my lady, I am glad to find you in good health. And the young master—what a happy face I see here. I am delighted. Since this month our late Lord Shigemori's soul will return to us, and today is the day for a memorial ceremony, I see you have put on your formal dress and are offering prayers.

NARRATOR: He faces toward the altar
And joins his hands in prayer.

KOKINGO: Because our Lord Shigemori was not with us, not only the whole Heike clan but we too have fallen on much hardship.

NARRATOR: For a moment he is overcome by tears.

KOKINGO: For myself, I hit upon the idea of selling these woven hats as a livelihood. Just think how you might feel if, like this young and inexperienced Kokingo here, you turned your hand to such an unfamiliar trade. But, there, I must tell you right away about the fate of our master, Lord Koremori. According to reliable report, he is still alive and is on Mount Kōya.[9] In any case, my plan is to escort my young Lord Rokudai to Mount Kōya and reunite him with his father. I want to see my lord again at least once. That is why I have come, to prepare us for the journey.

NARRATOR: Listening to him, Naishi feels
As though she were having a dream.

NAISHI: What's this? My husband has survived and is on Mount

---

Koremori's death by drowning in the sea in the third month of 1184. See *The Tale of the Heike*, 341, 346, 350–51.

9. A mountain in the northeastern portion of modern Wakayama prefecture (formerly part of ancient Kii province), made famous by the extensive temple complex there founded in the ninth century by the noted priest Kūkai (canonized as Kōbō Daishi).

Kōya? Oh, how happy, how thankful I am! Oh, don't say you'll take only Rokudai. I know that women aren't permitted on Mount Kōya, but please, Kokingo, accompany us both to the foot of the mountain.

NARRATOR: She is lost in joyous tears.

NUN: Oh, you have good reason to be happy. I would like to go with you, but an aged nun would just get in the way. Therefore, go quickly while it is still early in the day.

KOKINGO: Yes, you know what they say, "For every inch of good in this world there's a foot of evil," so before it catches up with us, both of you make haste and get ready to go. My specialty is these hats for travel, so we won't have to get any of those. Quickly, get your things together.

NARRATOR: As they prepare to leave,
From out front are heard
The fall of footsteps, sounds of people.
As she has done before,
The quick-witted nun
Pushes Lady Naishi and her child
Into the cupboard under the altar.
Hardly has she done so, when
Her brushwood gate is kicked aside,
And in a flurry Tomokata's man,
Inokuma Dainoshin,
Crowds in with his retinue.

*(Inokuma and his men storm into the house from SR.)*

INOKUMA: We have reports that Koremori's wife Wakaba no Naishi and his son Rokudai are both hiding in this hermitage, and we've come to arrest them. Tell us where you've concealed them!

NARRATOR: Realizing they've found out her secret,
The old nun gives a start
But feigns she does not know.

NUN: Oh my, more troublesome questions. I have nothing to do with Koremori's wife and no reason to hide her.

NARRATOR: Kokingo Takesato speaks up from nearby.

## Scene 2: The Hermitage at North Saga Village

KOKINGO: Surely you have the wrong hermitage. Please be good enough to conduct your inquiry elsewhere.

INOKUMA: I don't need any advice from an impertinent whippersnapper like you. And just who are you, anyway?

KOKINGO: Oh, I'm just a seller of sedge hats.

INOKUMA: Look here, if you're a tradesman, get out of here, and be quick about it.

NARRATOR: From his follower he takes
A sandal with a thong of silk.

INOKUMA: See, just so you wouldn't deny it, I had one of my men come here posing as a local runner, and he took this sandal as proof. An old bat of a nun like you would hardly be wearing a sandal with a red thong. Now, are you going to dispute this? *(To his followers:)* Take her inside and make her confess.

NARRATOR: A man takes her by the arm
And twists it upwards.

INOKUMA: All right, men. Let's torture the truth out of her.

NARRATOR: Roughly they march her off
Into the inner room.

*(Inokuma and his men push the nun off into the shōji room at SL. Kokingo is left on stage alone.)*

Kokingo frets; what can he do?
Through a crack between the doors
He peers into the inner room.
Then he has his lady and her son come out.
Good luck: he'll put them in his baskets.
He takes the narrow cord that binds his pack,
Flings it away, and puts the pair inside.
Into his cloth pack rolled for travel
He puts the portrait of Shigemori,
Pushes all down inside his pack,
And presses down again.
Just as he gets all in order,
Inokuma emerges from the room
Where the nun lies trussed in ropes.

INOKUMA: It's as I guessed, she's probably let them escape. You know anything about this, hat seller?
KOKINGO: Oh, indeed I do. Why, it must be that noble-looking woman with a child you're after. They ran off just now by the path at the back of the house.
NARRATOR: Inokuma's eyes flash as he listens.
INOKUMA: Oh! That must be them! A woman can go just so fast. Let's dash off and nab them. Two of you stay here, and don't let that nun inside get away.
NARRATOR: And off they run in pursuit.
"That did it!" thinks Kokingo.
Heart above the clouds in glee,
He lifts the load to his shoulder.
As he starts to go, the two men come up,
Each grabbing an end of his pole,
Refusing to let him move.
KOKINGO: Hey, what's going on?
FOLLOWER #1: What's going on? You look suspicious, that's what. There's a woman's garment sticking out of the bottom of your pack here.
KOKINGO: Oh, that's just part of a custom-made hat.
FOLLOWER #2: Come on, let's have the truth. Don't play innocent with us! That must be Lady Naishi and her child. Open this thing up so we can inspect it.
NARRATOR: The two begin to grapple with Kokingo,
But he grabs them by the shoulder
And pulls them away.
KOKINGO: Nothing doing, you wretches.
NARRATOR: In a flash they've drawn their swords
And started to slash away.
Kokingo dodges the attack
And brandishes his shoulder pole.
Striking where it hurts them most,
Left and right he lays them low.
So fiercely does he beat the pair,
Blood rushes from their noses, eyes.

## Scene 2: The Hermitage at North Saga Village

They writhe about in pain, then die.
Then, before the other foes return,
Kokingo shoulders his burden.
"Sedge hats, sedge hats,
Hats of woven rush," he calls out,
As through the hostile net they slip away.
*(Kokingo exits with his burden downstage SR.)*

SCENE 3

# THE HORIKAWA MANSION

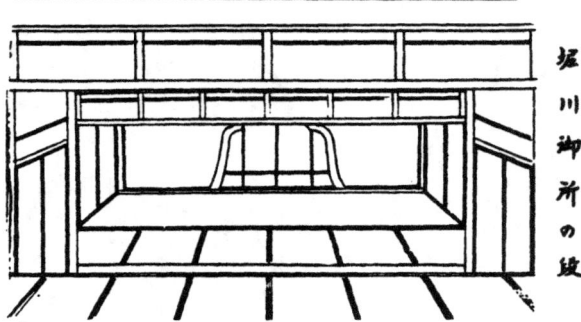

*(The scene is a large room, the illusion of spaciousness enhanced by two rows of flats across the forestage representing tatami mats. Upstage center is a series of six sliding panels decorated with navy blue crests on a silver ground. On either side of the sliding panels, the wall is painted with a representation of amorphous clouds in gold and white. SL of the panels a halberd hangs from the lintel, its blade inside a red brocade cover. As the scene opens, Shizuka is at center dancing for Yoshitsune, who is seated upstage center. Suruga sits at SL, Kamei at SR.)*

NARRATOR:

> The blossoms change their forms,
> Becoming lord and seven vassals
> Mounted on their steeds.
> The horses point the way
> To Tamuro Hill where, like flowers

### Scene 3: The Horikawa Mansion

That in their season bloom a second time,
Fortune smiles with favor once again.
So it was with Yoriyoshi
As he marched upon the far northeast.[1]
So too our master Yoshitsune
Has won a victory at Yashima,
Bringing peace to the country.
*(The foregoing is sung to Shizuka's dance.)*
Spontaneously the shouts ring out
In gathering applause,
Rising like a din of war cries
In praise of Shizuka's dance.
Such is the festive mansion in the Capital
At Horikawa and Nijō avenues,
Where the wife of Kurō Yoshitsune
Provides merry entertainment.
The middle chambers are for Kyō no Kimi,
The new apartments those of Yoshitsune.
Around him on one side, the ladies of his house,
While lined up on the other side
Are Suruga no Jirō, and next to him
The valorous Kamei no Rokurō,[2]
Then come the lesser retainers.
Though ignorant of dancing,
They prove a lively company,

---

1. Minamoto no Yoriyoshi (999–1075) was Yoshitsune's ancestor and a major figure in establishing Genji power in Japan's northeastern provinces. Preparing to attack the Abe clan in 1066, Yoriyoshi held a war council at Tamuro hill in what is today Miyagi prefecture. A dove flew over the camp and Yoriyoshi took this as a lucky omen. Afterward, his campaign, which had been plagued by losses, went on to victory. See Tsurumi, *Takeda Izumo shū*, 189, n. 2.

2. Kamei was one of Yoshitsune's "Four Guardian Kings," so called in imitation of the four heavenly protectors of Buddhism. He served Yoshitsune to the end, and was killed fighting to protect him. Suruga no Jirō also served Yoshitsune, but he was captured after Yoshitsune's death by Yoritomo's forces. His ultimate fate is not known.

>   Shouting out their compliments—
>   Praise to Shizuka, tributes to their lord.
>   From chamber to chamber
>   Move ladies bearing messages.
>   Another comes from Kamei,
>   Declaring all to be a fine diversion,
>   A rare and boundless joy.
>   The formalities concluded
>   Before Yoshitsune and his wife,
>   Shizuka comes from a dressing room,
>   Now changed to her courtly robes.
>   She steps out beneath the broad eaves,
>   Bows to Suruga and Kamei,
>   And turns to Kyō no Kimi.

SHIZUKA: As you wished, I have performed a dance for you, though most awkwardly I am afraid.

KYŌ NO KIMI: By no means. This is the first time I have seen you dance, and I found it quite pleasant. I have not been feeling well of late, even having treatment by a physician the other day. But today my lord urged me to see your dancing, and it has been surprisingly refreshing. I must thank you.

NARRATOR: Subdued by the lavish praise,
>   Shizuka bows low,
>   Then speaks most formally.

SHIZUKA: If you will permit me to presume on your good nature, my lady, there is a request I should like to make. Would you be so kind as to hear it?

KYŌ NO KIMI: You need hardly ask that; don't stand on ceremony so. Come closer and tell me what it is.

NARRATOR: The response makes Shizuka
>   Feel but more in awe.

SHIZUKA: Well, it is just this. It's such a sad thing, but I understand that Lord Musashibō Benkei made some sort of terrible blunder. He came to me in private and simply wept like a baby, asking me to do something for him. He has taken it all so seriously, and he's so . . . so sensitive, it was just too pitiful to watch him. He asked me to use my influence to restore him in our Lord Yoshitsune's good graces. This is what I beg most earnestly of you.

NARRATOR: Kyō no Kimi is amused,
And even Yoshitsune smiles.
Suruga wears a sour face.

SURUGA: That's really stupid, going to a woman for help. Rokurō, did you hear that? A rowdy like Musashibō Benkei goes weeping to one of our lord's ladies to get her to apologize for him. But, you know, he may have done just that. After the battle was over Ise and Kataoka, Kumai and Washinoō[3]—all of them Benkei's friends—went on leave back to their home provinces. And Satō Tadanobu[4] went off to Dewa in the far north because his mother was sick. You and I won't listen to him, and Benkei doesn't know whom to appeal to, so he ran off to get Shizuka to apologize for him. We should tease him a little bit more. Tell him that full head of hair of his makes him look like a clown.[5] That should make it more fun.

NARRATOR: This private chat is even more diverting,
And Kyō no Kimi stifles her amusement.

KYŌ NO KIMI *(to Yoshitsune)*: What sort of blunder did he make? This is a rather pathetic, if amusing, intercession.

YOSHITSUNE: He was unruly when he came to the imperial palace the other day. He was insulting to the Minister of the Left, Lord Tomokata, and he gave a thrashing to one of his retainers. I scolded him right there on the spot and told him he was not to appear in my presence anymore. Give that man

---

3. Ise no Saburō Yoshimori, Kataoka no Hachirō Tameharu, Kumai no Tarō Tadamoto, and Washinoō no Saburō Yoshihisa, respectively. All were Yoshitsune's retainers.

4. His full name is Satō no Shirōbyōe Tadanobu (the Shirōbyōe is pronounced Shirōbei throughout the play). Tadanobu and his brother Tsuginobu (also read Tsugunobu) personify the quintessence of loyalty to Yoshitsune. Tadanobu figures prominently in this play, particularly in the adventures later in the mountainous region of Yoshino.

5. Those in Buddhist orders normally shaved their heads, but Benkei has not.

an inch and he'll take a mile.⁶ Neither a noble nor a warrior would put up with him. I don't know what to do with him, he's such an uncouth bonze. All right, we'll tease him a bit.

NARRATOR: Seizing on his master's words,
Suruga no Jirō speaks up.

SURUGA: To begin with, those seven tools⁷ he has are a big nuisance. It's really shameful to us to hear people saying that the Genji have with them a priest who's a carpenter. You should tell him firmly to stop carrying those things around.

NARRATOR: Next to speak is Kamei no Rokurō.

KAMEI: No, those seven tools would still be useful in constructing a building. The troublesome item is that huge lance of his. The handle is four feet long, and the blade is four feet more. When he starts swinging all eight feet of that around, people find it really dangerous to be near him. He's just no use to us in an age of peace. He ought to be locked up for the time being.

NARRATOR: Varied are the opinions,
But Kyō no Kimi has pity.

KYŌ NO KIMI: If he hears you talk about him like this, he's going to get angry again. Both Shizuka and I apologize for him.

NARRATOR: At this intercession, Yoshitsune responds.

YOSHITSUNE: He is incorrigible. Be sure you remonstrate with him and repeat to him that he is to curb his rowdy behavior. And Shizuka, you tell him the same thing.

NARRATOR: Then he leaves his seat,
And with Suruga and Kamei
He enters the inner room.

*(They exit through the center doorway.)*

---

6. The text reads, "Release the reins on him and he's a man-eating horse."

7. Though there are other catalogs of the seven main weapons of a warrior, those associated in legend with Benkei are an odd assortment: a rake, a sickle, an iron staff, a mallet, a saw, a battle ax, and a *sasumata*—a long pole with a U-shaped blade at the end, used for apprehending criminals. Benkei is often depicted carrying this gallimaufry on his back, but in this play and in many other works he usually wields a sword or a long halberd.

### Scene 3: The Horikawa Mansion

Shizuka is elated.
SHIZUKA *(to her maid)*: Quickly now, summon Musashibō.
NARRATOR: She sends the maid running to fetch him.
SHIZUKA: My thanks to your ladyship for your good offices.
KYŌ NO KIMI: Oh no, it was all because of your request.
NARRATOR: They bow to one another,
 Each loyal and loving to her lord,
 Neither jealous of the other's place.
 As the bald-pated Musashibō[8]
 Comes crawling in, *(from the downstage SR curtain)*
 The maids cry out in fright
 As they see his seven-foot frame,
 The great sword over four feet long,
 Dragging along beside him.
 The maids all chatter together.
MAID #1: He's still an awfully stubborn priest. Oh look at him! He's so scared he's shrinking back in the corner.
BENKEI: Come on, don't make it so hard on me. You're all mean, taking unfair advantage. You'll get your retribution.
NARRATOR: He looks about the room.
MAID #2: Ooooh, there he goes again, glaring at us.
BENKEI: I'm not, I'm just squinting.
NARRATOR: He screws his face into a scowl
 And shrinks himself down small.
 Shizuka takes his hand
 And leads him to her ladyship.
SHIZUKA *(to Kyō no Kimi):* I entreat your ladyship to pardon him.
NARRATOR: Half smiling in her intercession,
 Kyō no Kimi is most suave.
KYŌ NO KIMI: A lord is a ship, his followers are the sea. If the sea billows up, it may itself capsize the ship.[9] It is no vindi-

---

8. So goes the text, but in performance Benkei has a great bushy head of black hair, tied with a thick rolled cloth (*oachimaki*) in bold red and white candy cane stripes.

9. An allusion to a passage from the Chinese classic *Hsun Tzu:* 'The ruler is

cation to say that one's actions were in the line of duty. My lord says to repeat to you that you must give up your uncivil ways and behave in a more gentle manner.

NARRATOR: She speaks to him as one would to a child.
Benkei can only wring his hands
And abjectly apologize,
"Yes, oh yes, I will."
But just at this instant,
Shinohara Tōnai, a tower lookout,
Hurriedly rushes in *(from SL)*.

TŌNAI: Just now as I was making a tour of inspection around Sakamoto in Otsu,[10] I saw some warriors from Kamakura sneaking into the Capital, and among the party were Tosabō Shōzon and Unno no Tarō Yukinaga.[11] They were pretending to be on a pilgrimage to the Kumano Shrine, but the rumor is that they are actually going to attack my Lord Yoshitsune. More particularly, the senior councillor to Yoritomo, Kawagoe Tarō Shigeyori,[12] has arrived, saying that he wishes to speak directly with my lord. He is presently in the antechamber. What should I tell him?

KYŌ NO KIMI: I don't understand what's going on here. This Kawagoe Tarō is one with whom I have . . . a certain connection. I wonder if he may have come to tell us about the

---

the boat and the common people are the water. It is the water that bears the boat up, and the water that capsizes it." See Burton Watson, tr., *Basic Writings of Mo Tzu, Hsun Tzu, and Han Fei Tzu*, 37 (pages numbered consecutively only in sections on each philosopher).

10. In modern Shiga prefecture, near Lake Biwa north of Kyoto.

11. Called Tosabō Shōzon in the play, his real name was Tosabō Shōshun (died 1185). A retainer of Yoritomo, he was ordered to attack Yoshitsune at the Horikawa mansion but was driven off and eventually killed by Benkei. See McCullough, *Yoshitsune*, 25–26, 139ff, 153–54. Unno may be modelled on figures in the *Heike monogatari* or the *Genpei seisuiki*. See Tsurumi, *Takeda Izumo shū*, 192, n. 35.

12. Kawagoe (died 1185) was an ally of Yoritomo, distinguishing himself in the battles against the Heike. When Yoshitsune lost favor with Yoritomo and was branded a rebel, Kawagoe also fell from grace because his daughter was Yoshitsune's wife.

planned attack of Tosabō and Unno. In any case, I know him. You may conduct him here. I will report this to his lordship. Musashi, you will go to him with me.

NARRATOR: She stands to leave . . .

BENKEI: An attacking party! Great! We're ready for them. This is wonderful! So it's Tosabō and Unno. Why, I'll grab them up in one fist and swallow them down in a gulp! I'll go out there and rip off their heads!!

*(He grabs his sword and is set to dash out.)*

NARRATOR: Shizuka stops his headlong rush.

SHIZUKA: No, that would be terrible, going out there without waiting to hear your master's wishes. You disgusting bonze!

NARRATOR: Forcibly she pulls him back.

They hurry to the inner room

Where Yoshitsune waits.

*(All exit through the center doorway.)*

# SCENE 4
## KAWAGOE TARŌ
## COMES AS ENVOY

*(The set remains as in the previous scene. The only change is that of narrator and his samisen accompanist, after the general exit at the end of the previous scene.)*

NARRATOR: Entering but a moment later:
　　Kawagoe Tarō Shigeyori,
　　Officer in the council
　　Of the Lord of Kamakura.
　　Distinguished, he is a bracing presence,
　　In his prime at fifty years of age,
　　Dressed in a flowing robe arrayed with
　　　　crests,
　　A pinched court hat upon his head.
　　As he enters from the heavy eaves.
*(Kawagoe enters slowly from SR, onto the forestage, which represents the courtyard.)*

### Scene 4: Kawagoe Tarō Comes as Envoy

NARRATOR: Lord Kurō Hōgan Yoshitsune,
  Now changed to formal robes,
  Slowly comes to meet his guest.
*(Yoshitsune enters the room from upstage center. Kawagoe ascends the center steps into the room, and the two men seat themselves formally, Yoshitsune slightly to SL of center, Kawagoe to SR.)*
YOSHITSUNE: Well, Shigeyori, this is a rare treat. I trust that my brother Yoritomo is, as ever, in good health, and that his retainers too are well.
NARRATOR: He bows deeply in respect.
KAWAGOE: May I first say that I am extremely pleased to find you robust and hearty. His lordship the General of the Right[1] is quite sound and secure with the various barons in daily attendance. Please be assured on that account.
YOSHITSUNE: I imagine that you have come in the same capacity as your cohorts Unno and Tosabō. But, what other business might you have?
KAWAGOE: Well, regarding that, there are three matters that have raised some questions, and I am to query you about each one. Depending on your response, my duty may be the same as that of Unno and Tosabō. Please forgive me if I overstate matters, but I would appreciate your answers in detail.
YOSHITSUNE: Ho hoo, most interesting. Yoshitsune is under suspicion, and his brother Yoritomo—through you as his representative—asks pardon for any exaggeration. Very well, go ahead and make your inquiries, and I will offer you my explanation. Feel perfectly free.
NARRATOR: Again he bows respectfully.
KAWAGOE *(bowing in return)*: You are too generous with me. Since we are about it, let me exchange seats with you.[2]

---

  1. Yoritomo, who held this office.
  2. Yoshitsune, as master in his own house and superior to Kawagoe, occupies the seat of honor. However, since Kawagoe represents Yoritomo, Yoshitsune's superior, formality dictates that the seat of honor be his. Such considerations

NARRATOR: He rises, and Yoshitsune moves
   To the lower seat, *(at SR)*
   As Kawagoe is ushered
   To the seat of honor. *(at SL)*
   Their positions thus arranged,
   Kawagoe begins his inquiry.
KAWAGOE: Tell me, Yoshitsune, though you distinguished yourself on the battlefield by defeating our enemy the Heike, are you resentful of the fact that you were turned away at Koshigoe and were refused an audience with Yoritomo? Or do you harbor no such bitterness?
NARRATOR: Yoshitsune arranges the sleeves of his robe.
YOSHITSUNE: I hold in esteem my respected elder brother's sense of propriety, and so I bear no resentment toward our continuing relationship.
KAWAGOE: Ah, but your words do not ring quite true. Among the Heike heads you sent to Kamakura, those of the New Middle Councillor Taira Tomomori, General of the Third Court Rank Taira Koremori, and Taira Noritsune, Lord of Noto, were false. Thus my second question to you: why would one who holds in esteem his respected elder brother's sense of propriety hand over misrepresented heads? What is your answer to this, a matter that has incurred Yoritomo's anger?
YOSHITSUNE: The answer to that is quite simple. One of the secrets of military strategy is to take something that is real and make it seem otherwise. I merely did the reverse and took false heads and made them appear to be those of others. The Heike were in their glory for twenty-four years. Now, even though they have been crushed, their old vassals and lesser followers are scattered throughout the country, just waiting for the time when the red banner of the Heike will

---

were important in a society where the observance of proper decorum was accorded great significance. Note Benkei's difficulties at court, due in part to his failure to observe appropriate etiquette.

again fly in the breeze. One member of the clan, the Middle General Koremori, was the son of Taira Shigemori and thus heir to the leadership of the Heike clan. And Shigemori, in particular, had won the hearts of his clansmen through his benevolence and humanity. The number of people indebted to him is countless. If Koremori survived, there is no question that remnants of the Heike would rally around him. Then there are the New Middle Councillor Tomomori and Noritsune, Lord of Noto, as cunning men as ever there were in any age. If generals of such ability put out a call for support, there are surely many who would rush to join them, and that would be a threat to the country. To spread the word that they all drowned or were killed has been a good thing. The people at large, believing that the entire Heike clan has been wiped out, have been fooled by those false heads. This was my plan for keeping the country at peace. Yet, we cannot simply disregard the fact that these men were formidable adversaries, and for that reason I pretended to give leave to my vassals Kumai, Washinoō, Ise, and Kataoka—some of my finest men—to return to their home provinces for a rest. In reality, it has been arranged for them secretly to capture these generals. Though I sit quietly here in the Capital, as you see me, my heart still suffers the worries of the battlefield. My brother Yoritomo amuses himself in the mountains of Kamakura, enjoys himself on nights of the stars and moon with all his barons in attendance, taking pleasure in the beauties of the seasons. Though we both spring from the same paternal line of the Seiwa Genji,[3] I go every morning to pay my respects at court, and in the evening I work to lay the basis for our clan's enduring rule.

---

3. Yoshitsune and Yoritomo had the same father—Yoshitomo—but different mothers. Several emperors, including Emperor Seiwa (reigned 858–76), established families bearing the clan name Genji as a means of providing for their proliferating offspring outside the expenses of the court itself. The Seiwa Genji clan became the most famous and consequential of these groups.

Perhaps someday I will rest peacefully on my pillow, but my lot right now is a miserable one.

NARRATOR: Yoshitsune is dispirited,
And while Shigeyori thinks
That what he's heard is true,
His duty is to pressure Yoshitsune.

KAWAGOE: Hmmm. Well then, if that is how you feel, are you contemplating rebellion?

NARRATOR: Hardly have the words been said
Than Yoshitsune is choked with emotion.

YOSHITSUNE: That is an odious thing to say! What would be my means, and what would be my purpose?

NARRATOR: Though his countenance has changed,
He displays no anger.

KAWAGOE: We have had an urgent report from Minister of the Left Lord Tomokata, that you sought from the Emperor a commission to overthrow Kamakura, that you accepted from him the Hatsune drum, understanding His Majesty's meaning that the back of the drum stood for Yoshitsune and the front represented Yoritomo, and that you were to strike the drum.

NARRATOR: Yoshitsune listens.

YOSHITSUNE: Then Tomokata lies. True, I had desired that drum for some time. I think it was Tomokata's plot to place upon that gift the meaning that the Emperor wanted me to rebel and to attack Kamakura. Thus, to refuse something given to me out of kindness by the Emperor would be to go against his wishes; to accept the drum was to mean that I was not demonstrating devotion to my brother Yoritomo. And to strike it was to mean that I would follow the Emperor's alleged command that I attack Kamakura. But, as you can see, it is merely an ornament that I gaze upon in the alcove. As the gods may bear me witness, I have not struck, not even touched, the drum.[4]

---

4. Yoshitsune's reasoning may be a rationalization: by merely keeping the

## Scene 4: Kawagoe Tarō Comes as Envoy

NARRATOR: Kawagoe laughs heartily and bows three times.

KAWAGOE: After such an oath as that, how could I have any doubts? Your answers to my first two questions have made matters quite clear. However, I have one more, and this may seem hard-hearted to you. Your wife, Kyō no Kimi, is the daughter of the Senior Councilor Taira Tokitada. Do you intend to form an alliance with the Heike?

YOSHITSUNE: What a ridiculous question! Yoritomo's own wife Masako is the daughter of Hōjō Tokimasa,[5] and he was on the Heike side, was he not?

KAWAGOE: Ah, but that was a marriage to form a strategic alliance with the Hōjō family when Yoritomo was at Itō in Izu Province.

YOSHITSUNE: Go on, I don't need you to tell me that. My wife, Kyō no Kimi, is originally *your* very own daughter. She was adopted and raised by Tokitada, but you are her real father. Why have you not gone so far as to tell Yoritomo *that*? Or is it that you have concealed it, thinking that a connection with Yoshitsune would be a blemish on your honor? Ah, Kawagoe, that is cowardly in the extreme.

NARRATOR: As he listens, Kawagoe abruptly stiffens.

KAWAGOE: Ah, that is unkind, Yoshitsune. To have Kurō Yoshitsune, a descendant of the Emperor Seiwa, as a son by marriage would doubtless make me a father-in-law without peer in all of Japan. Do you think that Kawagoe here, now past fifty, has such concern for his reputation? That he so

---

drum he accedes to part of the Emperor's wishes but by avoiding striking it he somehow holds in abeyance—but does not actually go against—the other part: a question of action in one instance, inaction in the other.

5. Tokimasa (1138–1215), a descendant of the Taira family, lived in Hōjō (in Izu province) when Yoritomo was exiled there by Taira Kiyomori in 1160. He was hospitable to Yoritomo, and sealed a family bond by having his daughter Masako marry Yoritomo, thus becoming an early ally of Yoritomo in the fight against the Heike. After Yoritomo's death, Tokimasa became a military adviser (*shikken*), holding the office from 1203 to 1205, in the process establishing a dynasty that continued its behind-the-scenes rule until the Hōjō family fell from power in 1333.

craves one of Yoritomo's fiefdoms? If I revealed my relationship to Kyō no Kimi, it would threaten the veracity of any explanations I might make on your behalf to Kamakura. It would show that I had a connection with you, so I have kept it to myself, kept it hidden. Though I've used all my powers of persuasion, both publicly and privately, those who would malign you to your brother have grown stronger. Even so clever and able a man as Hatakeyama Shigetada was unable to withstand the criticism about his having originally been on the Heike side.[6] As the situation now stands, do you think I could be convincing if I told people that she is my daughter? And your opinion that I am, as you put it, "cowardly in the extreme" fills me with shame. Therefore, as a memento of this visit I shall cut open this wrinkled belly of mine.

NARRATOR: Swiftly he draws his short sword.
KYŌ NO KIMI: No! Wait!
NARRATOR: Kyō no Kimi dashes in and seizes his arm.
KYŌ NO KIMI: Let me be your vindication!
NARRATOR: She wrenches away the blade,
  Thrusts it into her throat,
  And sinks to the floor.
  With a shout, Yoshitsune and Shizuka
  Rush to her, lift her in their arms,
  Calling out in a frenzy
  For medicine, for water.
  Amid their tears there is no room for words.
  Kawagoe will not look.
KAWAGOE: Ah, nobly done, daughter of Tokitada. With things as they were, my hope for harmony between Yoritomo and

---

6. Shigetada (1164–1205) was a descendant of the Taira family but sided with Yoritomo in the Genji-Heike wars. He distinguished himself in battle as a general under Yoshitsune, but he later took part in the attack against Yoshitsune, who was in hiding in the north. Yoshitsune died in that attack. Later, Shigetada became the object of Hōjō Tokimasa's machinations. Realizing Tokimasa's intentions, he refused an order to present himself in Kamakura. As a result, Tokimasa sent an army against him, and Shigetada died in the ensuing battle.

## Scene 4: Kawagoe Tarō Comes as Envoy

Yoshitsune would probably have gone unrealized. I had thought to summon you at once and kill you by my own hand, but I had meant to die with you—I wanted people to say after your death that you were a woman of constant virtue. I purposely pretended to kill myself, and you cleverly saw through this stratagem and took the sword from me. Well done, gallant girl.

NARRATOR: Though outwardly he praises her,
His heart within is filled with tears.
Yoshitsune approaches.

YOSHITSUNE *(to Kyō no Kimi)*: I feared that the issue might come to this, and so I deliberately revealed Kawagoe's relationship to you, hoping to cancel out any connection I might have with the Heike. What a meaningless death for you now. What a pity, how pointless now have been the tender vows we pledged with one another.

NARRATOR: At the sight of his welling tears,
Shizuka too begins to weep,
Her tender sympathy
Flowing out to Yoshitsune
And to Kyō no Kimi.
Lovingly, the dying girl
Gazes at her lord.

KYŌ NO KIMI: You were able to respond well to not only one but two of the questions put to you. As for the one that remains, the doubts about a marriage alliance with the Heike, the blame lies entirely with me. You have been most loving to me; remember that I have loved you. From this fleeting and indifferent world, where it is uncertain if fate will let us live to see the morrow, my parting words will be brief. Lady Shizuka, take good care of my lord, I beg you.

NARRATOR: She sobs convulsively.

KYŌ NO KIMI: Now, Lord Kawagoe, take the head of this daughter of Taira Tokitada and show it to Yoritomo. A reconciliation between the two brothers would be a fine gift for me to take to the world beyond.

NARRATOR: And with these words
   She stretches forth her head.
   So deep his feelings for her motives
   As he stands beside her,
   Kawagoe Tarō can but choke
   And swallow back
   The tears that fill his heart.
KAWAGOE: Perhaps this is not an entirely fitting example, but there is the Chinese story of Yang Kuei-fei, the empress of Hsuan Tsung, who was killed by Ko Shu-han on the plain of Ma Wei, thus sweeping away the troubles of the kingdom.[7] When there is discord between brothers, there are lamentations among the people. This honorable death will be for the sake of the country. Ah, nobly, nobly done. And now, one who to you is an utter stranger will serve as your second.[8]
NARRATOR: He slips his sword from its casing.
KYŌ NO KIMI: Ah, but to gain in my final moment the aid of an utter stranger means that there must be ties between us. As you do this service for me, might there be one word of parting?
KAWAGOE: Perhaps in a future life I will call you . . . "daughter."
KYŌ NO KIMI: Then, farewell to you.
KAWAGOE: Farewell, farewell.
NARRATOR: He strikes, and as the head rolls off,

---

7. Kawagoe is referring to a famous beauty and concubine of the sixth emperor of the T'ang dynasty, Tsuan Tsung (also called Ming Huang), who neglected his duties to be with her, thus leading to the rebellion of An Lu-shan in 755. The emperor fled to China's western province of Ssuch'uan, where on the plain of Ma Wei he was forced to witness Yang Kuei-fei's slaughter. She was not, however, killed by Ko Shu-han, one of Tsuan Tsung's generals, but by the emperor's favorite eunuch, Kao Li-shih. See Giles, *A Chinese Biographical Dictionary*, 365–66, 908–909. Kawagoe sees a parallel here: Yang Kuei-fei was killed to benefit the nation; Kyō no Kimi's death, though of a quite different order, is intended to serve Japan by aiding a reconciliation between Yoshitsune and Yoritomo.

8. Kawagoe is maintaining, for the sake of formality, the fiction that he is unrelated to Kyō no Kimi, possibly also suspecting that other ears may be listening.

### Scene 4: Kawagoe Tarō Comes as Envoy

Kawagoe slumps in despair,
Withered by his sorrow.
Both Shizuka and Yoshitsune
Are consumed in mournful tears,
Consoling him in his grief.
Then suddenly the sounds of gong
And drums assail their ears,
And there comes the rising sound of war cries.

SHIZUKA: What is this?

NARRATOR: Shizuka is filled with fright.
Her lord, too, is astonished.

YOSHITSUNE: I think those villains Unno and Tosabō have launched an attack. Kamei, Suruga!

NARRATOR: Even as their lord commands them,
Swiftly they draw their swords
And start to run out.
Kawagoe shouts to check their dash.

KAWAGOE: Wait! I had made the others hold off until I had heard your lord's explanations. That they now press their attack only shows that they are in league with those who would defame your master. Both of them are still deputies of the Lord of Kamakura. Do anything to injure them and it will be the same as declaring war on Kamakura. Can you just run them off quickly? Pretend to defend yourselves with arrows that will fly beyond them. If you don't, then you yourselves will bring on the swift ruin of Yoshitsune.

NARRATOR: Both men are quick to see
The logic of his orders.
"Quite right," the two men say
And dash off to the building's front.
Yoshitsune too sees reason
In Kawagoe's words,
But he's mindful of another man.

YOSHITSUNE: That reckless Benkei worries me. Musashi! Musashi!

NARRATOR: To his shouts a maid runs in.

MAID: Until just a moment ago Master Musashi was with us, sitting most dejectedly. But when he heard the war cries, he was elated, and he ran off in high excitement.

YOSHITSUNE: The lout! He's probably already started fighting. Shizuka, quickly go and stop him! Put on some armor; it will be dangerous with all those arrows.

NARRATOR: Acknowledging the command,
A maid brings armor out.
Then, taking the halberd from its hook,
Shizuka grips it tight beneath her arm,
And off into the fray
Dashes the woman warrior.
Thus, the tale of Shizuka's exploits
In the night raid at Horikawa
Will be told to ages yet unborn.
Now, just as Yoshitsune wonders
How the fight progresses,
Kamei and Suruga come running back.

KAMEI: My lord, we kept our men in check and had them shoot only blunt-pointed practice arrows. Then, just as we thought we had them on the run, that outrageous Musashibō came and crushed them with a battering ram. He cut the soldiers up with that huge saw of his, and the general of the attackers, Unno—well, he beat him to a pulp, head to toenails.

NARRATOR: Yoshitsune stares aghast,
And Kawagoe sighs in despair.

KAWAGOE: This is the end, he's gone and done it! If he has killed their general, then my hope for a reconciliation has vanished. What a wretched thing—my daughter's death has been to no avail. We seem to live in a world where everything is in vain.

NARRATOR: Lord Yoshitsune speaks through rueful tears.

YOSHITSUNE: Wise people of long ago did not hold grudges against others. They thought of things in terms of the way that fate worked, so they held no lasting resentment or rancor against other people. If I take advantage of Musashi's

### Scene 4: Kawagoe Tarō Comes as Envoy

insolence and flee the Capital, I will not be transgressing the Emperor's will, and it may placate Yoritomo's anger at the death of his deputy. Yet, in this light, how pitiable has been Kyō no Kimi's death. Everything is as insubstantial as a world of dreams. I have been abandoned by a fickle world. I seem to hear the tinkle of the little horse bells that betoken travel.[9] Kamei, Suruga, come.

NARRATOR: As he starts to leave,
  The despondent Kawagoe
  Stops him for a moment,
  And from the alcove takes the drum.

KAWAGOE: It would be unfortunate if, by leaving behind this precious drum that my lord has so long desired, people were to say that it was forgotten in your haste to run away. The report to you that it was the Emperor's wish that you strike the drum as a symbol of an attack on Yoritomo came from foul-mouthed slanderers I will investigate whether the Emperor in fact issued this command, and I will once again mediate between you and your brother. Here, take the drum with you as a consolation on your long journey.

NARRATOR: His heart filled with warmth,
  He hands over the drum
  To Yoshitsune's waiting hands.

YOSHITSUNE: Cut off now from warm relations with my brother, I seem to have exhausted my luck. Repair the damage for me, Kawagoe.

NARRATOR: With Suruga and Kamei at his side,
  Slowly, with a heavy heart,
  Yoshitsune leaves the hall.
  Watching Yoshitsune go, Kawagoe
  Feels his own heart laden full with woes,
  For he must now return to Kamakura.
  Such is the pathetic way of the world,

---

9. The reference is to the small bells that were given by the court to officials sent on tours of the provinces so that they might requisition horses at various way stations.

Small wonder he is so worn with care,
As behind him come the sounds
Of battle conchs and gongs
And the shouted cries of war.

*(As the narration continues, there is a scene change: as the Horikawa mansion set is pulled to the rear, a new one is lowered, depicting an area outside the wall surrounding the mansion. The wall is of tan mud with horizontal bands in white. At the center is a large wooden gate with black iron hardware and on each door a large crest of the leaves and blossoms of pampas grass.)* [10]

Meanwhile, Musashibō Benkei
Has cut down Unno no Tarō, and next
He seeks to do the same to Tosabō.
He dashes in pursuit,
Leaps on Tosabō's horse
And kicks and drives the beast
To the pebbled space before the house.

10. There is an alternate set, apparently not currently used. It is a perspective view of the courtyard outside the palace, a banded wall on SR, the outer facade of the palace on SL, both leading back in the distance to an imposing gateway topped by a large tiled roof. The gate may be flanked by tall pines. See Gidayū Nenpyō Hensan-kai, ed., *Gidayū nenpyō, Meiji-hen* (1956), 226, 400, 460 for variations.

## Scene 4: Kawagoe Tarō Comes as Envoy

Gongs and shouting shake the building.
*(Benkei enters from SR. He is astride a brown horse, Tosabō lying across the saddle in front of him.)*

BENKEI: Hey in there, I've confronted the raiders bent on harming our lord. Unno has been pulverized, and I've captured this villain Tosabō. Kamei, Suruga, where are you? Don't you want to have a look at this tidbit I've got left over from my recent entertainment?

NARRATOR: He shouts, but all is silent in the house.
Strange, he thinks, that none should answer,
And as he looks about, doughty Tosabō
Cuts away the sash around his waist,
Leaps to the ground and shouts.

TOSABŌ: Hey you men, over here!

NARRATOR: Several hundred underlings appear.
"Cut him down!" they cry,
And swarm around Benkei.
Down from atop his horse
Comes Benkei in a single bound.
He grabs their swords
As though with eagle claws,
Snatches at their heads
As would a bear or hawk,
And snaps them off, so many
That they fall like hail, like rain.
Spying his chance, Tosabō
Grabs Benkei around the waist.

BENKEI: Oh, you little urchin, that's good. A hip massage, eh? What'll it be, a pinch or a rub? C'mon, just give it a little massage!

NARRATOR: He swings his man from side to side,
Then down falls Benkei,
Tosabō beneath his buttocks.
But still the villain won't give up.
He charges with a great four-foot-long blade,
But Benkei dodges nimbly.

BENKEI (*pinning Tasabo under his right knee*): You've cost me so much time, running about trying to escape, that now I've missed accompanying my lord. Well, I'll just throw this head of yours, and where it lands will tell me which direction my master has gone. (Act I, scene 4)

---

As he slashes, Benkei takes it neatly
On the haft of his sword.
BENKEI: Ho ho ho ho. Well done, well done! Now that you've massaged my bottom for me, I'll just twist your head off for you!
NARRATOR: He flings Tosabō, his body twisting,
Kicks away the sword

### Scene 4: Kawagoe Tarō Comes as Envoy

And seizes his adversary by the head.
Benkei, with wrenching power,
Pulls Tosabō toward himself
And presses his head against his waist.

BENKEI: My lord! Madam Kyō no Kimi! Hey, Kamei, Suruga!

NARRATOR: He moves about, calls and searches,
But there is no one to be seen.

BENKEI: Have they fled the house? But why?

NARRATOR: Not an inkling has he
Of the harm he's done,
And no one comes in answer to his calls—
Only Tosabō, wailing out his misery
Like a crow cawing in a tree.
He shifts Tosabō
From his right hand to his left.

BENKEI *(to Tosabō):* You've cost me so much time, running about trying to escape, that now I've missed accompanying my lord. Well, I'll just throw this head of yours, and where it lands will tell me which direction my master has gone. Here goes!

NARRATOR: He snatches at Tosabō's head,
Covered by a cowl about the face,
Yanks it off his neck
And flings it into the air.
Down it tumbles in the southeast quarter.

BENKEI: They couldn't have gone toward Ubahara or Ohara.[11] My lord was known in his youth by the name Ushiwaka, so maybe it's to the northeast, the bull's quarter.[12] Maybe I

---

11. Tsurumi, *Takeda Izumo shū*, 190, n. 98 and n. 99, notes that both Ubahara and Ohara were in the old province of Tamba, which is to the west of Kyoto. Tamba is now part of the larger metropolitan district of Kyoto. Accordingly, there appears to be an error (Benkei's? The playwrights'?) in locating them to the southwest.

12. Yoshitsune's youthful name was indeed Ushiwaka, meaning something like "Young Bull." The Eastern zodiac is made up of twelve animals arranged graphically around a circle, giving to each position attributes of the hour of the day or night, year designations, compass directions, and so forth. The bull (*ushi*) occupies the position covered on the compass by the general northeast direction.

should look to the south; I'll bet they've gone to Yoshino.[13] They aren't here, and they wouldn't have gone west or northwest.[14] They haven't been gone very long. I'll take out after them. *(He mounts the horse.)*

NARRATOR: An act of loyalty, Benkei thought
His battle of defense;
But now with matters come to this,
All seems nullified.
Now, realizing his mistake,
The rowdy Benkei heads southwest,
Kicking up the pebbles underfoot,
And sending echoes rolling off,
In a rumbling, tumbling, booming din.
Firmly he plants each foot,
As in this predawn hour of the tiger[15]
He thrashes up a tiger-wind,
And stomps away pursuing Yoshitsune.

---

13. The general south to southeast direction is occupied by the snake (*mi*) and horse (*uma*), giving the pronunciation *mimuma*, which, according to the older phonetic orthography, produces the combination *mimu* (read as *min*), meaning "Maybe I should look."

14. Further puns on the zodiacal compass directions. Here *inu* (dog) and *i* (boar) point to the general northwesterly direction. *Inu* is also a homophone for the old verb meaning "not be here." Completing this quadrant of the compass is *tori* (bird = western direction). Hence the translation, "They aren't here, and they wouldn't have gone west or northwest."

15. The hour of the tiger (directionally standing to the northeast) is approximately 4 A.M.

# *Act Two*

## SCENE I
## BEFORE THE FUSHIMI INARI SHRINE

*(Three features dominate the forestage: at center is a small tree with white blossoms; at far SR is a similar tree with red blossoms; at far SL, and extending to center stage, is the entrance to the Fushimi Inari Shrine, marked by a large vermilion gateway (torii), with successive similarly painted torii continuing back to the inner precincts of the shrine. The first gateway stands on a stone base that extends to SL and SR and is topped with a vermilion picket fence. Directly behind the series of gateways rises a mountain covered with a thick stand of evergreen trees. At far SR and behind the red-blossomed tree are stands of tall pines. The near background is a vista of dun colored rice fields with tan pathways along the dikes separating the paddies. The distant background shows groves of pines*

*at the foot of rolling green mountains. It is night as the narration begins; the stage is empty.)*

NARRATOR: War cries sound upon the blowing wind,
 A fearsome prospect.
 Yesterday a protector of the palace,
 Today a fugitive fleeing the Capital,
 Such is the fate of Kurō Yoshitsune.
 His hosts of soldiers all dispersed,
 Now with but two followers—
 Kamei no Rokurō, Suruga no Jirō—
 He hastens toward the Yamato road,
 On a journey in the depths of night.
 Looking back, the Horikawa mansion
 Seems for the moment a billow of clouds,
 And the floating world about them,
 But this dreamlike road to Fushimi.
 As they reach the precincts
 Of the Inari Shrine,
 Kamei no Rokurō dashes in belatedly.

*(Kamei, Yoshitsune, and Suruga enter from SR.)*

KAMEI: Those war cries must come from the Kamakura forces. How it galls me to show them my back! With your permission, my lord, I'd like to take them on in battle.

YOSHITSUNE: I've told you no, Shigekiyo.[1] What my father-in-law Kawagoe Tarō told me in the Capital made perfectly clear my brother Yoritomo's anger. Kyō no Kimi's tragic death was to be an apology for me, but because of Benkei's rash attack on Unno no Tarō I've been obliged to get clear of the Capital. I wish to make peace with my brother, so from now on if any of you raise a sword against the Kamakura army it will be the end of your relationship with me.

NARRATOR: Clenching their fists in anger,
 The two men restrain their ardor for a fight.
 Just then in stumbles Lady Shizuka.

---

1. Kamei's full name is Kamei no Rokurō Shigekiyo.

## Scene 1: Before the Fushimi Inari Shrine

Before Yoshitsune sees her
She has clung to him
For whom she has so longed
Since he left the city.

*(She enters from SR and sinks down at Yoshitsune's feet.)*

SHIZUKA: Ah, my lord, you are too cruel.

NARRATOR: And for a moment she is choked with tears.

SHIZUKA: After you sent me to restrain Benkei, I heard that you had hurried away from the mansion. But such was my resolution that I chased after you even though I was three leagues behind. How unfeeling it was of you. You cast me aside, and even your two men wouldn't listen to me. *(To Suruga:)* Please, say something. Make him let me come with him too.

NARRATOR: As she cries out her lament,
Even Yoshitsune's heart
Is weakened by compassion.
Suruga no Jirō looks on.

SURUGA: We've heard no rumors as we've passed along the road, but our path will lead us among the enemy. In particular, we are headed for Mount Tō, where women are forbidden.[2] If a woman accompanies us, what do you suppose the people in the temple will think?

NARRATOR: As he coaxes and cajoles,
Up dashes Musashibō Benkei
Panting for breath. *(Enters from SR.)*

BENKEI: I stayed in the Capital to finish off Tosabō and Unno, and without realizing it I got left behind. I beg your . . .

NARRATOR: Before he can finish,
His general, Yoshitsune,
Beats him unrelentingly with his fan.

---

2. Located in modern Nara prefecture, the mountain is known also as Mount Tamu. The temple there was established in the seventh century and dedicated to the founder of the famous Fujiwara family, Fujiwara no Kamatari. Mention is made here of Jūjibō, whom I have been unable to identify. It may be the name of a priest, or possibly the name of a priestly office connected with the temple or monastery on Mount Tō.

Quite without compassion,
He strikes the headstrong priest about the face.

YOSHITSUNE: Just make a move, mister cleric, and I, Yoshitsune, will kill you with my own hands.

NARRATOR: Unprepared for such
A countenance of ire,
Benkei can only bow in trepidation.

BENKEI: You dismissed me a while ago and told me to attend you no longer because I spoke ill of Lord Tomokata in the mansion. But Shizuka's apology for me gained me your pardon. I am still smarting from that dismissal, and hardly have I gotten over that than it seems I have again given my lord offense. Yet, for myself, I cannot recall having been of disservice to you.

YOSHITSUNE: Ah, you say you do not remember. Disregarding the sincerity of Kawagoe's attempt to heal the discord between me and my brother in Kamakura, and even Kyō no Kimi's death, why did you kill members of the Kamakura force that was coming to attack me? Wasn't that a misjudgment on your part? Well, speak up, you miserable bonze.

NARRATOR: Under his master's glare,
Benkei remains speechless,
His head hung low.

BENKEI: Your pardon, my lord, I was not unaware of these things. But, however weighty may have been your wishes, surely I wasn't just supposed to sit there unconcerned about Tosabō coming to attack you in the mansion. No loyal warrior in Japan could put up with that. If I made a mistake, I offer you a thousand apologies. I am indeed your retainer, but your rebuke is too harsh. It must stem from the unsettled nature of my lord's life just now. How humiliating it all is!

NARRATOR: Benkei clenches his fists,
And though not one who easily weeps,
A few tears spill from his eyes,
Proof of his fidelity.
Shizuka perceives what's in his heart.

### Scene 1: Before the Fushimi Inari Shrine

SHIZUKA *(to Yoshitsune)*: He has told you what happened. Please, grant him your pardon.

NARRATOR: Hard upon her gentle plea,
Kamei and Suruga add their own—
"Your pardon, lord, your pardon."
Yoshitsune's countenance softens.

YOSHITSUNE: Shirōbei Tadanobu has returned home because his mother is ill. Since I will not have him in attendance, and our way will take us among the enemy, right now I will need the strength of every one of my good vassals. This time I will forgive him.

NARRATOR: At his words, Benkei breathes a sigh
And in embarrassment
Rubs his bald priest's pate.[3]

BENKEI *(speaking to himself)*: Let this be a lesson to you, Musashibō. *(Rubs his head again.)* Shizuka has repeatedly made apologies for you—more than you deserve.

SHIZUKA: I am happy for you that the apologies are over. Now, Benkei, it is for you to persuade my lord to let Shizuka accompany him.

NARRATOR: She seems to brood upon her thoughts.

BENKEI: Your apology on my behalf just now seems to have had an oblique purpose. I would like to speak as you wish, to return the favor, but I simply cannot agree with you. We've been separated from even our close followers, and we travel in secret. As you've heard, our destination is Mount Tō, and women are not permitted there. Since people's minds change constantly, it is impossible to gauge what those on Mount Tō are thinking.[4] From there our road changes: we pass through Yamazaki and go on to Amagasaki in Settsu province, where we'll take a boat from Daimotsu Bay.[5] Our lord

---

3. Again, in actual productions Benkei has a full and bushy head of black hair.
4. A body of armed priests was maintained on Mount Tō, and they may prove hostile to Yoshitsune and his party.
5. Yamazaki is a village south of Kyoto on the Yodo river, along which passenger boats traveled. Old Settsu province is now divided: the western portion

probably intends to seek refuge with the Ogata family in Buzen province,[6] and that means a long sea voyage. For all these reasons, you cannot go with us. Please give up this idea and remain in the Capital to await news of our lord.

NARRATOR: At his words, Shizuka bursts into tears.

SHIZUKA: Even when I have been with my lord, I would grow frantic if I lost sight of him for even a moment. How can I wait for him, even for a day, left behind as you all go off on a long journey into an unknown future? No matter what hardships we may encounter, I won't mind, Musashibō. Please take me with you.

NARRATOR: Weeping piteously,
She clings tightly to her lord,
Unable to let him go.
At this leavetaking from his love
Yoshitsune too blinks back his tears.

YOSHITSUNE: As Benkei has just told you, ours is a journey into an uncertain fate. You had best stay behind in the Capital and wait for the ship that will bring me back to you.

NARRATOR: He bids Kamei to hand him
The brocade bag he holds.

YOSHITSUNE: This is the Hatsune drum that I have wanted for so many years, and which the retired Emperor gave me. Though now it is mine, I cannot strike it even once, for by decree of the former Emperor if I do so it will mean that I must attack my brother Yoritomo. If I fail to strike it, I cannot escape censure for having gone against the imperial wish; if I do strike the drum, it will surely make my brother and me enemies. This drum, which presents me with such a

---

is in modern Hyōgo prefecture, the eastern section is now part of the city of Osaka. Daimotsu Bay is now part of Amagasaki, a town just northwest of modern Osaka on the eastern coast of the Inland Sea.

6. Buzen, in Kyushu, is encompassed today by Oita and Fukuoka prefectures. Ogata Saburō Koreyoshi was a power in Kyushu in the twelfth century and was originally allied to the Heike, later switching his allegiance to the Genji. When Yoshitsune fled the Capital at the end of 1185, he set sail from Daimotsu Bay to seek Koreyoshi's aid. See *The Tale of the Heike*, 208, 407–408.

## Scene 1: Before the Fushimi Inari Shrine

dilemma, I have kept close to me. But you take it as a keepsake till we meet again. Let it be a consolation to you each day as you think of me.[7]

NARRATOR: Though till now she had cherished hope,
The last of her dream is dashed
As she takes the drum he hands her.
Tightly she presses it to her breast,
Then suddenly sinks down in tears.
Kamei no Rokurō steps up.

KAMEI: This long discussion has taken much time. If the remnants of Tosabō's ruffians should attack us, we would be in trouble.

NARRATOR: Thus admonished, Yoshitsune rises,
Tears still streaming down his face,
Shizuka still clinging to his sleeve.

SHIZUKA: If you cast me aside all alone, rather than pine away for love of you, I shall throw myself into a river and there I'll die, I'll die!

NARRATOR: Her body is racked with sobbing,
And none knows what to do.
Should Yoshitsune weaken in his will,
Misfortune might befall his name.
Divining a solution,
Suruga no Jirō steps forth,
And lacking all compassion
Pulls her back.

SURUGA: Luckily, we have this cord. *(Takes the drum from Shizuka.)*

NARRATOR: He loosens the cord from the drum,
And swiftly, so she cannot get undone,
He binds up Shizuka's arms,
Then lashes her securely with the drum
To a withered tree beside the road.

*(He ties her to the white-blossomed tree at center stage.)*

---

7. This incident is drawn directly from the *Gikeiki*. See McCullough, *Yoshitsune*, 168.

SURUGA: There, that will take care of our trouble. Now, let us be on our way.
NARRATOR: And together they hasten down the road. *(They exit SL.)*
Behind them, Shizuka struggles.
As she watches her lord's retreating form,
She weeps, then watches, weeps again.
SHIZUKA: Oh, that heartless Suruga! How cruel this cord that binds me from my lord. Yet, should I escape my bonds, it would be sad to damage this keepsake drum. What shall I do? Oh, set me free and let me die!
NARRATOR: She cries out her lament,
But there is no one to observe her plight.
*(Hayami no Tōta enters from SR with several followers.)*
TŌTA *(to his men):* We'll not let the fugitive Yoshitsune get away.
NARRATOR: Tosabō's retainer, Hayami no Tōta, appears,
Followed by several men,
All bearing torches in their hands
And lanterns at their waists
To light the road in their pursuit.
They hear the sound of a woman weeping
In the shadow of a withered tree.
They approach, wondering who it is.
TŌTA: Hey! That sound we hear—it's that dancer Shizuka, Yoshitsune's mistress. We're in luck: she's already tied up with a rope. And this drum is Yoshitsune's prized possession. I'll bet it's the drum called Hatsune. Yoshitsune himself must be hiding somewhere along this road. What a stroke of fortune!
NARRATOR: Quickly Tōta cuts the cord.
He seizes the drum
And is about to drag Shizuka away
When along comes Shirōbei Tadanobu
Following after Yoshitsune.
Observing the scene, he springs forward,
Grabs Tōta by the shoulder
And takes back the Hatsune drum.

## Scene 1: Before the Fushimi Inari Shrine

He holds the drum aloft,
Sends Tōta reeling aside
And blocks the way to Shizuka.

SHIZUKA: Oh, that heartless Suruga! How cruel this cord that binds me from my lord. . . . What shall I do? Oh!, set me free and let me die.   (Act 2, scene 1)

---

Standing with his legs spread wide,
What a splendid sight!
SHIZUKA: Oh, Tadanobu, you've come just in time! How glad I am to see you.

TŌTA: Well now, if it isn't Tadanobu—a worthy opponent. I'll capture you and make a name for myself.
NARRATOR: His men spread out,
  Surrounding Tadanobu.
TADANOBU: Yaa, you feeble eaters of others' leavings![8] Come on, try for the distinction of capturing me!
NARRATOR: The words have hardly left his mouth
  Than from both sides they come,
  Crying, "Now we've got you!"
  Tadanobu parries their assault.
  With a shout he grabs each by the neck,
  And sends them somersaulting right and left.
  In a twinkling, from behind,
  Soldiers charge, swords drawn for attack.
  "So, you want a fight!" Tadanobu shouts,
  And he too draws his sword.
  His blade flashing silver
  Like a miscanthus leaf,
  He leaps among them like a flying bird,
  Slashing foes from head to collar bone.
  With a cry, they turn and flee.
  Tōta, slow in his escape,
  Is seized by the neck, thrown down,
  And trampled underfoot.
*(The fight is a vigorous, choreographed, melee with powerful action punctuated by strong poses. Tadanobu is prodigiously ferocious and athletic, flinging his adversaries bodily across the stage in an extraordinary display of strength.)*
TADANOBU: Scum, you're more brazenly thick-skinned than these drum heads if you think you can steal this drum! I'll smash you to bits!
NARRATOR: Angrily he tramples Tōta

---

8. Reviling his opponents, Tadanobu calls them *unzai*, short for *unzaigaki*, sinners sent after death to the hell of starving wraiths, where they are doomed to endless gnawing hunger and the vision of the plates of the living, whose leftovers they cannot eat.

## Scene 1: Before the Fushimi Inari Shrine

Till he falls face down.
With a shriek he meets his end,
His final breath cut short.
From the shadows
Beneath the gateway to the shrine
Yoshitsune and his men step forth.

YOSHITSUNE: I did not expect to see you here, Tadanobu.

NARRATOR: At his master's words,
Tadanobu is taken aback.

TADANOBU: I had not expected to see you, my lord.

NARRATOR: He leaps back and bows low.
Kamei, Suruga, and Benkei
Welcome their escape from capture.
Again Tadanobu bows his head.

TADANOBU: I am relieved to find my lord as well as ever. You gave me leave to visit my sick mother, and I went to my home province of Dewa,[9] where I took care of her for some time. Soon, however, she recovered fully. Just as I was thinking I should be returning to the Capital, I heard that you had been turned away at Koshigoe and that there was discord between you and your brother in Kamakura. I dropped everything to return to the Capital. Along the way I heard that a party of Tosabō's men were set to attack you, so I traveled night and day and just this evening arrived at the Horikawa Mansion. When I learned that you had fled the Capital, I followed after you. It is most gratifying to me to have been able to rescue Lady Shizuka from her unexpected difficulty.

NARRATOR: Yoshitsune is most pleased.

YOSHITSUNE: I came to pray at this shrine, so I have witnessed all of what you did just now. I had issued strict orders to my men not to raise a sword against any Kamakura warriors, but since Tosabō has been slain it does not trouble me that you have killed his retainer. Not for the first time, Tadanobu,

---

9. In the far northern part of the main island of Honshu, the area included in modern Yamagata and Akita prefectures.

have I been much impressed with your prowess. Your older brother Tsuginobu was a loyal retainer of uncommon valor. He shielded me from an arrow and gave his life to save me.[10] In you his younger brother I have the same confidence. I now bestow on you my name: you will be called by a name descended from the Emperor Seiwa, Minamoto Kurō Yoshitsune. In times of emergency, you will take my place in order to deceive the enemy. This is my reward to you now; your name will go down in history.

NARRATOR: He bids his retainer
To bring his suit of armor,
And this he bestows on Tadanobu,
Who receives it gratefully,
Bowing low to the ground.[11]

*(Kamei brings the armor and hands it to Tadanobu.)*

TADANOBU: To receive from my lord this armor for chasing off the men of Tosabō, and more, to be given your revered name, is an honor that will last through many lives and many worlds. I have achieved a warrior's highest desire.[12]

NARRATOR: Giving thanks to heaven,
Making obeisances to the earth,
He is choked with tears of joy.
Yoshitsune continues.

YOSHITSUNE: I go on from here to Kyushu to seek the aid of the Ogata family in Buzen province. You will accompany Shizuka and stay with her in the Capital. See that all is well with her.

NARRATOR: Grievous for Yoshitsune
This parting from his love.

SHIZUKA: Are we truly now to say farewell?

NARRATOR: As Shizuka approaches her lord,

---

10. See *The Tale of the Heike*, 364–66.

11. Yoshitsune's bestowal of his name on Tadanobu and the gift of his armor are based on an incident involving different circumstances, recounted in *Gikeiki*. See McCullough, *Yoshitsune*, 177–78.

12. That is, the honor to be permitted to die in one's master's stead on the battlefield.

## Scene 1: Before the Fushimi Inari Shrine

Benkei, Kamei, and Suruga
Step forth and stand between them.
Tadanobu too bids his lord farewell,
And to each other they nod godspeed.
Pushing the grieving Shizuka aside,
Lord and vassals, four in all,
Move confidently away,
To pass through Yamazaki,
Bound for Amagasaki
And Daimotsu Bay. *(Yoshitsune, Benkei, Kamei, and Suruga exit SL.)*

SHIZUKA: Oh please, wait, stay with me yet a little longer!

NARRATOR: She tries to stop them,
But they continue on.

SHIZUKA: It's as though I can still see his face. How dear he is to me!

NARRATOR: She sinks prostrate upon the ground,
Insensate in her sorrow.

TADANOBU: Ah, I understand your grief. You are parted from your master, but he has given you this drum as a keepsake. Think of it as your lord and keep it close to you to help dispel your misery.

NARRATOR: Tadanobu takes the suit of armor
And lightly throws it on his shoulder.
Soothing and consoling her,
He takes Shizuka's hand.
Weeping as she goes,
She holds close the keepsake drum.
Choking back her sorrow
At this parting all too brief,
In tears she makes her way
Along the road
Beneath the nighttime sky.

# SCENE 2
# THE TOKAIYA

*(The scene is the house of Ginpei, who operates a hostelry and freight office called the Tokaiya at Daimotsu Bay in the city of Amagasaki. The building, raised on short posts above the ground, stretches from SL about three-quarters of the way across the stage, its main room at center stage and open to the audience. To SL of the open room is a smaller chamber enclosed by shōji panels. Near the center of the main room is a doorway leading to inner rooms, its opening hung with a curtain decorated with bamboo stalks and leaves. Next to the doorway is a small shrine containing a vertical scroll indicating that it is dedicated to the god of ship captains. Next to the shrine is another set of three shōji panels. Downstage of the house is a combination yard and beach, a cloth of blue and white waves at far SL indicating the water's edge. At SR of the house is a gateway. The far background behind the house is the ocean, seen at SR. The stage appears unoccupied as the*

*narration begins, but Oyasu is sleeping unseen behind a low folding screen near centerstage.)*

NARRATOR: Busy the beaches at Amagasaki town,
　　As ships sail in each night, each day.
　　And known to all at Daimotsu Bay
　　Is the shipping agent Ginpei.
　　His shop, facing toward the sea,
　　Is filled with stores like anchors
　　And stout cotton cloth for sails.
　　Ginpei's life is prosperous,
　　His seaport inn ever bustling
　　With captains and with pilots
　　Bearing cargoes north and south.
*(Ginpei's wife, Oryū, wearing an apron, enters through the center stage curtained doorway and begins slicing a daikon (large radish) for supper.)*
　　While Ginpei makes the warehouse rounds,
　　His wife, Oryū, who manages the house,
　　Prepares her lodgers a meal,
　　A fare, in keeping with the place,
　　Of creatures caught in nets,
　　Flavored by the salt-smack of the sea.
　　More sweetly brought up,
　　The couple's only daughter,
　　Oyasu, now catches a cat-nap.
　　To ward away the breeze,
　　Oryū adjusts her coverlet.
　　Noisily an inner door slides open,
　　And abruptly enters a traveling priest,
　　A cloth-wrapped bundle slung across his back.
*(Benkei enters from the SL room. On his head is a large white kerchief, peaked at left and right; around his neck is a Buddhist rosary, and he carries across his back an elongated bundle containing a sword and wrapped in black cloth.)*

ORYŪ: Oh, sir priest, I was just about to bring you your tray. Where might you be going?

ACT TWO

BENKEI: Ah . . . well . . . I find my companions rather tedious as we just sit around waiting for fair weather to travel to the western provinces. Rather than stay in inside, I . . . ah . . . I think I'll just go over to Nishimachi for some shopping.

ORYŪ: Oh, what a pity. There's a cockle salad for the other guests, but I made a vegetarian dish especially for you. Won't you try some?

BENKEI: No, no, I'm a mountain priest,[1] so I'm not a vegetarian. A cockle salad will be fine for me.

ORYŪ: But, today is the twenty-eighth, a commemorative day for the god Fudō.

BENKEI: Oh, good heavens, you're right. It's an important day of abstinence. What shall I do? Well, no help for it if I forgot. I've something to attend to, so I'll just be on my way.

NARRATOR: He rises hastily. *(Picking up his bundle, Benkei stands and tries to step over Oyasu asleep behind the screen. There is a rapid beating of drums.)* [2]

BENKEI: Oh! Ow, ouch! *(Sits down, rubbing his right knee. He peeps behind the screen.)*

ORYŪ: Oh sir, what happened?

BENKEI: Ah, it's nothing. Is this your daughter sleeping here? I suddenly got a cramp in my leg when I stepped over her. Ah, I've got it! *(Slaps his knee, puts his right hand to his forehead in a gesture of understanding.)* She's still just a little thing, but she's a girl, and it must be that she had some feeling I was going to step over her and she became tense. *(Stops and listens to the rain.)* Well, I'd better go before the rain starts coming down hard.

NARRATOR: Musashibō Benkei takes a large umbrella
Made of bamboo bark,

---

1. Mountain priests, *Yamabushi*, were members of an ascetic Buddhist sect who spent much of their time in mountainous regions, often dedicating mountain peaks to the Buddha. One of their special subjects of veneration was the guardian deity Fudō (Achala in Sanskrit), a fiery figure who was defender of the Buddhist law. Dietary abstinence was customary on days commemorating Fudō.

2. Deep, rolling drum beats usually signal supernatural occurrences, in this case a divine warning of insult to an emperor.

## Scene 2: The Tokaiya

Spreads it above his head,
And hurries off. *(Exits downstage right.)*
The mother goes to her daughter's side.
*(She brings Oyasu out from behind the screen and caresses her hair.)*
ORYŪ: Here, Oyasu, don't catch yourself a cold napping like that.
NARRATOR: As she's held in her mother's arms,
The young child rubs her eyes.
OYASU: Oh, mother. I was watching you at work, and I just dozed off.
ORYŪ: But now you're awake. Run along now and write out nicely the writing lesson you learned this morning. We must show it to your father.
NARRATOR: Blind are parents when it comes to their child.
The mother takes her hand
And leads her to the inner room.
*(Both exit through the curtained doorway.)*
Arriving just that moment,
An unknown warrior from Kamakura,
Retainers following in his retinue.
*(Sagami Gorō, holding aloft an umbrella, enters from SR with two followers.)*
SAGAMI *(calling out gruffly)*: I want to see the master.
NARRATOR: . . . And into the house he marches.
Startled, Oryū rushes out.
ORYŪ: My husband is away just now. What can I do for you?
SAGAMI *(arrogantly)*: I am Sagami Gorō, retainer of the Hōjō. My lord Tokimasa in Kamakura has heard that Yoshitsune has appealed for help to Ogata Saburō Koreyoshi and is fleeing to Kyushu. My master has given me orders to act as his deputy, and I have just now come from Kamakura to attack Yoshitsune. But with this continuing rain and wind, there hasn't been a single boat for passage. Fortunately, I've heard that at this house there is a boat for hire which will set out as soon as the weather clears. I insist that you man that vessel and hire it out to me. If any travelers show up, either

chase them away or open up the guest room and let them wait in there. Quickly, be about it!
NARRATOR: He delivers his blustering order,
Flaunting his authority.
Embarrassed for an answer,
Oryū moves near the man.
ORYŪ: I'm sure it is inconvenient for you not to have a ship for your important business. Our guests *(gestures toward the SL room)* have taken lodging with us here for two or three days now awaiting fair weather. As things now stand, I really cannot deny them a boat in order to accommodate your needs. And especially, since our guests too are warriors, I cannot ask them to share their boat with you. *(Bowing.)* If you will just be patient, sir, and wait tonight, the weather will surely clear up in the meantime, and then there will be plenty of boats. Let us engage one for you from among those coming in.
SAGAMI: Shut up, woman! If we had time to take lodgings, I wouldn't be giving you an order. I command you, in the name of the official constable of this area. If you're afraid of the warriors in that room, then I'll talk to them directly myself.
NARRATOR: He springs to his feet,
But Oryū clings to his robe.
*(Sagami jumps up and takes his sheathed sword in his left hand. Oryū holds onto the hem of his kimono.)*
ORYŪ: Sir, I can understand your impatience, but if you go in there to speak with those people, it will make trouble for our hostelry. Please, sir, wait till my husband returns.
NARRATOR: She wrings her hands contritely.
SAGAMI: Obstinate wench! If you won't let me see those men inside, that suggests to me that they may be Heike fugitives. No slips now, men! Be on your guard! *(He readies his sword for drawing and with his men moves toward the SL room. Oryū attempts to stop them.)*
NARRATOR: Oryū, trying to block their way,
Is pushed and shoved aside.

*Scene 2: The Tokaiya*

When she grabs at them again,
She's roughly kicked away.
Ginpei now returns.
Seeing the struggle, he dashes in
And seizes the samurai's arm.

*(Carrying a large anchor on his shoulder, Ginpei comes in from SR. He drops the anchor, enters the house and throws Sagami's two henchmen into the yard. He then grabs Sagami by the arm and drags him over to SR, then seats himself on the floor and bows. Sagami thrusts his sword into his left hand and glowers.)*

GINPEI: I must beg your humble pardon, sir. I am Ginpei, master of this house. You seem to be vexed about something. Perhaps you had best explain matters to me.

NARRATOR: On his knees, he bows.

SAGAMI: Hmmm, since you're the master, I'll tell you. I am a retainer of the Hōjō family, and I'm under orders to attack Yoshitsune. I was about to go into that room and speak to those warriors inside to see that the boat they reserved is turned over to me when your wife blocked my way. That was the cause of the ruckus.

GINPEI *(speaking very deferentially)*: I see. You'll excuse me, but I think you are being somewhat presumptuous. I say this because, . . . well, is it not unreasonable to try and force someone who has already engaged a boat to give it up to you? Moreover, you say that my wife refused to let you barge into my guest's room, and for that you trample her and kick her around. I think that's, shall we say, rather unbecoming a samurai. Why, I'd never be able to face any of my merchant customers, even for a night, if I just let people storm into their rooms like that. *(Bowing again.)* I beg your indulgence in this, sir, and ask that you please take your leave.

SAGAMI *(blustering)*: A miserable townsman telling a Kamakura warrior to get out . . . why, that's an insult! I don't care what you say, I'm going into that room!

*(He claps his right hand on his long sword, loosening it menacingly in its scabbard several times.)*

NARRATOR: He readies his sword for action

And advances intimidatingly.
GINPEI *(holding up his right hand):* Oh, master samurai, you're letting your temper get the better of you. I may run a seaport inn, but I've learned a thing or two. Your long and short swords are not, I believe, just for killing people. A samurai's two swords are to be used for protection. It's my understanding that they are implements to protect people from unruly ruffians. It would seem that's the reason why one of the Chinese characters for "warrior" is written with the two elements that mean "stop the thrust of the lance."[3]
SAGAMI *(angry and speaking rapidly):* Impudent lout! I'll slice off your offensive tongue!
NARRATOR: Sword drawn, he lunges.
But Ginpei dodges back
And grabs Sagami's sword arm
In a steel-like grip.
GINPEI *(forcefully):* I've had just about enough of this! To a townsman his home is the same as a castle is to a warrior. It isn't enough that you've barged into my house with muddy feet; just who are you going to strike with this sword? *(He twists Sagami's sword upward.)* And this talk about Heike fugitives; and, of all things, people connected with Yoshitsune—are you threatening these travelers? All right, let it be Lord Hōgan himself. And if I, the well-known Mazuna Ginpei of Daimotsu Bay, am hiding him, what are you going to do about it? Well, I'm waiting. Just try and make a move! I'll bash in your lousy skull! I'll steer your life to starboard, and that'll be your voyage out of this world.[4]
NARRATOR: Ginpei wrenches the sword away.
He waves it up on high,
Advancing on his adversary,
And sends him tripping on the gate sill,
Somersaulting out.

---

3. The word for "warrior" is *bushi*. The *bu* of *bushi* is written with two elements meaning "a spear" and the verb "to stop (something)."

4. In keeping with his maritime vocation, Ginpei spices his speech with nautical vocabulary.

## Scene 2: The Tokaiya

*(As Sagami tries to flee, Ginpei raps him with the back edge of the sword. Crawling, Sagami gets out of the house. Ginpei throws the sword into the yard, where it hits Sagami on the head and then is retrieved by one of his followers.)*

Enduring his pain, Sagami rises,
A scowl upon his face.

SAGAMI: Remember me well, you rotten innkeeper. For my revenge I'll have your head. P-p-prepare yourself to lose it! *(He trembles with rage.)*

GINPEI: Are you still flapping your chin? *(Goes down into the yard.)*

NARRATOR: With a grunt, Ginpei heaves up high
A heavy anchor lying in the yard.
Fearing to be crushed beneath its weight,
Sagami and his minions
Flee without a backward glance—
Sails unfurled upon their buttocks,
Like little boats before a storm.

*(They exit at SR. Ginpei returns to the house and seats himself.)*

Ginpei pulls over his tobacco tray. *(Lights pipe.)*

GINPEI: Ha ha ha. Great! That was wonderful! Oryū, I suppose our guests inside have heard all the fuss.

NARRATOR: The couple's hushed tones
Seem to have been overheard.
The sliding panels of the room
Are pushed aside
Revealing Lord Yoshitsune.
His noble face is thin
And shows the strain of travel.
He emerges from the room,
And in his wake come Suruga and Kamei.

GINPEI *(recognizing Yoshitsune)*: Oh! This is most unexpected.

NARRATOR: Even Ginpei quickly
Assumes a formal posture.
He and his wife bow low,
As Yoshitsune surveys the room.

YOSHITSUNE: "Nothing is more visible than what is secret,"

goes the saying.[5] When I incurred the displeasure of my older brother Yoritomo, I sent to the Ogata family a request for assistance. Tokimasa counted on this and, knowing that I would stop over here, has sent his men to pursue me. Your admirable effort in rescuing me from this difficulty, Ginpei, is something I would not have expected from one of your calling. When I attacked the Heike at Ichinotani, I had a young woodcutter named Washinoō[6] guide me over the mountain path. Mountain dwellers are strong people, so I made him a warrior and took him into my service. But you have distinguished yourself far more. Well done! In former times I, Yoshitsune, would have made you a samurai and elevated you into my service. But I am now a wanderer whose life is hardly worth living. *(Stands dejectedly.)*

NARRATOR: At such rueful words
By so gallant and fierce a general,
Both Suruga and Kamei
Clench their fists in helpless rage.

GINPEI: Ah, I am most grateful for your kind words. People around here know me as Mazuna Ginpei, but I am a mere townsman. When you come down to it, my actions just now were only those of what you might call a "household general" defending his hearth. It is far more than I deserve that you should take note of so small a thing and bestow such gracious words. I remember in particular seeing you, my lord, when you went to Yashima.[7] You ordered vessels for your soldiers from the anchorages of Watanabe and Fukushima,[8] and my own boat proved to be of service to you. Thus, not once, but

---

5. From the Confucian classic, *The Doctrine of the Mean* (in Chinese *Chung Yung*). See James Legge, tr., *The Chinese Classics*, Part 1, 124.

6. On the battle at Ichinotani, see *The Tale of the Heike*, 310–14; on Washinoō, see McCullough, *Yoshitsune*, 32.

7. Yashima is in the modern city of Takamatsu on the northeast coast of the island of Shikoku. For an account of the battle at Yashima, see *The Tale of the Heike*, 359–70.

8. Both located at the mouth of the Yodo River that flows through Osaka and empties into Osaka Bay.

## Scene 2: The Tokaiya

now again we meet. By some strange fate you have stayed in my house, so there seems to be a deep bond between us. I must tell you, however, that it will be very dangerous for you should the Hōjō men return. You had best board your boat right away.

NARRATOR: Before he can finish, Suruga Jirō speaks.

SURUGA *(jumping up):* We are of the same mind, my lord. *(To Ginpei.)* What if we set sail in this weather?

GINPEI: Oh, we should not miss such a good opportunity. The use of weapons is your calling. Keeping an eye on ships and the weather is the job of a shipping agent like myself. *(Looks up at the sky.)* Yesterday and today the wind has been southwesterly. During the night the rain will cease, and it will turn stormy by dawn. From my years of experience, I would say that now is the best time to depart.

NARRATOR: By the way he speaks,
   As one who sees into the future,
   Clearly he knows his calling.
   Kamei Rokurō rises resolutely.

KAMEI: Well done, Ginpei. As you say, we should leave at once during this break in the rain. We will accompany our lord.

YOSHITSUNE: Ginpei, I shall leave shipboard matters to you.

NARRATOR: Ginpei bows in assent.

GINPEI: As I have just told you, I have been schooled in naval matters since my youth, so I will see you off as far as Suma and Akashi in my own boat. The main vessel lies some five hundred yards offshore. It's an auspicious day when one decides on a course of action, goes the saying; and the ship bears a lucky name—*Hiyoshi*, "Day of Fortune." I'll get the rain gear ready and follow after you. Wife, see our lord off.

*(He leaves through the curtained doorway. Oryū moves outside the house to get straw raincoats.)*

NARRATOR: Oryū nods and brings out straw rainwear
   To hide them from the eyes of a prying world.

YOSHITSUNE: I shall not forget your kindness.

NARRATOR: Both Kamei and Suruga

Take and don their coats of straw,
Quickly fastening the neck cords.
KAMEI: My lord, let us go.
NARRATOR: Retainers in attendance,
Their master walks to the water's edge.
*(As they dress, a small boat has been drawn up alongside Ginpei's house. After Kamei has helped Yoshitsune put on his straw raincoat, the latter walks across a plank to board the boat.)*
With Yoshitsune in the skiff,
Kamei and Suruga spring aboard.
SURUGA: All right oarsman, get going.
*(Flanked by his two retainers, Yoshitsune stands amidship, holding up a conical straw hat to shield himself from the rain. A boatman at the stern, his kimono pulled away from his upper body, works a sculling oar.)*
NARRATOR: The mooring line is loosed;
From the gate Oryū bids farewell.
*(She bows as the boat is rowed off to disappear at SL.)*
ORYŪ: May the fortunes of war be yours. If fate will have it so, we will meet again. Farewell.
KAMEI AND SURUGA: Farewell.
NARRATOR: The oarsman leans upon his oar.
The boat moves off,
Leaving Oryū with bated breath
As she re-enters the house
And the evening bell peals forth.
*(Oryū disappears through the curtained doorway. As the bell sounds, she re-emerges and peers around outside the house. At this point, there is usually a change of narrator and his samisen accompanist.)*
ORYŪ: Oh, I feel so restless.
NARRATOR: She clicks a flint against a stone,
Lights the lamp, and illumines
The room and the shelf of the gods.
ORYŪ *(looks toward the curtained door, claps her hands)*: Daughter, Oyasu, Oyasu. You've been so diligent, studying your writing right up till evening. Your father is seeing our samurai

## Scene 2. The Tokaiya

guests off to the main ship tonight, I'll be here with you till you go to sleep. *(She calls out to Ginpei.)* My husband, you seem to be preparing yourself for a journey of a thousand or more leagues. It's getting late. If you're ready, you should be going. *(She cocks her head and listens for an answer.)*

NARRATOR: She calls, but there comes no answer.

ORYŪ: I wonder if he might be weary from the day's work and taking a nap. Ginpei, Ginpei!

*(Ginpei, now appearing in his true identity of Taira no Tomomori, utters his first line offstage in the chanting style of the Nō theater. The opening line itself is drawn intact from the Nō play* Funa Benkei.*)* [9]

TOMOMORI:     What you will now behold
    Is the ghost of Taira no Tomomori,
    Scion in the ninth generation
    Of the Emperor Kammu.

*(The shōji of the SL room are removed, revealing Tomomori seated on a stool, dressed in white armor and a white tunic, holding upright in his left hand a long halberd wrapped in white cloth. He continues, speaking with a slow and solemn dignity.)*

    Ginpei the shipping agent—that was but a temporary name. Now that I have revealed my true name, New Middle Councilor Taira no Tomomori, I now stand in reverence and awe.

NARRATOR: He takes his daughter's hand,
    And reverently he places her
    In the seat of honor.

*(Holding his halberd in his left hand, he moves to the center of the room and sits. Taking a straw mat from the room's alcove, he spreads it on the floor and with great deference places her on it. He then moves back, kneels and bows deeply.)*

TOMOMORI: My liege, you are in truth our sovereign in the eighty-first generation, Emperor Antoku. Yet, the world has become the narrow domain of the Genji. When it became clear that we could not win in battle, your grandmother, the nun Nii, clasped your precious person in her arms, and we

---

9. For a full translation of *Funa Benkei*, see Nihon Gakujutsu Shinkōkai, ed., *Japanese Noh Drama*, 167–82.

deceived the enemy into believing that you sank along with Tomomori to the bottom of the sea.[10] Throughout these years and months I have stayed in attendance upon you, pretending that Tsubone here, your wet nurse, is my wife Oryū and that you, Your Majesty, are my child. It has been worth the wait! For within the space of this night I will kill Kurō Daibu Yoshitsune,[11] and my long-cherished desire will be fulfilled. Haa haa haa! What joy! What happiness! Rejoice, Tsubone, rejoice!

NARRATOR: Standing there before them,
Brave of countenance,
Fierce and lofty in his bearing—
The Heike general Tomomori!

TSUBONE: It has always been your wish to do this, and indeed you seem resolved this night. But Yoshitsune is, above all, a clever man. Take care you make no mistakes.

TOMOMORI: Ho ho ho ho ho! I have a strategy that will take care of matters. The man calling himself Sagami Gorō, a retainer of the Hōjō, is a boatmen under my own command. I had him pretend to be part of a party pursuing Yoshitsune and to pick a fight with me. I've thrown Yoshitsune off his guard and made him think I'm on his side. I've deceived him into thinking that tonight's storm will be fair weather, and I will attack him in his boat. But, if the rumor goes around that Tomomori is still alive and that he has killed Yoshitsune, then I will be unable to protect and care for you, my lord. Moreover, I will not be able to take my revenge on Yoritomo. I have therefore placed my men in position, and we will follow after Yoshitsune in a boat. When we do battle in the open sea, we will appear to him to be the evil spirits of

---

10. The emperor, his grandmother, Tomomori, and other important Heike clan characters in the play did indeed drown at the final great conflict of the Heike-Genji wars, the battle of Dannoura. For an account of the historical event, see *The Tale of the Heike*, 372–83.

11. *Daibu* was a title of the fifth rank in the imperial court. As a lieutenant in the imperial police (*Kebiishi*), Yoshitsune held the junior fifth court rank, lower grade.

## Scene 2: The Tokaiya

the Heike who perished in the western sea; and I, Tomomori, will be taken for a vengeful apparition.[12] Fortunately, the rain and wind will make it hard for them to see us, and

Tomomori, clad in white armor, prepares to leave to do battle with Yoshitsune at sea. Note the crossed eyes, a dramatic convention denoting intense emotion. (Act 2, scene 2)

---

so that we may carry out the deception I've dressed as you see me now—my armor plating laced with white cord, to give me an unearthly appearance. See here, with this lance wrapped in white cloth I shall take Yoshitsune's head and bring it back with me! But, as a signal whether we have met victory or defeat, if the lanterns and torches on the boat go out all at once, it will mean that Tomomori has fallen. *(Turns to Tsubone.)* In that event, you should have our lord prepare to meet his fate . . . so that his body will not be desecrated.

12. In the Nō play *Funa Benkei*, the ghost of Tomomori rises from the waters in an attempt to take revenge on Yoshitsune for his defeat of the Heike clan.

TSUBONE: Oh, do not worry about us. Just send us good tidings.
EMPEROR: Be quick, Tomomori.
TOMOMORI: At once, my lord. My thanks. *(Draws back and bows.)*
NARRATOR: He gazes on the royal countenance,
    So grown up for the young lad's eight short years.
    Then comes the sound of eight drumbeats
    Telling the small hours of the night.[13]
*(The samisen sounds the eight drumbeats, Tomomori counting the last of them off on his fingers.)*
TOMOMORI: Swiftly, I take my leave.
*(The following several lines by the narrator are adapted from the Nō play Funa Benkei and are chanted in the style of the Nō theater.)* [14]
NARRATOR: In the evening waves, in the evening waves,
    He grips again his lance and cleaves the air
    And swirls the sea to billows.
    Then, kicking sand into the air
    So gusting blasts of wind
    Blow it stinging in the eyes,
    He runs off as though flying.
*(Tomomori comes out of the house to downstage center. He waves the halberd above his head; then holding it high he moves up and down, suggesting the motion of the waves. Finally, after several more flourishes with the halberd, he exits SL. Tsubone retires through the curtained doorway. At this point there is customarily a change of narrator*

---

13. *Yatsudoki;* it corresponds approximately to 2 A.M.
14. The lines in *Funa Benkei* are as follows:

    Floating on the evening waves,
    He grips his lance anew
    And cleaves the air,
    Swirling waves in billows,
    Kicking water into the air,
    And blowing up an evil wind.
    He blinds their eyes
    And makes their minds distraught,
    So none know where they are.

See Nomura Hachirō, ed., *Yōkyoku shū*, 1: 533.

*and his accompanist. After a somber and ominous samisen interlude, Tsubone returns.)*
NARRATOR: Tsubone watches him depart,
   Then moves to the Emperor's side.
TSUBONE: Did you mark well what Tomomori said? Though you are a child, you are the Emperor, lord of the ten virtues.[15] Dressed so miserably as you are would be an affront to the gods of warriors. Let us dress you in your royal robes.
NARRATOR: Determined, should a crisis come,
   That both be fitly clothed
   For a journey to the nether world,
   She rises and, concealing tears,
   Enters the inner room.
   Quickly now the night has spread its dark,
   And fiercely sound the wind and rain.
EMPEROR: Tomomori should be undertaking his difficult task about now. My heart goes out to him.
NARRATOR: Mature beyond his years,
   Upon his face one reads his keen torment.
   Soon Tsubone returns,
   Bearing reverently on a plain wood tray
   A coronet of state,
   The royal raiment, yellow tinged with blue,
   The color of the mountain dove.
   Tsubone too has changed her robe.
*(From her earlier simple kimono of dark lavender with black around the collar, Tsubone has changed to light purple court robes dominated by geometric figures in gold. She carries a folding fan with ribs of unpainted wood and long colored ribbons hanging from its ends.)*
TSUBONE: Quickly now, your royal gown.
*(She bows. The Emperor goes off through the curtained doorway, followed by Tsubone. The narration, describing her dressing the Em-*

---

15. In Buddhism, possession of the ten virtues (*Jūzen*) means one has not perpetrated any of the ten cardinal sins (*Jūaku*): rebellion, desecration of sacred tombs, treason, treachery, irrationality or inhumanity, blasphemy, disobedience to parents, disharmony, immorality, and civil insurrection. The emperor, by virtue of his exalted status, *ipso facto* possesses the ten virtues.

*peror, continues while they are offstage. About midway through the recitativo, first the Emperor and then Tsubone re-enter the room through the same doorway.)*

NARRATOR: She draws near and helps remove
    His unpretentious tunic,
    Then arrays him in his under-robes of silk,
    His silken over-gown and royal mantle
    And majestic coronet of state.
    When all is finished, how splendid is he—
    In his noble mien,
    So different from his former self,
    He seems to bear the markings
    Of a scion of some god.

*(When the Emperor re-enters, he is dressed in a white robe with scarlet underlining, a golden coronet on his head, and a flat baton of state in his hands. As he goes to his former seat at SL, Tsubone re-enters.)*

TSUBONE: Now, we have but to await good news from Tomomori.

NARRATOR: Then come the drumbeats, bells
    That set the heart to racing—
    Can those far off sounds be tidings?
    They must be in midbattle now, she thinks,
    And swiftly to her young lord's side she moves.
    As she anticipates an imminent report,
    In rushes Tomomori's man, Sagami Gorō,
    Fairly choked for breath.

*(Sagami runs in from SR, a rolled towel bound about his head, clad in armor and holding a drawn sword. Catching a deep breath, he crouches in obeisance on the ground.)*

TSUBONE: How goes the battle? Quickly, tell us, tell us!

NARRATOR: Rising, Tsubone urges his report.

*(Sagami's monologue is accompanied by energetic and choreographed posturing as he gestures and acts out the story he reports.)*

SAGAMI: Just as we had planned earlier, after dark our men all put to sea in their skiffs. Then, as we rowed up close to the main ship where Yoshitsune was aboard, down from Mount

Muko[16] came a fierce storm, thundering and deluging us with rain. All of us being expert swimmers, we thought that now was our chance, and one after the other we leaped into the water. We shouted out, "The Heike clan, that perished in the western sea, now comes to take its vengeance on Yoshitsune!" But the enemy must have been prepared for us. They boarded our boats, scattering the lanterns and torches about and fighting as though it were a last-ditch battle. Most of the men we'd mustered were cut down, and the situation appears in doubt. I must return now and see how fares my Lord Tomomori.

NARRATOR: Hardly has he finished than away he runs. *(Sagami exits SR.)*

TSUBONE: Oh, something terrible has happened! I fear for Tomomori's fate. What can be going on out there on the sea?

NARRATOR: She slides the shōji open, and there,
Lanterns, torches glow like stars,
Brightening the sky
As the endless sea comes into view.

*(Holding a candle in her hand, Tsubone slides open the three shōji panels at the rear of the room, revealing a seascape with two tiny ships off in the distance, showing lights. The sounds of conch, drums, and bells suggest the battle in progress.)*

Numbers of tiny vessels
Weave and swerve among each other.
With shipboard watchtowers[17] as their shields,
Friend and foe mingle in the melee,
Leap and spring from boat to boat,
Pursuing, slashing one another,
War cries bursting from their throats.
So vivid are their shadows,
Their embattled voices

---

16. The old name for Mount Rokkō, rising to the east of the modern city of Kōbe.

17. Part of the play's subtitle comes from this scene.

Borne in upon the wind,
They seem to be within the very room.
*(More sounds of conchs, drums, and bells suggesting battle.)*
TSUBONE: Oh look, Your Majesty. Tomomori is in the midst of all that.
EMPEROR: Oh, where?
NARRATOR: As he stretches up to see,
One by one the lamps and torches die,
The action out at sea turns still.
Can it be the signal of Tomomori's death?
Tsubone, so dazed she cannot weep,
Stands gazing in bewilderment.
Suddenly, Irie Tanzō returns,
All bloody from the fight.
*(Sword in hand, Irie staggers in from SR.)*
IRIE: Yoshitsune and his men have fought fiercely, and every one of ours has fallen. Our lord Tomomori too was surrounded by a large force. It seemed the end for him, and he has disappeared completely. I am sure he jumped into the sea and ended his life. I shall go now and serve him on the road to the other world.
NARRATOR: Quick as his words, he loosens his armor.
Into his midriff he thrusts his blade
And leaps into the depths of the tide.
TSUBONE: Ah, so Tomomori too has met a tragic end!?
NARRATOR: She sinks down with a cry;
Confounded by her grief, she weeps.
In the intermingled sadness and the horror
Of what he sees and hears,
The Emperor also joins her in his tears.
Rather than be submerged in sorrow,
Tsubone takes the youthful sovereign
On her knee and looks at him intently.
TSUBONE: For over two years now you have made this miserable house your home, thinking of it as your jeweled palace. Even your morning and evening meals have been the coarse stuff

of the lower folk. Yet, in your heart you have considered it the fine fare of imperial halls. But now that Tomomori has met his death we too have reached the end. No longer shall we hide in this lowly hovel. Are you finally to become a part of the earth here in this bay? Has it come to that? For you who stand above all others, how misfortunes have pursued you one upon the other! Ah, but these are worthless lamentations. Come, my lord, prepare yourself.

NARRATOR: Tears flowing, she takes his hand
And leads him to the water's edge.

*(There is a samisen interlude as Tsubone leads the Emperor from the house. She unrolls a long bolt of white cloth from the house to the water's edge, and as the Emperor walks along it she holds aloft her fan to protect him from the rain. While this is taking place, the set undergoes a change, the house moving roughly half its length to SL, thus revealing more of the ocean's expanse. The Emperor seats himself on a rock, and the recitative resumes.)*

Must, she thinks, so fine a youth
Sink from sight beneath this sea?
At the thought, her head is in a whirl,
A turmoil in her heart,
Her body all atremble.

The lad is clever, but the thought of death
Is distant from his mind.

EMPEROR: Tell me, nurse, you say I am to prepare myself, but where are you going to take me?

TSUBONE *(speaking to him gently)*: Ah, of course you wonder. Now listen to me carefully. Our land has become a fearful place, overrun by warriors of the Genji. But beneath these very waves lies a splendid city called the paradise of the pure land. Your grandmother, the Lady Nii, and all of the Heike clan, and Tomomori too are in that city, so let me take you there and we will escape from the sorrows of this bitter world.

NARRATOR: As she gazes on him,
He seems disheartened.

EMPEROR: Am I to go all by myself beneath these frightening waves?

TSUBONE: Oh, such a loss, what a pity! Why, what sort of world would it be if I, your wet nurse who has taken such loving care of you, should send you off alone to the thousand fathom depths of these rolling waves? No, I shall accompany you. My beloved lord, whom I've raised so tenderly, how could I send you off alone?

EMPEROR: Then, I am happy. As long as you are with me, I will go anywhere.

TSUBONE *(sinking down in tears)*: Oh, well spoken, well spoken!

NARRATOR: She draws him to her,
Clasps him in her arms.

TSUBONE: We may leap into the flames or drown in the water, but ordained for us from a previous life there is the promise of a world to come. Now, say your prayers for your rebirth in paradise, and make your farewell to the goddess of the Sun.

NARRATOR: She has him face toward the east.[18]

---

18. The Ise Shrine, sacred to the sun goddess Amaterasu, lay to the east. A few lines later, Tsubone has the emperor face in the opposite direction, the place of the western paradise of the pure land.

## Scene 2· The Tokaiya

*(Tsubone has him face to SL, and they both hold their hands in prayer.)*

He clasps his lovely hands before him
And bows in supplication.
As Tsubone gazes on, her heart grows faint.
*(During the narration, she brings from the house a low table bearing an ink stone, a brush, and a narrow strip of paper for writing a poem.)*
TSUBONE: Ah, you have performed your leavetaking well. Now, the Buddha's land is in this direction.
NARRATOR: She faces him toward where she points.
*(Toward SR.)*
EMPEROR *(reciting his poem)*:

> Now at last I realize!
> In that flowing river
> Before the Ise Shrine
> A city lies beneath the waves.[19]

*(As he speaks, Tsubone takes up the brush and writes the poem on the strip of paper. A stage assistant then removes the table and writing materials.)*
TSUBONE: Oh, well done. A fine poem you've composed. Had you created such a poem long ago at one of the elegant parties in the palace, how happy everyone would have been— your father the Emperor, your grandfather Lord Kiyomori, your grandmother the nun Lady Nii, and especially your mother Lady Kenreimon'in.[20] Yet now, at the moment of death, it goes for nothing.

---

19. The poem comes, with hardly any change, from another chronicle of the Genji-Heike wars, *Genpei seisuiki*, a work of unknown authorship probably dating from the middle years of the thirteenth century. In *Genpei seisuiki*, the Lady Nii recites the poem to the young emperor just before they leap to their deaths in the water. See Yūda, *Bunraku jōruri shū*, 379, n. 11. Here the poem is to be the emperor's *jisei*, his final poem as a commemoration of his death.

20. The emperor mentioned is Takakura (reigned 1168–80). His consort, and the mother of young Emperor Antoku, was Tokuko, a daughter of the Heike leader Kiyomori. After the Genji victory over the Heike, Tokuko survived but

NARRATOR: Well may our hearts go out to her
    As she struggles with her grief
    Till her tears are spent,
    Her lamenting voice grows weak.
*(Weeping, she rises on unsteady legs and goes to the Emperor.)*
    In moments between her wrenching tears,
    She strokes and smooths the Emperor's hair.
TSUBONE: Quickly now, let us hurry on our way to the land of bliss. *(She lifts the Emperor and holds him in her left arm.)*
NARRATOR: Grasping the Emperor fast,
    She lets the hem of her robe grow moist
    In the wavelets at the water's edge,
    As she gazes out, far out,
    Across the face of the sea.
TSUBONE: Hear me, you eight great dragon kings of the sea, you myriad creatures bearing fins, the Emperor comes forth! Grant him your protection.
*(Taking the Emperor in her arms, she moves toward SR. Suddenly, from downstage SL, Yoshitsune rushes in, a sedge hat held to hide his face. Seeing Tsubone and the Emperor, he flings his hat aside and hurries to them.)*
NARRATOR: Just as she is poised
    To leap into the swirling waves—
    From where can he have come?
    Yoshitsune dashes in
    And grabs her in his arms.
TSUBONE: Oh, good heavens! Leave us alone and let us die, I beg you!
NARRATOR: She looks behind her.
TSUBONE *(recognizing Yoshitsune)*: Oh, it's you!

---

was obliged to spend her remaining years as a Buddhist nun, taking the name of Kenreimon'in. Lady Nii, Antoku's grandmother, was known as Tokiko when she was Kiyomori's wife. She too became a nun, adopting the name Nii. According to *The Tale of the Heike*, at the battle of Dannoura, Lady Nii took the young Antoku, then seven years old, into her arms and leaped into the sea, where both perished.

YOSHITSUNE: Be still!
NARRATOR: He pulls the Emperor away
And holds him under his arm,
As upward he twists Tsubone's wrist
And forces her with him into the house.
*(They enter from the SL room; the shōji close behind them. Benkei, a straw hat held aloft, enters from downstage SR and covertly moves upstage.)*
At this moment Tomomori returns,
His hair unbound and flying free,
Arrows sprouting hairlike from his armor,
Its lacings stained with blood.
*(Tomomori staggers in from SR, leaning on his halberd for support. Arrows bristle from his armor; his clothing is pulled back at the left shoulder, revealing red beneath, evidence of a deep wound.)*
Unaware that behind him
Benkei has emerged and listens,
Tomomori lifts his voice.
TOMOMORI: Your Majesty, where are you? And your wet nurse, Tsubone, where is she?
*(Soldiers rush in from SR, striking at him. He sweeps them away with his halberd. More soldiers attack from SL, and he flings them off to SR. Again he staggers and leans on his upright halberd.)*
NARRATOR: Again he calls their names
And then sinks down.
TOMOMORI *(weaving about as he stands):* Oh, plague and torment! Such a wound as this will not weaken me!
NARRATOR: The halberd as his staff, he rises.
TOMOMORI: Tsubone! My lord! *(More soldiers attack him. He cuts them down.)*
NARRATOR: As on unsteady legs he moves about,
The door of the inner room opens
And Yoshitsune stands before him,
Pulling Tsubone forward
And cradling in his left arm at the hip
The youthful Emperor.

*(Yoshitsune is followed from the room by Kamei and Suruga.)*
TOMOMORI: Ah, well met, Yoshitsune! I hadn't expected to find you here. Just as Tomomori sank beneath those well remembered waves at Dannoura, now he will smash Yoshitsune to bits!
NARRATOR: He takes a firmer grip upon his lance.
*(Benkei moves forward, placing himself between Tomomori and Yoshitsune.)*
TOMOMORI: To the finish, Yoshitsune! Have at you!
NARRATOR: He advances on his adversary,
But Yoshitsune firmly stands his ground.
YOSHITSUNE: Control your temper, Tomomori. I, Yoshitsune, have something to say to you.
NARRATOR: He hands the Emperor to Tsubone,
And slowly he approaches.
YOSHITSUNE: It was brave and praiseworthy of you to pretend to drown yourself in the western sea, then conceal yourself in this place while protecting the Emperor and seeking to take vengeance on the enemy of your clan. As soon as I took up my stay here, I could tell that you were a man of no ordinary character and stature, and I perceived that you were a fugitive of the Heike clan. I explained things to Benkei, and we laid a plan for seeking out the Emperor. When by accident Benkei happened to step over that child, he felt a pain shoot through his body.[21] Moreover, I saw through your scheme to feign friendship, put me off my guard, and then capture me. So, I threw the boat's captain into the sea, turned the boat back to the shore, and reached here before you. Then I kept a careful eye on all that was happening. Though the Emperor is now in my hands, what good reason would one such as I, Yoshitsune, have to make a prisoner of

---

21. Stepping across a person's outstretched legs is a breach of etiquette, the insult being far greater when committed against an emperor. Moreover, the divinity that surrounds the emperor guarantees that such an act will bring some form of retribution. Earlier in the scene Benkei unwittingly stepped across Oyasu's legs and experienced a severe pain, evidence that helps Yoshitsune to realize that there were grounds for his suspicions about the Tokaiya and Ginpei.

our supreme lord, the true ruler of Japan? Since His Majesty's temporary difficulties stem only from the fact that he is a blood relative of the Heike clan, if I now give him assistance, not even my estranged brother Yoritomo will find fault with me. Have no anxiety about the safety of His Majesty, Tomomori.

NARRATOR: Tsubone is joyous at these words.

TSUBONE: Oh, there is no doubt about what he says, Tomomori. A little while ago, with many expressions of his compassion, he made a warrior's oath to hand over the Emperor to one of his relatives. Rejoice, Tomomori!

NARRATOR: Hearing this, Tomomori
Bristles with fury.
He grabs Tsubone and thrusts her aside.

TOMOMORI: Ah, how all this galls me! After all my labors to take vengeance on the enemy of my clan, it must be heaven's will that this very night my plan has been exposed so quickly, that even my identity has become known. *(To Tsubone.)* Just because you think it a heaven-sent blessing that Yoshitsune will protect the Emperor, that does not mean that Tomomori must therefore be grateful. Now, Yoshitsune, as an offering to the departed spirits of my clansmen, I will slice you in two with a single stroke!

NARRATOR: Staggering with his wound,
Tomomori urges his legs forward.
Snatching up his lance,
He confronts his adversary.
Benkei steps between them.

BENKEI: Listen to me, Tomomori! We anticipated all of this, and since this morning I too have been preparing for a naval battle against you. We have thwarted your designs, so give up the evil in your heart that thirsts for revenge. Embrace the way of the Buddha!

NARRATOR: Nimbly Benkei throws his rosary
So it lands round Tomomori's neck.

TOMOMORI: Come now, Benkei. By throwing this rosary at me,

I suppose you mean to suggest that I enter the priesthood. Eh! Take the filthy thing away! *(He takes off the rosary and flings it back.)* Since the beginnings of the four noble families,[22] it has been the lot of the Genji and the Heike to clash with one another. Whether I live or die, do you think I set aside my rancor?

NARRATOR: Wrathful his countenance—
Eyes shot with blood,
Hair flying in wild disarray—
Tomomori's face is that
Of a hateful wraith not of this world.
As he speaks, Suruga and Kamei,
Fearful for their lord,
Dash out to deal with Tomomori.
Though but a youth, the Emperor
Has heard and comprehended all.
He turns to Tomomori.

EMPEROR *(still held in Yoshitsune's arms)*: You, Tomomori, have been most gallant in your attendance and the care you have given me for so long. And today, by saving my life, Yoshitsune has shown his compassion. Bear no ill will against him, Tomomori.

NARRATOR: Tears well up within his eyes,
And Tsubone too is choked with weeping.

TSUBONE: Oh, well spoken, my lord. I'm sure Your Majesty will never forget Yoshitsune's kindness. People know that the Genji and the Heike are enemies, and it may be that people later will doubt the sincerity of my own heart toward His Majesty. I can thus serve him no more by living on. Take good care of my lord, I beg you Yoshitsune.

NARRATOR: Into her throat she plunges
A dagger she has kept in readiness.
Wretched at this parting,
She gazes on the Emperor's face,

---

22. The Minamoto (Genji), Taira (Heike), Fujiwara, and Tachibana families.

*Scene 2. The Tokaiya*

Her only word, "Farewell."
As to this world she bids adieu
And sadly breathes her last.
Tsubone's death, so unforeseen,
Wrenches the Emperor's heart.
Yet even more, Tomomori,
For whom such miseries
Come hard upon each other,
So crushed is he in spirit
That for a moment he can find no words.
Tears in full course,
He draws near to the Emperor.

TOMOMORI: Great is your good fortune, sire, that your were born an Emperor, the lord of heaven. Yet, as we drifted in the western sea and gazed across its waves, in those tides there was no water for us to drink. Our thirst was like that in the hell of starving wraiths. Once we encountered a storm, and your vessel was driven onto a wave-lashed, rock-strewn shore. When all the ladies of your court lifted their voices in lamentation, thinking your life had come to an end, the sound was like the wailing chorus of those in the hell of endless torture. Our battles with the Genji on land were a torment like nothing so much as the hell of contending demons. And the neighing of the countless horses in all of the Genji camps was like the din in the hell of ferocious beasts. Now, my Emperor, you have fallen to humble circumstances, experienced the hardships of mortal men, with the six roads to hell[23] revealed before your very eyes. And all

---

23. The Buddhist *Rokudō*, the six roads to hell, find frequent mention in the puppet theater. Each road represents a way of life that leads one to a specific place and form of treatment after death. The highest is *Tenjōdō*, a celestial existence of pleasure, akin to the concept of a blissful Christian heaven. Below that is *Ningendō*, the way of human beings, meaning broadly that one in this category could at least expect karmic rebirth as a human being rather than as some lower order of life. The remaining four roads are places of suffering and torment. Moving progressively to the most fearsome, these are: *Shuradō*, a place of perpetual strife; *Chikushōdō*, a hell of torment by ferocious beasts; *Gakidō*, a hell of eternally

of this has been due to my father Kiyomori's ambition to become connected with the imperial house. He spread abroad the story that a princess was a prince; and through his power he tried to outwit providence, making you, his grandson, the Emperor.[24] His treacherous lies to the Sun goddess have gathered one upon the other. It was inevitable that all his sins should finally be visited on the entire Heike clan! Mortally wounded as I am, I can go on no longer. Now Tomomori will sink into the sea, leaving behind a name to be known by later ages. Let it be said that he who sought revenge against Yoshitsune in the offing at Daimotsu Bay was but the unforgiving ghost of Tomomori. Now, now quickly, while breath is still in me, I beseech you, Yoshitsune, take care of His Majesty.

NARRATOR: He rises on tottering legs.

YOSHITSUNE: I head now for the Ogata house in Kyushu, and I shall attend the Emperor wherever I go.

NARRATOR: Yoshitsune takes the Emperor's hand.
Followed by Kamei, Suruga, and Benkei,
He begins to move away.
A wry smile forms on Tomomori's lips.

TOMOMORI: Yesterday's enemy is today's ally. But now my heart is at peace. I am happy. And so, I take my leave of this world.

*(After an obeisance toward Yoshitsune and the Emperor, Tomomori weakly pulls himself up by his lance.)*

---

starving wraiths; and finally *Jigokudō,* a hell of endless and excruciating pain and torture.

24. Kiyomori followed the earlier practice of the Fujiwara nobility of marrying a daughter to an emperor, thus gaining influence in imperial affairs. Kiyomori's daughter was Kenreimon'in; her child, and hence Kiyomori's grandson, became the young Emperor Antoku. The statement in the text, that Kiyomori tried to make it appear that a princess was a prince, is unclear, and there is no reference to this later in the play. Indeed, this line apparently is often deleted in performance . See headnote for line 27 of the text in Yūda, *Bunraku jōruri shū,* 167. *Gassaku,* or multiple authorship, may have led to some inconsistencies from act to act; this mention of a deception of identity may reflect some lack of coordination between the three playwrights of this play.

## Scene 2. The Tokaiya

TOMOMORI: Yesterday's enemy is today's ally. But now my heart is at peace. (Act 2, secene 2)

NARRATOR: Tearfully he casts back
   A glance to see his Emperor's face.
   The Emperor too turns back
   To look upon him in this last farewell
   Before he too takes leave.
   For Tomomori, left behind,
   His will be a journey setting sail
   To a realm whence none return.

(*Kamei, Suruga, and Benkei have already entered the inner portion of the house. Yoshitsune, still carrying the Emperor, now follows them. Tomomori, alone on stage, moves off to downstage SR. A samisen ensemble plays a lively interlude suggesting the restless waves, during which a curtain descends across the stage. When it rises, the set is dominated at mid-stage by a great rock outcropping at the sea's edge, a huge anchor on the sand before it.*[25] *A smaller rock is at SR. The foreground is the beach at Daimotsu Bay, the background the wave-swept sea stretching to the horizon. The narration resumes. Slowly and painfully, Tomomori heaves the anchor up to his shoulder and climbs to the top of the large rock. There he winds the anchor rope around his waist and knots it. He then hoists the anchor high above his head and heaves it over behind him. Tomomori poses grimly as the line plays out. The rope draws taut. For a moment Tomomori resists its pull. Then it drags him backwards into the sea.*)

    To plumb those briny depths
    Known as the Three Ways Sea,[26]

---

25. In some productions the rock is offshore in the water, and Tomomori sculls a small boat carrying the anchor out to it. The remainder of the action follows as described here.

26. The reference is to the Sanzu River (*Sanzu no kawa*), the river of three ways, the Eastern equivalent of the river Styx. The earlier imagery of the ocean is continued here with the Sanzu River spoken of as the Sanzu Sea.

## Scene 2: The Tokaiya

NARRATOR: To plumb these briny depths
    Known as the Three Ways Sea,
    He lifts an anchor above his head,
    And calling out, "Farewell, farewell,"
    He plunges into the swirling waves.
(*Tomomori drowns himself at Daimotsu Bay.*)
                              (Act 2, scene 2)

---

He lifts an anchor above his head,
And calling out "Farewell, farewell,"
He plunges into the swirling waves.
To his sovereign a noble liege,
Faithful servant to his lord,
The ill-starred Tomomori fades from view.
There a thousand fathoms deep
Beneath the Daimotsu moorings
His lifeless form will waste away.
Whither goes his name, his fame,[27]

27. These last lines are taken almost verbatim from

Drawn by restless tides
And flowing on, flowing ever on,
Amid the foaming billows?
No one may know.

---

the closing phrases of the Nō play *Funa Benkei*. See Nomura Hachirō, ed., *Yōkyoku shū*, 1:534.

# Act Three

## SCENE 1

## THE PASANIA TREE

(*At SR is a simple hut where tea is sold to drink. A woven straw mat has been unrolled and leans against its front as a shade. Near the center is a tall pasania tree with wide outstretched branches and full foliage. Beneath the tree are two simple benches draped in red cloth. The near background is a landscape of paddy fields and their dikes. Beyond the paddies are groves of trees at the base of low earth-colored mountains, green shrubbery mottling their peaks. As the narration commences, the stage is unoccupied.*)

NARRATOR: Three places there are, known as Yoshino:
In Tango, in Musashi, and along the Yamato Road,[1]

---

1. The old Tango province is now part of the metropolitan district of Kyoto. Musashi is the old provincial name

ACT THREE

>Where famed Mount Kimbu and its temple stand,
>Its precious treasure
>The statue of Miroku in the Zaō Hall.[2]
>On days this figure is unveiled,
>People throng from fields and hills alike,
>And tea stalls stand along the roads,
>The aroma of their brewing teas
>As fragrant as the flowers.
>And like a flower too, the young wife
>At her pinnacle of beauty,
>Tending the tea stall
>In her pale blue apron.

*(Kosen emerges from the tea stall and begins to arrange the benches. She is soon joined from the stall by her son Zenta, who begins to play in the sand.)*

>But with a boy of five or six
>Crying "Mama" at her side—
>Like tea grown cold, the fragrance fades.
>Now Wakaba no Naishi comes along
>With her young son Rokudai
>And retainer Kokingo.
>Parted from her husband Koremori
>And left to wither away,
>Now is she all the more
>So like a broken branch bereft of buds.

---

for what is today part of metropolitan Tokyo and neighboring Saitama prefecture. The town of Yoshino located along the Yamato Road is in Nara prefecture, some forty kilometers south of the city of Nara. The action of this act takes place in this last region.

2. Mount Kimbu is also known as Mount Yoshino, where the famous seventh century priest En no Gyōja is believed to have founded a temple dedicated to the Buddha Zaō, a central figure venerated by the austere *yamabushi* sect of mountain priests. The present temple dates from its rebuilding in 1456. Zaō is a deity of Indian origin, believed variously to be associated with Miroku (Maitreya, the Buddha of the future) and to be an incarnation of the historical Sakyamuni Buddha.

## Scene 1: The Pasania Tree

Having fled from Saga, their hopes are set
On finding Koremori on Mount Kōya.
With traveling bundles wrapped in cloth
And tied across their backs,
They have passed through Oshiumi
And come to Shimoichi Village
Here in Yoshino.[3]
Young Rokudai has been ill,
And luck has brought them to this tea house.
Kokingo urges Naishi to rest.

*(With Rokudai leading the way, Naishi enters from SR, a thin bamboo cane in her right hand, a black lacquered hat with red cords in her left. Kokingo brings up the rear, carrying their rolls of baggage slung front and back diagonally across his shoulder, a straw hat in his right hand. As Rokudai rubs his ailing stomach, Naishi comforts him, and the two sit on one of the benches. Kokingo seats himself on the ground.)*

KOKINGO: Here, rest on this bench for a while.

NARRATOR: He lowers the bundle from his back
And signals for tea.
The maid responds with cordiality
As Naishi looks around with care.

*(Kosen brings out a tray with two cups, Zenta at her heels. Naishi takes one cup and has Rokudai drink. Kokingo takes the other, drinks a bit and spits it out.)*

NAISHI *(spying Zenta)*: Ah, I see you have a child too. I have this one with me, a forgotten memento of his father. He's fallen ill with a stomachache along the way, and we have just exhausted our supply of medicine. As a mother yourself, I'm sure you can sympathize. If you have any medicine put aside, I wonder if I might request some.

---

3. Oshiumi (now Oshimi) is a village in modern Nara prefecture. Shimoichi village is situated along the Yoshino River in Nara prefecture, some two or three kilometers west of the city of Yoshino. Popular legend claims that Taira Koremori lived in hiding there after the Heike defeat. See Yūda, *Bunraku jōruri shū*, 308, n. 22.

KOSEN: Oh, that's a terrible thing to happen. But my boy here has never had a stomachache, so I'm afraid I haven't a thing.

NAISHI: Oh my, I don't know what I'm going to do.

KOSEN: Oh, wait a moment. Fortunately, in front of the village temple there's a person who sells darasuke medicine made over in Dorogawa.[4] That young man with you could get some in no time.

KOKINGO: No, wait. I'm not familiar with this place. I'm sorry to trouble you, but couldn't you get it for us?

KOSEN: Oh, that's easy enough. I'll fetch you some. Zenta, will you stay here, or do you want to go with me?

ZENTA *(clinging to his mother, and in a piping voice)*: I want to go with you.

*(Kosen and Zenta exit SL.)*

NARRATOR: A pretty thing is Kosen,
    Taking her child in hand,
    And noble is her heart as off she goes
    To buy medicine at the temple.
    Naishi watches her leave.

NAISHI: What a pleasant girl. Oh look, Rokudai. There are lots of nuts here from this big tree. Wouldn't you like to have fun picking them up? Kokingo, you don't mind picking some up, do you?

NARRATOR: Encouraged by her cheerful words . . .

KOKINGO: Yes, I'll pick some up too.

NARRATOR: Rokudai gets up,
    His illness half forgotten in the game,
    As Naishi too joins in.

NAISHI: Here, let's gather them up.

KOKINGO *(solicitously)*: No, I'll get them for you.

NARRATOR: Kokingo, a young man close to twenty,
    Behaves unlike a grownup
    To cheer the child, as they gather

---

4. Dorogawa was a small town not far from Yoshino. The *darasuke* medicine, a dark bitter potion used to treat stomachaches, was well known in the area. See Yūda, *Bunraku jōruri shū*, 380, n. 23.

## Scene 1: The Pasania Tree

Horse chestnuts and *kaya* nuts.[5]
Just then a young man comes in,
Walking briskly on weary legs.
He too carries dangling from his shoulder
A traveler's bundle wrapped in cloth.
He spies the tea house.
*(Gonta enters quickly from SR. He carries the same sort of pack over his shoulder as Kokingo had been carrying. He wears a light rain cape and has a cloth wrapped about his head, a wicker hat in his hand. The others take no notice of him as he sits on one of the benches and places his cloth bundle next to Kokingo's pack.)*
GONTA: Well, I guess I'll take a rest here and have a smoke.
*(He takes out a pipe with a thimblelike bowl and packs some tobacco into it.)*
NARRATOR: With a thump, he drops his bundle on the bench.
GONTA *(speaking into the tea hut):* Excuse me, but I'll just help myself to a light.
NARRATOR: He puffs away at his pipe.
GONTA: Eh, are all of you folks going to the unveiling of the statue?[6] The young master here stopping off for a spell? He's not like the country children where I come from. My, but isn't he a handsome lad.
NARRATOR: Though he offers praise
And tries to strike up a chat,
The others are reserved,
And without exchanging words
Continue gathering nuts.
After a short rest, the man speaks up again.
GONTA: Look here, all those nuts that have fallen from the tree have worms in them. They may look all right, but there's nothing inside. Get the ones on the tree.

---

5. *Kaya* nuts (also called *tochi* nuts, or horse chestnuts) are from the tree known botanically as *torreya nucifera* (a member of the yew family). It is curious that these are the nuts being gathered, since the tree in the scene is a pasania.

6. The unveiling of religious statues normally kept from view was an occasion for pilgrimages.

KOKINGO: What are you talking about? This tree is over twenty feet tall. We haven't got claws to climb with.
GONTA: Ah, there's an easy way to get them.
KOKINGO: What's that?
GONTA *(tapping the tobacco from his pipe and putting it away in his tobacco case)*: Here, let me show you what skill can do.
NARRATOR: He picks up a stone,
 Throws it at a branch,
 And down the nuts fall.
*(Gonta starts picking up nuts himself, putting them into his wicker hat, which he then dumps into Rokudai's hat.)*
 So happy is Rokudai
 He quite forgets his discomfort.
ROKUDAI: Oh, pick them up, Kokingo.
NARRATOR: Her spirits lifted,
 Naishi too is delighted.
NAISHI: Oh, what a nice thing you've done for us. Thank you, thank you.
NARRATOR: She bows to him, a gesture that
 He knows is more than he deserves,
 But he keeps this knowledge to himself
 And shows a proud demeanor.
GONTA: Heh, heh, see how well I did it? Well, I'd like to demonstrate it a little more, but I've got a long road ahead, can't entertain you any longer. I've got to be off.
*(He jumps up, grabs the pack Kokingo had left on the bench, hiding the pack with his hat.)*
NARRATOR: He hoists the bundle to his back.
GONTA: Perhaps we'll meet again.
NARRATOR: So saying, he takes his leave. *(Gonta exits SL.)*
 Kokingo completes his nut gathering.
KOKINGO: Madam, I think this is enough. That man just now was a clever one.
NARRATOR: As he watches the departing man,
 He notices the bundle on the bench. *(Startled.)*
 Though of the same color,

## Scene 1: The Pasania Tree

It seems somehow different.
To the bench he dashes
And examines the contents.
But the things inside are unfamiliar.
In this one is a leather covered basket,
While his had been of wisteria vine.

KOKINGO *(musing):* I wonder, did he purposely go off with our bundle while we were preoccupied with the nuts, or was he just careless? *(He reties the bundle loosely and replaces it on the bench.)* In any case, I'll run after him and exchange it.

NARRATOR: Kokingo is set to dash off in pursuit,
When the man comes clattering back
From the direction he had gone.

GONTA *(bowing):* Oh, my apologies. I made a mistake.

NARRATOR: He holds out the bundle.

GONTA: It was beginning to get dark, and I was impatient to be off. Your bundle was the same color, so I didn't pay attention to whether it was heavy or light. I just carelessly took the wrong one and suddenly realized the mistake on the road. I've come back to return it and offer my apologies. I'm terribly sorry. *(He lowers himself to the ground and bows.)*

NARRATOR: He begs with an earnestness
That belies his looks.
Kokingo breathes a sigh of relief.

KOKINGO: If it was a mistake, there's no need for an apology. As long as nothing happens to be missing. All right?

GONTA: Why, if there were to be any discrepancy, I wouldn't be able to face you. Please, examine it carefully.

KOKINGO: Hmmm. All right then, if you say so. I don't have any doubts, mind you, but I'll just take a look.

NARRATOR: He opens and checks the bundle
And finds nothing amiss.

*(Kokingo examines the contents, sees the portrait of Koremori and quickly tucks it into his sleeve. He then returns Gonta's bag to him.)*

KOKINGO: Let's just say it was an inadvertent error. I'm quite satisfied. Here, you may take yours and be on your way.

NARRATOR: As he hands back
   The cloth wrapped bundle on the bench,
   The man's face grows suspicious.
GONTA: Um, I see you untied the inner package.
KOKINGO: Well, it looked different from mine at first, but just in case I might be wrong, I glanced through it.
NARRATOR: As Kokingo speaks,
   The man opens the inner basket,
   Scatters things about,
   Pulls out a lined gown,
   Searches an unlined cotton kimono.
   Astonished, he holds the basket up
   And shakes it violently.
GONTA: What's this? Hey, it's gone, gone, it's gone!
NARRATOR: He rolls his eyes about.
KOKINGO: What's gone? What is it you can't find?
NARRATOR: Kokingo stands worriedly by,
   Looking all around.
   Having planned it all,
   The quarrelsome man
   Tucks up his sleeves belligerently.
GONTA: Look here, young man, this basket contained twenty ryō[7] in gold that someone gave me to pay for a prayer service at a temple up on Mount Kōya. You took it! You're trying to cheat me! Give it to me. Come on, let's have it! GIVE IT BACK!!
NARRATOR: At this unlooked for predicament,
   Kokingo is roused to fury
   And readies his sword for a fight.
*(He whips the cloth traveling cover from the hilt of his sword, pulls it slightly from the scabbard and strikes a stance of readiness.)*
KOKINGO: Listen, you low life, if you've got something to say to a samurai, let's hear it!
NARRATOR: Kokingo's face wears a look of threat,

---

7. The gold ryō coin was a common high denomination currency during the eighteenth century. Twenty ryō constituted a considerable sum.

## Scene 1: The Pasania Tree

But the man remains undaunted.

GONTA *(impudently)*: Ha ha ha ha ha. The thief always puts on a bold face, they say. Well, I won't be put off by your high-handed posturings, not me. Are your trying to intimidate

KOKINO: I've tolerated you all I'm going to! (Gonta cringes before the threatening Kokingo.) (Act 3, scene 1)

me, drawing that rusty-as-a-red-sardine sword of yours? Save your cute act for some nice spring afternoon. It's only twenty ryō. Stop quibbling and hand it over, before you're arrested as a common criminal.

*(At this point, Kosen and her child return from their errand and, unnoticed by the others, quietly enter the tea hut.)*

NARRATOR: Kokingo recognizes him
  For the crooked swindler that he is.
KOKINGO: I've tolerated you all I'm going to!
NARRATOR: About to draw his sword,
  Kokingo looks at his two companions.
  Sternly he endures the insolence
  And takes a breath to control himself.

*(In the interplay between Kokingo and Gonta, when Kokingo threatens to use his sword Gonta cringes; as soon as Kokingo controls himself, Gonta resumes his strutting truculence.)*

KOKINGO *(in forced levity)*: Ah ha ha ha ha ha. Young man, you've made a mistake. As you can see, I am accompanying these two leg-weary travelers here, so even if thousands of gold coins spilled out of your pack, I wouldn't think to pay it any attention. Go ahead, ask them.

GONTA: Now wait, wait, just wait a minute! You've brought along these tired travelers just for the purpose of robbing people. Nobody would suspect you. Makes it easier. It's the latest thing these days. Now, there weren't thousands of gold coins in that bundle, just . . . heh heh . . . just twenty ryō.

KOKINGO: And you've made up your mind that I stole it.

GONTA: Well, its obvious!

KOKINGO: And your proof that I took it?

GONTA *(sputtering)*: Well . . . why . . . why the hell did you untie the basket inside the bundle? Look here, this basket's mine. "As long as there's nothing missing," you said about your own parcel, didn't you? That was just an empty quibble. All right, let's have it! HAND IT OVER!

NARRATOR: He draws close to Kokingo.

*(Gonta waves the two parts of the basket about, then advances on Kokingo and pokes him in the chest.)*

KOKINGO: That does it!

NARRATOR: As Kokingo draws his sword,
   Naishi, all afluster, holds him back.

*(As Kokingo brandishes his sword, Gonta tips one of the benches on end and hides cringing behind it. Naishi comes up behind Kokingo to restrain him.)*

NAISHI: Kokingo, your anger is quite justified, I understand. But if you lose your temper, it will make things difficult for me and for the child. I know you must be angry, but be patient. Give in to what the fellow wants and settle the matter quietly. Think of the disaster that might befall me and the boy, and calm yourself, I beg you.

NARRATOR: As she speaks, she is overcome by tears.
Kokingo, his blood running hot,
Cannot bear to see her weep.

KOKINGO *(with great emotion):* If these were better days for us, it wouldn't give me satisfaction even to cut off the arms and legs of such a lout. But we are like fugitives, who take fright even from the wind blowing through a field of miscanthus, thinking it might be a pursuing party. I'll do as you wish. But it really does gall me.

*(Gonta remains quaking in fear behind the shield he has made of the bench.)*

NARRATOR: Kokingo must serve as escort
For his two precious companions,
And so he grits his teeth
And bears his deep chagrin.
Seeing this, the other man
Is filled again with impudence.

GONTA: Now that you've warmed your pocket with my twenty ryō, what kind of a face is that? *(Teasing:)* Oh, I'm scared, I'm so scared. Ha ha ha ha ha. So you're going to kill me with that red sardine of a sword? Trying to intimidate me with that scowl on your face? I'm going to pull out those hairs on the front of your head, one by one. And the money, have you already hidden it? Well, I'll search for it, starting with that wench who's with you.

NARRATOR: As the man moves toward Naishi,
Kokingo grabs him by the neck
And drags him back.
From the money for their journey
Kokingo, glaring, pays the man as asked.

KOKINGO: Since I have to accompany these people here, who are important to me, here's the twenty ryō you've swindled from me. Take it now and get out!

*(Kokingo throws a packet of money in Gonta's face, knocking him down.)*

NARRATOR: Kokingo throws the money packet at him,

But as it is with swindlers,
The man is blinded by the sight of gold,
And swiftly he snatches it up,
Counting the coins as they clink by his ear.
GONTA *(speaking as though to himself but actually for Kokingo's benefit)*: Oh, that was a close call. If I hadn't had my wits about me, this young hooligan would've swiped even more.
NARRATOR: His words are filled with bitter spite.
KOKINGO: I'll smash your insulting jaw!
*(Kokingo again puts his hand to the hilt of his sword, and Gonta again cringes, trying to hide behind his wicker hat.)*
NARRATOR: Naishi holds back the threatening Kokingo.
NAISHI: Come, before anything else happens.
NARRATOR: Young Rokudai in tow, she leaves,
And Kokingo too is dragged away,
Helplessly nursing his ire
As they hurry off
To lodgings in Kamiichi.[8] *(The three exit SL.)*
GONTA: Ha ha ha ha ha. He could glare at me a hundred times, I wouldn't care. Why each time would be worth one bu, wouldn't it?[9] Nice piece of work!
NARRATOR: The crooked Gonta tucks away the gold
Into the fold of his kimono.
As he's set to race off to the gambling den,
His wife at the tea house bars his way.
KOSEN: Gonta, where are you going?
GONTA: Oh, Kosen. You left the shop open. Where've you been?
KOSEN: I went over to Sakamoto[10] to buy some medicine for some travelers.
GONTA: Oh, that was a good move. If I'd been here I'd probably have just been a nuisance. Good thing I slipped away.

    8. A town in modern Nara prefecture some eight kilometers east of the village of Shimoichi.
    9. Gonta's calculation is a bit off. One ryō equaled four bu; one hundred bu would be twenty-five ryō.
    10. There were several places in the region with Sakamoto in their names. Yūda (*Bunraku jōruri shū*, 381, n. 26) speculates as to which one was Kosen's destination.

### Scene 1: The Pasania Tree

NARRATOR: She grabs him by the front of his robe
And pulls him to her.
KOSEN: Gonta, you're trying to pull some wool over my eyes. You didn't slip away. You were just making a great fuss about something when I came back a little while ago. If you swindled somebody, show me what you cheated them out of. I don't know what it might be, but I was listening in the shadow of that pine over there. Oh, you . . . you do some awful things. You may look like your parents, but you're not like them at all. Your father is Yazaemon, the former Yasuke, of the Tsurube Sushi Shop[11], and he's a man of influence in this village, but the way you behave one would think you'd been disowned by him. We were some distance away when we lived in Gose.[12] But even after we came to live nearer, here in Shimoichi, he hasn't come near me, your wife, or even his grandchild here. You've got a reputation among people for being "Crooked Gonta" and "Swindler Gonta" because of the way you behave. Don't you love your son Zenta? If you need money for your gambling so much, you could get it by selling off your wife and child. I ask you again, please give it up. What karma has made you so frightening?
NARRATOR: She clings to him, lamenting,
But he sends her reeling away.
GONTA: Hey, you'll tear my clothes. You're always nagging me with the same old line. Look here, any stealing or swindling I do is because of you.
KOSEN: Oh, such outrageous things I have to listen to. Why do you say that?
GONTA: Why do I say it? You know why. I went through the

---

11. There is indeed a Tsurube Sushi Shop in Shimoichi today, and the proprietor possesses documents showing that it has existed there at least as far back as the middle years of the seventeenth century, enjoying a high reputation for its sushi in several nearby provinces. See Yūda, *Bunraku jōruri shū*, 381, n. 27. A *tsurube* is a wooden pail used to draw water from a well. A similar pail is used at the Tsurube Sushi Shop in the making of its sushi.

12. A town in modern Nara prefecture, about ten kilometers north of Shimoichi.

coming of age ceremony when I was fifteen. On instructions from my old man I went to Gose and set up a sushi house. Then I found you there working as one of the unlicensed whores, and once I got to like you I couldn't give you up. To get money, I took to stealing my mother's savings—she snores like a shark, but she sleeps like a Buddha. Then I embezzled all of the savings of the shop and the money from the clients' accounts, and I used up half of all I owned—you understand? With that, the old man threw me out of the house, he *did* disown me. I was just too much for him to handle. As fate would have it, you were pregnant with this brat at the time, and your boss demanded money to pay off your indenture. So, I stole the rice set aside for the land tax and used that to pay off your boss. Then the village headman, that ass, he came complaining about it, said he'd have my head. Said I had to pay it all back in annual installments. He came damn near every day dunning me, so to settle that account I turned to gambling. I moved up in the world, to small-time extortion and swindling. In the meantime, I cut a hole through the wall of the old man's storehouse to see what I could take from there. But my sister Osato and that guy living in my father's house were crooning at each other the whole night, so I lost that chance altogether. Now that fortune has come my way today, I'm going to go with my luck and give my mother a fleecing—I can take her for two or three kamme.[13] You go out and buy some sake and wait for me. Hey, Zenta, don't you fall asleep on me as soon as the sun goes down. If you can't stay up all night, I won't hand the trade on to you.

(*During his monologue, Gonta variously mimes the action he describes. While talking to Kosen, he takes his rain cape and spreads it on the ground. From his tobacco pouch he produces a set of dice and starts to*

---

13. The kamme, or kan, was a unit both of money and of weight. In southwestern Japan, where the play is set, the preferred currency was silver, which usually traded by weight. In Edo, gold was the more common large denomination coin. Four kamme of silver equaled one gold ryō coin.

## Scene 1: The Pasania Tree

teach Zenta how to gamble. In the course of this instruction, he alternately praises and cuffs Zenta. Finally, he takes up the cape and tucks it under his left arm.)

NARRATOR: As he stands up, his wife holds him back.
KOSEN: What a terrible thing to do, cheating even your own mother. Please, come on home.
NARRATOR: She clings to him, but he throws her aside.
KOSEN: Oh, Zenta, make him stay.
NARRATOR: As his mother bids him,
　The clever boy speaks up.
ZENTA *(in a high piping voice)*: Papa, come home, come!
NARRATOR: Like a creeping vine,
　Zenta wraps himself
　About his father's arm.
　No good, thinks Gonta,
　For the lad to follow after him.
　Against his will
　He is drawn back by the child,
　Bound all the more by ties of blood.
*(Zenta buries his head in Gonta's stomach, holding to him and pushing him back. Gonta, his attitude softening, gives him a couple of gentle taps on the rump.)*
GONTA: Ah, all of this has put me off. Maybe I can make a new start.
NARRATOR: Even an ogre would be moved by the child.
GONTA *(speaking gently)*: What cold hands you have.
*(He holds Zenta's hands in his to warm them.)*
NARRATOR: He takes the lad by the hand,
　And with his wife they start for home.
*(Holding hands, they exit to SR as the clappers signal a change of scene.)*

SCENE 2

# THE DEATH OF KOKINGO

*(Dusk gathers along a roadway through a bamboo grove surrounding rice paddies. At SR and SL are stands of bamboo, a thicker grove visible in the far background beyond a foreground of tan rice fields. At center is a single small pine tree. A sloping roadway descends to the stage from between the bamboo stalks at SR. As the narration begins, there is no one on stage.)*

NARRATOR: As the sun is sinking in the west,
    Kokingo Takesato escorts
    Lady Naishi and her young son Rokudai.
*(To the excited slap of the clappers, Naishi stumbles in along the road that enters at SR, pulling Rokudai after her. She looks behind her anxiously, then leads Rokudai off SL.)*
    In the village of Kamiichi
    Kokingo was surrounded

## Scene 2: The Death of Kokingo

By scores of Tomokata's men,
And now he suffers many wounds.
Yet still he thinks only
To return with his charges to the Capital.
In pursuit come several hundred men,
Crying that the fugitives shan't escape.

*(Inokuma Dainoshin appears from downstage SR. As he advances onto the stage, he looks back at the stand of bamboo. He takes a stalk and fashions it into a spear, then hides himself in the bamboo thicket at SL. Soon after, Kokingo comes in from SR, fighting furiously with four pursuers. Kokingo's upper garment has been pulled down, and his formerly dressed hair has been loosened in the battle and now flies in a wild shock about his head. As the narration continues, he slashes left and right, killing three of his attackers and putting the fourth to flight SL.)*

Though he bears the wounds of battle,
Kokingo's spirit remains
As strong as iron, firm as stone.
His sword lashes out in reckless fury,
Downing here three, there seven, men
As he slashes through the horde,
Leaving behind the bodies of his foes
Like fallen maple leaves
And flowers of the autumn.
Now the pursuing party's chief,
Inokuma Dainoshin, belatedly comes out. *(From his hiding place at SR.)*

INOKUMA: Yaa, Kokingo! You escaped death once. Now where do you think you're going? My master, Lord Tomokata, was in a towering rage when we let you escape earlier at North Saga, and I felt so low that I couldn't return to his mansion. We made a priest back at the hermitage confess, and since then we've been following you along this road. Now then, hand over Koremori's wife and child. It's time for you to give up and kill yourself!

NARRATOR: At his shouts, Kokingo grits his teeth,

Smarting at his bleeding wounds.
KOKINGO: Never! So long as I, Kokingo Takesato, son of Shume
  Hōgan, draw a breath!
INOKUMA: Those words seal your death!
NARRATOR: Up springs Inokuma, slashing out,
  But with his own blade Kokingo
  Parries the blows with a clang.
  Displaying nimble footwork,
  He swings around to dodge a strike.
  Yet however sharp his skill,
  His wounds have their effect.
*(Naishi and Rokudai re-enter from SL.)*
  Naishi and Rokudai, terrified, uncertain,
  Pick pebbles from the ground,
  And with a will they fling them at their foe.
  Into stubborn Inokuma's eyes they fly.
  Now, with his foe's eyesight confused,
  Kokingo slashes in and cuts him twixt the eyes,
  And down he topples with a thud.
  As Kokingo leaps upon him,
  Inokuma thrusts upward with his sword,
  Running Kokingo through the ribs,
  Pitching him in a backward bend.
  When Inokuma tries to rise,
  Again Naishi hurls sand in his face.
  Inokuma has been slashed, but Kokingo too
  Struggles painfully with his wound,
  On the verge of passing
  To the realm beyond.
  Yet steadfast in fidelity,
  Kokingo with no trouble holds his rival down.
  Then with a push he delivers the lethal thrust.
KOKINGO *(bearing up under his pain)*: There, I'm glad I finally
  finished him off.
NARRATOR: Now, heavy is his weary heart,

## Scene 2: The Death of Kokingo

And with a groan he sinks down to the ground.
Naishi and Rokudai console him
And take him in their arms.

NAISHI *(in tears)*: Oh, Kingo, Kingo, don't leave us. Come back, I beg you. If you die, what's to become of this child? Oh, how wretched, my heart is broken.

NARRATOR: Her wailing voice reaches Kokingo's ears;
He lifts his head.

KOKINGO *(slowly and painfully)*: Oh, Lady Naishi, Master Rokudai, please forget about me. My heart is fearless still, but I can't go on. My young lord, your humble Kokingo in his last breath has something he must tell you. Listen carefully. My lord Koremori had earlier wished to enter the priesthood, and as I was to meet someone at Kumano Bay, I was to escort you two safely to Mount Kōya. But wounded as I am, I simply cannot take another step. Young master, you accompany Lady Naishi to the Kamiya way station and leave her there.[1] Have someone take you up the mountain. Don't mention your father's name; just say you've come to see a novice who has recently entered the priesthood. We are in the midst of our enemies both to the west and to the east, so don't let them know you are a noble of the Heike. If later when you have grown to manhood you should remember Kokingo, then as one drop of water can nourish a single flower it will sustain me on the road to the world beyond. I will be waiting to hear how you have grown up. Ah, how bitter is this parting from you. *(He weeps.)*

NARRATOR: He speaks with labored breath,
As Rokudai clings to him.

ROKUDAI: Don't die, Kokingo! If you die, I'll never see my father.

---

1. Kamiya, in modern Wakayama prefecture, was a way station at the entry to Fudō Slope leading up to Mount Kōya. Since women were not permitted on Mount Kōya, Naishi would have to wait there while Rokudai went up the mountain to see his father.

NARRATOR: Naishi, in tears,
Comes quickly to his side.
NAISHI: Listen to him, Kokingo, even though he's only a child. We look to you alone. Just think to yourself, "I won't die, I won't die till I've seen Koremori." All of the Heike clan has perished; the whole wide world is in the hands of our enemies. How can we survive much longer? Kill us too!
NARRATOR: Small wonder that she grieves,
And the injured Kokingo
Is choked with tears.
KOKINGO: Our former lord Shigemori is a saint of Japan. My young master here is his grandson, so it cannot be that he is without the blessings of all the gods and Buddhas. Believe that he has a promising future, and put such ill-considered thoughts from your mind. *(He staggers to his feet and points SL with his sword.)* Oh look, the lights of lanterns over there. Another search party is probably on its way after us. Quickly, take the young master and go.
NAISHI: No, no, I will not abandon you wounded here. Where would I go? If you die, I shall die with you.
NARRATOR: She sits beside him on the ground.
KOKINGO: Ah, what faint-hearted words. Isn't Master Rokudai important? Kokingo is not one to die from such wounds as these. If you won't listen to me, I will kill myself right now. (He points his sword at his abdomen.)
NAISHI: No, please, wait. If you care so deeply for us, then we will go on ahead. Kokingo, don't die, I beg you.
KOKINGO: Don't worry about me. I'm lucky. I'll follow after you.
NAISHI: We will surely be waiting for you.
NARRATOR: While she speaks, nearer draw
The threatening lantern lights.
Now with bitter sadness in her breast
Naishi takes the young child's hand
And leads him off in flight.

## Scene 2: The Death of Kokingo

How piteous her warmth of heart.
The wounded man watches them depart.
*(With many glances back, Naishi and Rokudai exit SL.)*
KOKINGO *(in great pain):* I lied when I said I wouldn't die. Even if I had the strength of all the Buddhas of the universe, how could I survive with all these wounds? *(Gasping:)* Lady Naishi, Master Rokudai, this is my last farewell.
NARRATOR: On the point of death,
Now past six of the deepening night—
The very hour of his birth—
He takes his final breath,
And like the morning dew he fades away.
*(Still on his feet, Kokingo sways and lurches backward against the pine tree at center stage. He swings around with his sword, cutting a branch from the tree, and then he sinks to the ground and lies still.)*
The lanterns that soon arrive
Are those of the village's five-man group,[2]
Who chat noisily among themselves
Along the mountain road.
The village headman Saku draws to a halt.
*(Saku and another villager, with Yazaemon between them, enter SR along the sloping road and stop where it joins the stage. Each carries a paper lantern.)*
SAKU: Say, Yazaemon, you're a sushi presser, and that brings something to my mind. Those samurai from Kamakura who swarmed in on us just now and pressed[3] us into service—they whispered into my ear, rustling like so many centipedes. Said things that would scare a person bald. We bowed and scraped and agreed to everything they said without thinking about it. Do you know what it was all about?

---

2. As a means of insuring social order during the Tokugawa period, communities were organized into five-man groups having collective responsibility for their members.

3. Yazaemon's sushi shop makes *oshizushi*, a sushi made by pressing the finished product with a weighted lid. Hence the pun here on the verb *osu*, "press."

YAZAEMON: Oh, it's perfectly clear. Haven't you all measured me up by now? This is Yazaemon here. When I finally gave up on my own son, I wouldn't let him even come close to my door. Once I've figured things out, I'm not one to sit around and let my legs fall asleep. The last thing the samurai said to us gives us a wonderful chance. The search party told us that a young man and a woman with a child had escaped from Saga and had come to this village. At that point, the chief creep of the search party said that there'd be a reward if the fugitives were caught. So there, we've got a golden opportunity in this. Every one of you keep a good watch.

VILLAGER: Oh, yeah, and for a thing like this we ought to go get that ill-tempered son of yours Gon . . . I mean Master Gontarō to help out.[4]

NARRATOR: As the rest of the group goes off
Along the mountain road,
Yazaemon descends the slope.
Then, just ahead of him,
He comes upon a wounded man.
With a gasp he jumps aside.
The feeling is an eerie one,
But he lifts the lantern high
And slowly, slowly draws near.

*(As he moves across the stage toward SL, Yazaemon stumbles in the dark on Kokingo's body and leaps back. He then inches forward for a better look with the aid of his lantern.)*

YAZAEMON: My, he's been cut up something brutal. Looks like a traveler. If this had been done by a highwayman, he'd have stripped the man naked. Maybe it's the work of some ruffian after his traveling money.

NARRATOR: As father of a no-good son himself,
His anxiety rises apace.

YAZAEMON: Hey, young man, young man.

---

4. The full name of Yazaemon's son Gonta is Gontarō. The villager refers to him as Good-for-Nothing Gonta (Igami no Gonta), switching in mid-phrase to the more polite form of his name out of deference to his father.

## Scene 2: The Death of Kokingo

NARRATOR: From the still form
No answer to his call.
YAZAEMON: So, he's already breathed his last? What a pity. I wonder where he comes from. Looks a bit old for that sort of hair style.[5] Ah, all of our meetings in this life, even the chance touching of sleeves, all are foreordained by a previous existence. *(He joins his hands and offers a Buddhist prayer.)* Namu Amida Butsu, Namu Amida, Namu Amida Butsu.
NARRATOR: So goes his prayer for the dead.
YAZAEMON *(stepping over the body and starting to move off to SL):* Ah, such is this transient world that life is uncertain for both old and young. Even seeing such a melancholy sight as this is an admonition from the Buddha. It's important to sow the right seeds in this life if one's to proceed straightaway to a better hereafter.
NARRATOR: Such are his ruminations
As he moves away.
*(Yazaemon stops and thinks.)*
But then, what thought
Has brought him to a halt?
Suddenly struck by a notion,
He hesitates, stands still.
Slowly, pensively, he returns.
Carefully looking around,
He picks up the unsheathed sword.
Then quickly, in a single stroke,
He cuts off the dead man's head.
A puff blows out the lantern's light,
And in his hand he holds the severed head.
*(There is the sound of insects in the bushes, then the deep gong of a bell tolling the late hour. During the narration, Yazaemon hangs his lantern on the pine tree, takes off his cloak and cautiously draws*

---

5. Kokingo has not yet had his pate shaved, part of a boy's initiation into adulthood and usually performed between the ages of eleven and sixteen. Kokingo is about twenty, rather late to be wearing such a hair style. The preceding five years of warfare may have interfered with his undergoing such a ceremony.

*Kokingo's sword to him with his foot. Carefully surveying his surroundings, he cuts off the head and wraps it in his cloak, which he then tucks under his right arm.)*

YAZAEMON: For this, much thanks.

NARRATOR: Off he hastens, straight
 Along the road to home.

*(Tottering in his haste, Yazaemon exits SL.)*

SCENE 3

THE SUSHI SHOP

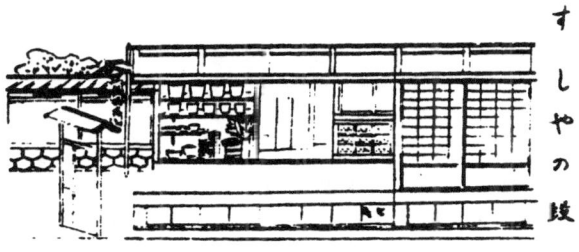

(*The scene is the Tsurube Sushi Shop of Yazaemon. The interior of a house extends from SL about two-thirds of the way across the stage, its far SL portion a room enclosed by shōji panels. The other room, open toward the audience, has a curtained doorway at center. At the SR side of the room is an alcove for wooden sushi pails, several of which are on their racks. The house is raised about two feet off the ground in typical Japanese fashion. The entrance to the main room is at SR, where a sign hangs advertising the business. Outside the entry is a simple gateway. The distant background at SR is of green mountains, groves of trees at their bases, and tan-colored rice paddies with pathways along their dikes in the nearer foreground. As the narration begins, Osato and her Mother emerge from the curtained doorway and seat themselves before the rack holding the sushi pails. Osato is dressed in a lavender and*

gray checked kimono with red floral patterned sleeve linings, and a red cord to hold back her flowing sleeves. On her head is a large white kerchief. Her Mother is dressed in a brown kimono. Soon after they sit down, villagers come ordering sushi and the women attend to them.)

NARRATOR: When sushi's made by a fair young maid—
So lovely that she makes the flowers bloom
Though spring has yet to come—
The seasoning is fine and people come to buy.
Just right the sushi's tang
At the Tsurube Sushi Shop,
Whose wares are widely sold
In Yoshino's Shimoichi.

(As the Mother hands out sushi wrapped in bamboo bark to the village customers, they are noticeably less appreciative than when Osato serves them.)

While Yazaemon, the master,
Is absent from his sushi shop,
His wife—herself a shrewd shopkeeper—
Tends to the quick-work sushi,[1]
While her daughter Osato,
Her sleeves tied back with cords
And over her skirt an apron,
Smiles with such a winsome charm
It draws the customers in
To eat this sushi made of river fish.
The sushi at its pinnacle of taste,
A young girl in the freshness
Of her maidenhood—
Who would wonder that the Tsurube Shop
Enjoys a happy reputation.
As she drives the wedges
Around the wooden covers

---

1. At the Tsurube shop, sushi is made with seasoned rice packed into a wooden tub. Fish flavored with salt or vinegar is placed on top, then a weighted lid is wedged in place and the fish is left to cure. Sushi made in this way and ready for sale in four or five days is known as *hayazume*, or quick-work, sushi.

### Scene 3: The Sushi Shop

And puts away the sushi tubs,
Osato speaks.

OSATO: Oh, mother, yesterday father said that Yasuke and I would be married this evening. Since then, how bright the world has become. We'll be man and wife, he said, but it's dusk and father hasn't come back. I wonder if he was fibbing to me.

MOTHER: What are you talking about? Why would he tell you a fib? Why, Yasuke's a fine young man with lots of promise. Your father brought him back from a pilgrimage to the Kumano Shrine. He said that he could read the young man's mind and heart, and he's given him his own name of Yasuke, your father now calling himself Yazaemon. When he said that he was going to turn over the business of the shop to the young man, it meant that he already intended for you to marry him. Today your father had a sudden call to go to the village office. It's taking more time than I expected it would, but there's nobody here we can send to meet him.

OSATO: You're right, that's too bad. Yasuke said there were several orders for sushi and he didn't think we had enough tubs to go around, so he went out to get some of the empty ones. He ought to be returning by now.

NARRATOR: In the midst of their gossiping
A man returns, upon his shoulder
A balance pole supporting empty tubs.

*(Yasuke enters from SR with a balance pole holding empty sushi tubs across his shoulder.)*

By his look he's quick of wit
And dapper in his dress.
Of whom but such a charming man
Would the poem of old have spoken:

> . . . .only you can savor both
> The color and the fragrance.[2]

---

2. An allusion to a poem (number 38) by Ki no Tomomori from the poetic anthology *Kokin waka shū* (comp. 905):

With his thick sidelocks—
The kind the young girls love—
Even if made to wear a hat,
He would cut a handsome figure.
Even before he enters the house,
The eagerly waiting Osato
Finds herself ecstatic.

*(She runs to the doorway, and as Yasuke enters she takes one end of the balance pole to help him in.)*

OSATO *(sweetly)*: Oh, Yasuke, you've come back. I've been waiting for you. You're so late. *(Coyly)* I was worried, thinking that you might have stopped off somewhere.

NARRATOR: She tries to give herself a wifely look.

Predictably, a daughter of a sushi man
Whose trade requires swift work,
It seems she's grown up quickly.

*(Yasuke puts down the pole, enters the room and sits at SR near the doorway. Osato goes and sits next to him.)*

Her mother stifles her amusement.

MOTHER: Pay no attention to her, Master Yasuke. Here in the Yoshino district there's a teaching from the goddess Benzaiten[3] that says, "Hold your husband dear, as though he were a god or a Buddha." Jealousy, however, runs deep. But, that old

---

To whom if not you, my love,
Should I show them,
These flowers of the plum?
For only you can savor both
The color and the fragrance.
Saeki Umetomo, ed., *Kokin waka shū*, 111.

The poem is quoted to suggest that Yasuke is a man of finely honed sensibilities. For other translations, see Helen Craig McCullough, *Kokin Wakashū: The First Imperial Anthology of Japanese Poetry*, 21; and Earl Miner, *An Introduction to Japanese Court Poetry*, 10.

3. Benzaiten (also known as Benten) is a female deity of speech and learning, often depicted holding a stringed musical instrument.

saying in Yazaemon's family—"a melon vine produces no eggplant"—there's really nothing to that.[4]

NARRATOR: So wags her clever honeyed tongue.

YASUKE: All of this . . . well . . . you may not care for what I'm going to say, but now on top of all your many kindnesses you're even going to give me your daughter you prize so highly. *(Growing somewhat impatient.)* I just can't find any way of showing my appreciation. And you're still in the habit of calling me Master Yasuke this and Master Yasuke that, putting "Master" on my name all the time. I get embarrassed about it. Couldn't we be a little more informal, like "How about this, Yasuke?" or "Do it this way, Yasuke"?

*(The Mother holds her head down, Yasuke is embarrassed, and Osato is sullen.)*

MOTHER: Oh, you must forgive me.

YASUKE: Why is that?

MOTHER: Well, you see, the name Yasuke was the one my husband used till recently, and I just couldn't bring myself to say things to him so informally. So, please, let me add "Master" to your name as I'm used to doing.

NARRATOR: Truly, in her voice
There's tenderness of heart
As she seizes on her daughter's presence
To speak of Benzaiten's teaching
To hold a husband dear.
Then, as Osato and Yasuke
Arrange the empty sushi tubs
On the wooden racks,
The elder son of the family,
Good-For-Nothing Gonta,[5]

---

4. Meaning that ordinary parents will not produce outstanding children. By discounting the saying, the mother is suggesting that even though she and Yazaemon may be ordinary, they have a lovely daughter in Osato.

5. Throughout the text, Gonta is usually called *Igami no Gonta*, "Quarrelsome Gonta" or "Ill-tempered Gonta." For simplicity and consistency, however, I have generally called him either Good-for-Nothing Gonta, or simply Gonta.

Calls out softly from the gate.
*(Gonta enters from SR, both hands drawn inside his kimono. He peeps into the room, then pushes the door open with his right foot.)*
GONTA *(entering the house and calling softly):* Mother, mother.
NARRATOR: His entry startles Osato.
*(Yasuke, embarrassed, moves nearer the Mother.)*
OSATO: Oh, it's you again. *(More cordially.)* Ah . . . welcome home.
NARRATOR: Nervously, she rubs her hands together.
GONTA *(glaring at Osato):* Well, what are you looking at me so curiously for? You said welcome back. Why so startled? Well now, you seem . . . heh heh . . . awfully friendly with Yasuke here. Hey, listen to me Yasuke. I may have been kicked out of the house, but everything here, right down to the ashes under the stove, it's mine. I heard that my caterpillar of an old man had gone off to the village office today, so I just came by to talk over something with my mother. Since it's just between the two of us, get off to the other room.
NARRATOR: He glares about with menace.
Gently saying, "Take your time,"
Yasuke slowly moves away,
And taking Osato with him
They enter the inner room.
*(Yasuke and Osato move off to the inner room, Osato intimidated by Gonta's manner. As they leave, Gonta closes the door with his foot and shoots the bolt home. He then sits and bows to his mother.)*
Left behind, Gonta's mother heaves a sigh.
MOTHER: Have you come again to beg for money while your father's away? You're absolutely incorrigible. I can't do a thing with you! You have a wife and child, but we won't let them come near us because you're so wicked. I hear they are in the village, but your wife and I have never met; even if we passed in the street, we'd be like two blind people who wouldn't recognize each other. People say I'm blind as a bat about you, and I feel I can't hold up my head. You're such an unfilial son! *(She strikes the floor vehemently for emphasis.)*

## Scene 3: The Sushi Shop

NARRATOR: As she looks daggers at him,
   Gonta sees her displeasure
   Will not so quickly soften,
   And he changes his approach.
*(He edges up closer to her.)*
GONTA: Look, mother, I didn't come here tonight to beg money from you. I came to say goodbye.
MOTHER: What do you mean?
GONTA: I'm going somewhere a long way from here, and so I just came to wish father and you good health.
NARRATOR: He speaks, head drooping in dejection.
   His mother is astonished.
*(She moves closer to him, her concern evident.)*
MOTHER: Where is this far place? Why are you going? What are you going to do there?
NARRATOR: As she fires her questions at him,
   Thus begins the deception.
   "Now she's hooked,"
   Gonta says to himself.
   Eyes cast down, he blinks back tears.
*(He takes a small towel and presses its end to his eyes, blubbering like a baby.)*
GONTA: What belongs to a parent belongs to his child, goes the saying, and so I've begged money from you in the past. Until today I haven't taken even a single chopstick that belonged to someone else. And I haven't done a single crooked thing. Maybe it's punishment for being so unfilial. Last night I met up with a terrible robber.
MOTHER: Oh no!
GONTA: And I was robbed of three kamme in silver that I was to give to the government deputy's office for the land tax. I've no excuse to offer, and there's nothing left for me to do, so I've made up my mind to kill myself rather than face the punishment. What a miserable thing to happen to me.
*(He gets up, takes a carving knife from the shelf and thrusts it toward his throat. Noting that his mother is not looking at him, Gonta nudges*

*her and repeats the performance. Once she sees what he is doing, she becomes agitated and quickly takes the knife from him.)*

NARRATOR: He presses his sleeve to his face
    For the tears that fail to flow.
    To aid the semblance of grief,
    With his tongue he'd lick
    The margins of his eyes,
    But there, how irksome:
    His nose is in the way.
    His mother believes his words,
    Letting her indulgence
    Come before resentment,
    And she too rubs her watery eyes.

*(Gonta struggles ineffectually to produce some tears. He lifts up his left sleeve to hide the fact that with his right he is wiping saliva on his eyes. He peeks furtively at his mother, then rolls on the floor toward the room's entry, pretending to weep convulsively.)*

MOTHER: The gods themselves may slip from the path of righteousness, they say. Still, I'm proud of your readiness to give up your life for being robbed of the tax money. When you run into trouble, it's a punishment on your parents. I hope you realize that.

GONTA: Oh, I do, I do realize it. But I'll still probably have to die.

*(He gets up on one knee, takes his towel and twists it around his neck, pulling upward as though hanging himself.)*

MOTHER: Oh, this is terrible!

*(She tries to take the towel from him. He clings to it and rolls onto the floor, face upward.)*

GONTA: Yes, yes it is!

*(He rolls from side to side, kicking his feet.)*

MOTHER: I know what you're like all the time, and you may still be up to one of your tricks, but there's some money we were to leave all of you to divide up when we died. Don't tell your father. Take it, and mend your ways.

*(She wipes her eyes once more then goes to the cupboard set into the back wall. Behind her, Gonta waves his arms in obvious joy.)*

### Scene 3: The Sushi Shop

NARRATOR: Slowly she moves to the cupboard.
   An indulgent mother,
   Who'd even steal from her husband
   For the sake of a son,
   She cannot work the easily opened lock.
GONTA *(miming the act of breaking the lock with his pipe case)*:
   Here, you can knock it open with the end of my pipe case.
NARRATOR: The unfilial son instructs her
   In the tricks to which he's so accustomed.
   Later she will smooth things out,
   But now, doting on her darling son,
   She brings out three silver kamme
   That in the end will send
   The young man straight to hell.
MOTHER: I'd like to wrap this up in something.
NARRATOR: The mother's foolish fondness
   Knows no bounds.
GONTA: Ah, you're a sweetheart.
NARRATOR: . . . says Gonta, his eye upon
   An empty sushi tub to hold it.
GONTA: Here, put it in this. *(Holds out a sushi tub.)*
NARRATOR: Thus mother and son
   Put silver in a pickling tub,
   Perhaps to turn it into golden sushi.
   Then on goes the lid, in go the wedges.
MOTHER *(pats Gonta on the shoulder)*: There, that's a good boy.
   Now take it away where it won't be seen.
*(The sushi tub under his arm, Gonta heads for the doorway.)*
NARRATOR: Just as the two feel satisfied
   They've managed things so well,
   Back comes the father Yazaemon,
   Much less doting than his wife.
   To the gate he comes in feverish haste,
   Stricken by the pangs of conscience.
*(Yazaemon enters hurriedly from SR, with the head wrapped in his cloak under his left arm. He pulls down his robe and knocks on the gate.)*

YAZAEMON: I'm back. Open up.
NARRATOR: He pounds upon the gate.
GONTA *(surprised, trembling, trying to hide the sushi tub between his legs)*: Good heavens, it's the old man!
NARRATOR: He loses his head in utter confusion.
MOTHER *(whispering in Gonta's ear)*: Here, put the tub over here.
NARRATOR: He puts the tub among the empty ones.
> Then mother and son,
> Each with bated breath,
> Leave on muffled feet—
> She to the adjoining room,
> He to the inner portion of the house.

*(Mother goes into the SL room and closes the shōji behind her. Gonta disappears into the center curtained doorway.)*

YAZAEMON: Hey, why don't you open up? *(Hammers the gate harder.)*
NARRATOR: So noisy is the pounding,
> Yasuke comes running out
> And opens up the gate.
> Yazaemon enters and peers about,
> His face a picture of irritation.

YAZAEMON: What's the matter? Is everyone here asleep? Has all the sushi I ordered been fixed?
NARRATOR: He rattles the tubs about,
> Lifting them, opening them.

*(In the process, Yazaemon puts the head wrapped in his cloak into one of the tubs.)*

YAZAEMON: Humph, you haven't made as much progress as I'd have thought. What are my wife and that lazy Osato doing?
YASUKE: Uh, they're inside. I'll go and call them.
NARRATOR: As he moves to go,
> Yazaemon holds him back.
> Inside the house and out
> The old man peers about.
> He closes the front gate,
> Arranges a seat of honor,
> And makes a deep obeisance.

## Scene 3: The Sushi Shop

YAZAEMON *(bowing):* I owe a great debt of gratitude to your father the Komatsu Minister, Lord Shigemori.[6] I wished to find his son, and that is you, my lord Koremori. I came upon you at Kumano Bay. I had you shave your head in the townsman's style, and I brought you to live with us in this house, making you a low-ranking apprentice to keep you from the prying eyes of others. I may have gone too far, and that is a pity, but I have discussed the matter in detail only with my wife. Your wedding ceremony this evening is meant to place my daughter in service at the court of a noble gentleman. I even passed on to you my humble name and called you Yasuke, because the characters used to write that name have the auspicious meaning of "safe at last." I thought others would not know who you were, but today Kajiwara Heizō Kagetoki[7] arrived from Kamakura. He conducted a thoroughgoing investigation, telling me that he thought I was concealing lord Koremori. I was evasive, and I talked myself blue in the face trying to convince him otherwise. That Kagetoki, though, he's a sly one, and he just may come around looking for you. But I already have a plan in mind. In any case, as they say, carelessness can lead one to harm. Tomorrow I am going to retire from the shop. You should move to Kamiichi Village.

NARRATOR: Lord Koremori responds.

KOREMORI: Among the countless thousands of those shown favor by my father Shigemori, can there be any so faithful as you? What sort of person were you in the past?

*(Assuming the formal manner of a nobleman, Koremori looks affectionately at Yazaemon.)*

---

6. Yazaemon refers to Shigemori's title of *Komatsu no Daifu*. The ministry of the Inner Precincts was one of several governmental offices Shigemori held. His apartments in the Heike's headquarters in Rokuhara in Kyoto bore the name Komatsu. He is referred to both as the Minister of the Inner Precincts and as *Komatsu no Daifu*, "The Komatsu Minister."

7. Kagetoki (died 1200) was originally from the Heike clan but became one of Yoritomo's most trusted advisers. He is described as "a haughty, vindictive, and unscrupulous man, with a slanderous tongue," and his antagonism to Yoshitsune led to several clashes between the two men during the wars with the Heike. See McCullough, *Yoshitsune*, 17–22, 135–37.

YAZAEMON: By your leave, my lord, in the days of the glory of the Heike clan, when Lord Shigemori dispatched a gift of three thousand gold ryō coins to Iwōzan in China,[8] it was my misfortune, as the official handling the matter, to be robbed of that money in the narrow straits of Ondo.[9] I was on the point of killing myself as an apology, and it was Lord Shigemori who came to my aid. He said to me, "I, who would send Japan's gold off to China, I indeed am the one who robs Japan." And he lamented what he had done. Moreover, he did not blame me at all. Instead, he granted me leave to go. I returned to the place of my parents and took over a sushi business that had a long history. Up until today I have been able to live in comfort and ease, but my son Gonta is a thief and a cheat. I realize that it must be retribution because I have killed living things.[10] Such is my confession, of which I am much ashamed.

NARRATOR: As he speaks, Koremori too
Recalls the days of glories past,
Thinks about his father.
How pitiful indeed the tears
That fall upon his knee.

(*Both men touch their sleeves to their eyes. The shōji door of the SL room now opens, revealing Osato inside arranging the bridal bed for herself and Yasuke. She pauses, moves the pillows closer together, pauses and blushes, then moves them a bit closer.*)

The daughter Osato comes out,
The bedding in her arms
As she awaits the moon tonight

---

8. This is apparently based on an incident related in the *Heike monogatari*, in which Shigemori sent 3,000 *ryō* in gold to the Sung court in China, asking that 1,000 *ryō* be distributed to the priests at Mount Yu-wang so that services might be conducted for his spirit after his death. See *The Tale of the Heike*, 119.

9. The Ondo Strait is located near the modern city of Hiroshima in Japan's Inland Sea. The *Heike monogatari* does not mention the bearer of Shigemori's gold being robbed.

10. A Buddhist inspired sentiment, this may refer to the deaths Yazaemon caused during the preceding years of warfare; or it may refer to the fish he uses in the making of sushi.

### Scene 3: The Sushi Shop

When she will welcome
Her handsome husband.
Her father, startled,
Hides his tearful eyes.

*(Yazaemon abruptly stands, tightens his sash and moves to SL. Koremori, assuming again his subservient demeanor as Yasuke moves to SR.)*

YAZAEMON: Yasuke, be sure, be absolutely sure you don't forget what I told you just now about going to Kamiichi Village. You make yourself at home here tonight with Osato. Her mother and I will be in the far room. Best we be out of earshot; you'll be more at ease with us not around, eh.

NARRATOR: He gives a laugh
And heads for the inside of the house.
His daughter is delighted.

OSATO: What a considerate father. With them in the far room, we won't even know they're there. He and mother will be as comfy as two little rice cakes. Oh, ho ho ho, that's silly. We can sleep here. *(She moves close to Koremori, points to the pillows in the SL room and then steps invitingly into the room.)* We can do just as we please and enjoy our bridal bed.

NARRATOR[11]: She spreads out the bedding.
Lord Koremori feels most keenly
How fate has dealt with him.
He can think only of the sky
Spread above the Capital,
Of Wakaba no Naishi, his wife,
And his young child Rokudai.
He cannot feel elated;
Cheerless are his spirits.
Seeing him sit in such dejection,
Osato moves to him and tries
To enliven him with her coquetry.

OSATO *(seductively)*: See? Oh look . . . Oh, I'm so impatient.

---

11. From this point on the narrator's lines show a distinctly heightened deference to Koremori (honorifics, titles, and the like), now that his true identity has become known to the audience.

You're so innocent and inexperienced, I worry about you. The vows we make on the pillow we'll share together will last through two lives, even three.[12] *(Pointing to the pillows.)* See, there they are, side by side. Come, let's go to bed.

NARRATOR: The way she's first to tumble into bed
And curl up as though asleep
Seems so like a lover's guile.
Koremori moves toward the pillow.

*(He crawls across the main room to the doorway of the SL room.)*

KOREMORI: Osato, up till now this has been but a temporary affair. If we are to be man and wife, it is a relationship that will join us through two lives. But I have a difficult apology to make. I have been keeping something from you. I have a wife and a child whom I left behind in my home province. The injunction that a faithful wife does not marry a second time holds true also for a husband. Please release me from my pledge to marry you.

NARRATOR: True to his noble lineage
As a son of Shigemori,
Something of his father's noble air
Yet remains within him,
Even in the way he bares his heart.

Wakaba no Naishi knows no more
Of these events than does she of
The unfamiliar road on which she's strayed,
Seeking lodgings where
She may leave young Rokudai
And seek aid for the wounded Kokingo.

*(Naishi, cane and lacquered straw hat in hand, enters from SR, with Rokudai in the lead.)*

Thus through a strange affinity
She happens upon this very house.

---

12. Buddhism teaches that the ties of man and wife last through the present life and the next one to come. Osato's enthusiasm leads her to hope for yet another existence together.

## Scene 3: The Sushi Shop

She knocks upon the gate
And calls out,
"Please, a lodging for the night."
Koremori, thankful for the chance
To escape from Osato's side,
Comes to the front of the house.
He speaks toward the gate,
Whence comes the sound of knocking.

KOREMORI: This is a sushi shop, not an inn.
NARRATOR: Brusque is his response,
But not without civility.
NAISHI: Oh please, I am a woman traveling with a young child.
I beg you lodging for the night.
NARRATOR: About to refuse and send her on her way,
Koremori pushes open the gate.
There in the shadowy moonlight
He spies Naishi and Rokudai.
A startled gasp; he shuts the gate
And looks about inside.
Troubled at what Osato must think,
Back he goes on careful feet and peers,
But she seems already wrapped in dreams.
Outside the gate Naishi is mystified.
NAISHI: That person just now, I thought somehow he bore a resemblance to my husband. But, his dress, the way his head was shaved, like a servant. Surely it wasn't . . .

*(Inside, Koremori tiptoes to the curtained doorway at center, peers in, then quietly moves back to the gate.)*

NARRATOR: As Naishi mulls the matter in her mind,
Again the gate draws open,
And there stands Koremori.
KOREMORI: My wife, is it Naishi? And Rokudai?
NAISHI: Oh! It *is* my husband after all!
ROKUDAI *(running to Koremori):* Is it father?
NAISHI *(going to Koremori and embracing him):* Oh, how we've missed you! *(Koremori embraces them both.)*

NARRATOR: They cling to one another.
  No words are possible,
  All they can do is weep.
KOREMORI: Now now, come inside.
NARRATOR: Quietly, they follow him in.
*(Koremori leads them inside the house. Naishi and Rokudai sit at SL as Koremori sits at SR.)*
KOREMORI: How strange to be seeing you on this very night, when I was thinking especially of the time when we lived in the Capital and wondering if my wife and child were safe. But, who told you I was here? I've no idea how you got all the way here with no one to help you.
NARRATOR: To his questions, Lady Naishi responds.
NAISHI: After we parted in the Capital, I worried about what happened in the battles at Suma[13] and Yashima. After hearing that the whole Heike clan had perished, I was left hiding in Saga with nothing to do but weep. Then someone said that you might be somewhere around Mount Kōya, so Kokingo came with us and we set out to find where you were. We ran into a search party from Kamakura, and I parted from Kokingo after he was wounded. *(Weeps.)* Now, with no one to rely on and no strength left in me, oh how happy I am that I've found you. But Koremori, you are a Middle Imperial Attendant of the Third Rank. Why do you look like this—sleeveless jacket, your head shaved on top?
*(She goes to him, puts her hand on his shoulder, then sinks in tears at his knee.)*
NARRATOR: She clings to him
  And chokes upon her tears,
  As though all is past endurance.
  Koremori, in shame,
  Puts hand to head and sleeve to face,
  And he too is consumed with grief.

---

13. Suma refers to the famous battle at Ichi no Tani. See *The Tale of the Heike*, 310–12.

## Scene 3: The Sushi Shop

> Yet even as she weeps,
> Naishi spies the sleeping Osato.

*(Naishi draws back from Koremori.)*

NAISHI: A young girl asleep, and two pillows there. *(Speaking rapidly and accusingly.)* Oh, of course, she must be an attendant to your comforts. *(Osato hears and quickly tries to hide the pillow beneath the covers.)* Living such a life of ease here, and yet you still long for the Capital, eh? You might have sent me some tidings, but instead you've cast me aside. Oh, how cruel.

NARRATOR: Bitter are her words.

KOREMORI: Oh no, I thought of writing to you, but I was afraid the letter might go astray. But more to the point is the master of this house, Yazaemon. To repay his debt of gratitude to my father Shigemori, he has aided me, and he and his wife have since then repeatedly shown me many kindnesses. I wished to express my own thanks to them, and so I engaged in a romance with their daughter. I see now that I have made an inconsiderate mistake. The gratitude I meant to repay has, on the contrary, done harm. I made passing pledges to the girl, but Yazaemon sealed my lips and would not let me tell her about myself. He said that a woman in her jealousy might reveal to others matters of importance. My heart was not in this relationship. I have done it all out of an obligation to her parents.

NARRATOR: As he speaks—can it be because
> The sleeping girl cannot bear it?—
> Osato breaks into heart-rending sobs.

*(Osato burrows down under the bedclothes, covering her head. The convulsive movements of the covers shows that she is weeping.)*

NAISHI: Oh, what's that?

NARRATOR: The startled Naishi grabs Rokudai,
> And is about to flee.

OSATO: No, please wait.

NARRATOR: Out runs the sobbing Osato.

*(Osato throws off the covers and runs into the room.)*

OSATO: First, please come here.
*(Osato has Koremori move over to his wife and child at SL. Then she goes to SR and kneels and bows to them.)*
NARRATOR: She bids Naishi and the young lord
  To assume the honored seat.
OSATO: I am Osato, the daughter in this house. You must think me capricious and hateful, and I ask your forgiveness.
*(At this point, Osato's monologue becomes song.)*

> Around last year's spring,
> To this village so remote
> It rests amid tall grass,
> There came a gentleman *(bows to Koremori)*
> Of beauty seldom seen,
> Like someone from a painting.
> To this young girl's heart,
> Who knew him not as Koremori,
> How gentle was he, how sweet;
> And from this my affection grew.

*(Hands inside her long sleeves, she claps them together in joy.)*

> My father told me nothing *(weeps)*.
> Even mother never dreamed the truth.
> Had I but been told,
> Though I might have died
> In yearning for him,
> Think you that the daughter
> Of a lowly sushi shop
> Would presume to love so fine a man,
> One who attends the nobles of the court—
> Those who dwell above the clouds?

*(She hides her face in her sleeve.)*

> To spend the rest of my life
> With this handsome gentleman—
> On that I had set my heart.
> But now our vow of love,
> A love to last beyond this life,
> Is a thing that may not be.

## Scene 3: The Sushi Shop

*(Addressing Koremori:)*
>You say you pledged yourself
>Out of duty to my parents.
>What a heartless thing!
>For in your love
>I had placed my trust.

NARRATOR: She sinks down, engulfed in tears,
>Her body racked by sobbing.
>Lord Koremori is at a loss;
>And Naishi, in her sympathy,
>Sheds tears that seek forgiveness.
>Yet, ere the grieving tears have dried,
>In rushes a village officer
>To pound upon the gate.

*(Officer enters from SR.)*

OFFICER: See here, Master Kajiwara has come. Clean up this place!

NARRATOR: He spits out the words and leaves.
>For those within the house,
>In an instant weeping eyes are dry,
>As suddenly all are startled
>And wonder what is afoot.
>Quickly Osato remembers something
>And speaks excitedly.

OSATO *(to Koremori)*: Oh quickly, you're to go to father's retirement villa in Kamiichi Village.

KOREMORI: You're right. Yazaemon reminded me of that. But now the final fate of the Heike has been sealed. I'll handle the investigating party and show them a manly death as I rip my belly open.

*(He grabs a knife carried by Rokudai.)*

NARRATOR: As he starts to prepare himself,
>Naishi cries out in grief.

NAISHI: Wait! Think of this child here, so lovely in his youth. Quickly, we must get out of here.

NARRATOR: She seizes him against his will
  And starts to lead him off.
  Koremori's heart is also with the child,
  And, loath to part with him,
  He also leaves, as in the balance
  Still hangs his fate.

*(Koremori, Naishi, and Rokudai go out into the courtyard at center stage and exit SR. At this point there is usually a change of narrator and his samisen accompanist.)*

  Now from the back door—
  Perhaps he's heard everything—
  Good-For-Nothing Gonta prances in.

*(Stripped to the waist, Gonta enters through the center curtained doorway.)*

GONTA *(to Osato)*: There's a warrant out for Naishi and Rokudai and that Koremori, alias Yasuke. I'm turning them all in.

NARRATOR: He tucks the hem of his robe
  Into his sash and starts off.

OSATO: Wait!

NARRATOR: Osato grabs hold of him.

OSATO: Gonta, this is the plea of my life. Please, let them go.

NARRATOR: She begs, but he will not listen,
  And flings her aside.

GONTA: This is a big thing, worth a lot of money to me. Don't get in my way!

NARRATOR: Osato claws at him,
  But he kicks her down
  And sends her flying.
  He grabs the sushi tub
  Into which he'd placed the money.

GONTA: Oh, mustn't forget this.

NARRATOR: Then hard upon his victim's heels
  He dashes in pursuit.

*(In muscular movements, Gonta runs out at SR.)*

OSATO *(running to the curtained doorway)*: Oh, father, mother, father, mother!

### Scene 3: The Sushi Shop

NARRATOR: At her frenzied summons,
   In rush Yazaemon and his wife.
*(Yazaemon enters from the curtained doorway, the Mother from the SL room.)*
MOTHER: What's happened?
OSATO: Oh, listen to me! Koremori's wife and son wandered in here from the Capital. We were in the midst of a long talk when we heard that a search party had come. I had them run off to Kamiichi, but—oh what a wretch he is!—Gonta had been listening. He said he was either going to kill them or capture them for a reward. And just now he ran off after them!
NARRATOR: Yazaemon is dumbfounded.
YAZAEMON: This is terrible!
*(He pulls down his robe from his right shoulder to free his sword arm, tucks the hem of his skirts into his sash at his back. He grabs a short sword and thrusts that into the sash, then he leaves the house and heads off toward SR.)*
NARRATOR: Into his sash he thrusts his sword,
   Ever at hand in its crimson scabbard.
   As he starts to dash away,
   Shouts come from outside.
*(To the sound of a drum, four soldiers enter SR carrying lanterns emblazoned with crests and hung on tall poles.)*
SOLDIERS: Hai, hai, hai!
NARRATOR: Truncheons in hand,
   And bearing lanterns painted
   With an arrow fletching crest,[14]
   The men of Kajiwara Kagetoki
   Swarm in and block the way.
*(As Kajiwara also enters from SR, Yazaemon bumps into him.)*
KAJIWARA: Yaaa, you old gaffer, where do you think you're going? Think I'd let you get away?

---

14. Kajiwara Kagetoki's family crest was a herringbone pattern of arrow fletching.

(*Yazaemon runs this way and that trying to escape, each time blocked by the soldiers. Again he runs into Kajiwara, then falls down, breathing heavily.*)

NARRATOR: Surrounded and surprised,
  Worried what will happen next
  Yet unable to escape,
  Yazaemon squirms in agony,
  Heart pounding like a fire alarm,
  For now, it seems, his time has come.

KAJIWARA: Yaaa, insolent wretch! When I questioned you today about Koremori, you dodged about saying you had no idea where he was, knew nothing about him. I let you go home so I could break in on you when you weren't expecting me. We know that Koremori is hidden in this house, because someone from here informed the authorities. Right away I sent off a dispatch to Kamakura, and those who'll take him will be here in short order. If there are any slip-ups, I'm not going to escape punishment myself. So, are you going to hand over his head, or are you going to put up a fight? Let's have an answer!

(*He glares down at Yazaemon, who cringes on the ground in dejection.*)

NARRATOR: Thus pressed, resistance is hopeless.
  Yazaemon comes to a decision.

(*Yazaemon stands, removes the towel tied about his head and squares his shoulders.*)

YAZAEMON: I see. Yes, I did tell you he wasn't hiding here, but so forceful was your interrogation that I knew I couldn't possibly keep him hidden. I've already cut off his head, and now I'll show it to you. This way please.

(*Yazaemon leads Kajiwara into the house, where he sits on a stool at SL. Osato and her Mother watch anxiously from the center curtained doorway.*)

NARRATOR: As Kajiwara follows him inside,
  Mother and daughter are anxious

## Scene 3. The Sushi Shop

As to what will now unfold.
Yazaemon picks up
One of the sushi tubs.
Then, slowly he comes back
And places it in the middle of the room.

YAZAEMON *(to Kajiwara):* Here is the head of Koremori. Please take it.

NARRATOR: He is about to remove the lid
When his wife comes running in
And stays his hand.

MOTHER: Oh wait! I put something rather important in that tub. What am I going to do if you open it?

YAZAEMON: Humph, I don't know. A little while ago I put the head of Lord Koremori in here.

MOTHER: No no no! There's something in here I can't let you see!

NARRATOR: She pulls the tub to herself,
Yazaemon pulls it back.

YAZAEMON: Huh, I don't know what you're talking about, so . . .

MOTHER: It's just *because* you don't know . . .

NARRATOR: His wife, thinking of the money,
Struggles with her husband,
Till finally Kajiwara intervenes.

KAJIWARA: They've arranged all of this in advance to evade me. Bind them! Tie them up!

SOLDIERS: We've got you!

*(As Kajiwara waves his war fan, the soldiers run out, brandishing their truncheons. The Mother moves back to the curtained doorway.)*

NARRATOR: The soldiers surround Yazaemon.
Just then a voice calls out.

*(Gonta, still stripped to the waist, enters from SR, leading by a rope a woman and a child. They are bound with their hands behind them and gagged in a manner that partially obscures their faces. Gonta pulls them in roughly.)*

## ACT THREE

NARRATOR: Solemnly, the pugnacious Gonta
   Leads in Rokudai and Naishi.
   Both trussed up like monkeys.
   He drags them in so roughly
   Their feet hardly touch the ground. . .
   (Act 3, scene 3)

GONTA: I, the one people call Good-For-Nothing Gonta, I've caught both Koremori and his wife, and the brat too. These here I've taken alive; I killed the other.
NARRATOR: Yazaemon is stunned.
   His wife and daughter stand transfixed,
   Their minds in a frenzy.
   Solemnly, the pugnacious Gonta
   Leads in Rokudai and Naishi,
   Both trussed up like monkeys.
   He drags them in so roughly
   Their feet hardly touch the ground,
   Then forces them to squat
   As though awaiting an audience.

GONTA: My liar of a father brought Koremori here from Kumano Bay. On the road back he had him shave his head to make him look like a young whippersnapper, then changed his name to Yasuke. The other day the old man chose the damn strumpet-chaser to be his son-in-law. Koremori knew he'd be disgraced if I took him alive, and he turned out to be a tougher customer than I thought. But I got some villagers to help me and we finally struck him down. I cut off his head and brought it with me. Here, make your inspection.

*(He takes the sushi tub, pulls out Kokingo's head and moves toward Kajiwara. As he does so, Yazaemon makes a move to intercept him. Gonta draws back, and Yazaemon is clearly hesitant as to what to do. Two soldiers take Yazaemon away through the center curtained doorway.)*

NARRATOR: He presents the severed head.

*(Gonta places the head before Kajiwara. He then unties the towel around his head and begins elaborately wiping the sweat from his face and shoulders and back.)*

KAJIWARA: Ah, I see. I knew about the Yasuke business and the shaven head, but I didn't say anything earlier so as not to provoke any suspicions by that Yazaemon fellow. From what has reached my ears about you, Gonta, I understand that you're a bad one. To your superiors, however, you are loyal. You've captured Naishi and Rokudai. Well done, well done. *(Gonta, sitting between his prisoners and bowing, steals a peek at Kajiwara, then with his arms on the backs of the woman and child he closes his eyes, momentarily overcome with emotion. Kajiwara looks over his fan at the woman.)* Hah, she's a good looking one. Right off she reminds me of the Dreamfield Deer.[15] So, you've caught the doe and the fawn. A splendid

---

15. The reference is to a story in the eighth-century Japanese history *Nihongi* (or *Nihon shoki*) in which a man goes to sleep on the moor at Toga. Two deer, a male and a female, lie down beside him. The male deer tells the female of a dream he has had, and the female interprets it as a portent that he will die. At dawn the following morning, the male deer is killed by a hunter. From this arose the saying, "Even a belling deer relies on the interpretation of dreams." See W. G.

piece of work. As a reward to you, I'll spare the life of your father Yazaemon.

GONTA: Ah . . . no no, wait. I didn't do all this hoping to spare my father's life.

KAJIWARA: Then, even if your father's life is forfeit, you still want a reward?

GONTA: What becomes of him is something between the two of you. As for me, well . . . I'd like some money.

KAJIWARA: Ha ha ha ha ha. Well, you're an agreeable type to deal with. You'll get your reward.

NARRATOR: He removes the cloak he wears
And gives it to Gonta,
But Gonta's face is sullen.

*(Kajiwara throws the cloak to Gonta. Gonta is nonplused.)*

KAJIWARA: Look here, that cloak belonged to Lord Yoritomo. Bring it to Kamakura anytime and you can exchange it for money. That'll be your tally to prove you're to get the reward.

*(Gonta brightens.)*

NARRATOR: At this, Gonta lifts the cloak
To his head in thanks.

GONTA: I've done it, I've done it! There's a lot of hoodwinking going on nowadays, but this way no one can cheat me out of the reward! Ah, you're really clever. *(Delighted, Gonta stands up, puts on the cloak and struts about the room.)*

NARRATOR: In exchange, he hands over
The prisoners in their bonds.
Kajiwara accepts them,
And has the head returned to the tub.

KAJIWARA: Well then, Gonta, for the time being I'll leave Yazaemon and the rest of his family in your hands.

GONTA: Oh, you don't have to worry about them. I won't let 'em budge an inch!

---

Aston, tr., *Nihongi*, 289–90. Introduction of the reference here seems to have no relevance other than to introduce the metaphors of doe and fawn that follow.

KAJIWARA: You're an admirable fellow.
NARRATOR: Singing Gonta's praises,
   Kajiwara picks up the prisoners' rope
   And leaves.
*(Kajiwara pulls the prisoners as they exit SR. Gonta removes the cloak.)*
GONTA *(calling after Kajiwara)*: Next comes my reward of money. Don't forget!
*(Yazaemon peeks out from the curtained doorway, then ducks back inside the curtain.)*
NARRATOR: As Gonta bids Kajiwara farewell,
   Yazaemon sees an instant
   When Gonta's off his guard.
*(Yazaemon re-emerges from the curtained doorway, his outer robe pulled down from both shoulders, a drawn sword in his right hand.)*
   Nursing a bitter hate,
   He plunges his rancorous blade
   Into his son.
   Back topples Gonta,
   His face to the sky.
*(Gonta falls backward, his hair now loosened to fly about his head. Osato and her Mother rush out from the curtained doorway and run to Gonta.)*
   Mother and daughter, as they watch,
   Utter an astonished cry.
   Hateful though her son may be,
   Instinctively the mother runs to him.
MOTHER: You know it's heaven's punishment! You realize your guilt as an unfilial child!
NARRATOR: She censures him, but not before
   The tears have started to fall,
   And she collapses sobbing away.
   But not Yazaemon,
   Who gnashes his teeth in rage.
YAZAEMON *(still holding the sword thrust into Gonta's belly)*: Don't cry for him, wife! What are you howling about? If I let this

kind of wretch live, saying he was piteous or dear to me, why he'd be an affliction to the whole world! I ordered you never to let him set foot in here, and yet you let him in. How could he kill our precious, precious Koremori, and hand over Lady Naishi and young Rokudai to Kamakura?! Oh, it . . . it . . . it sends me into a rage, a rage! I weep for them, it t-t-tears at my breast! In all the three thousand Buddha worlds,[16] I must be the only father who would kill his own son. *(Ironically.)* You, Gonta, must be the bringer of retribution on me for my sins in another life. Bravo! You've done your vile work well!

NARRATOR: Fiercely he grips the handle
Of the naked sword,
As though to crush it.
He gouges the sword in Gonta's wound,
But in his heart are tears.
Though crooked to the heart,
Gonta pushes back the blade.

GONTA *(slowly, in great pain)*: Father.

YAZAEMON *(irritably)*: What is it?

GONTA *(still painfully)*: It was . . . beyond your power . . . alone . . . to save Koremori.

YAZAEMON: Don't say that! As luck would have it, today I found at the side of the crossroad a man who had died of his wounds. His head was to be a perfect substitute for Koremori's head, so I cut it off and brought it home and hid it in this tub here. *(He takes the tub from the rack holding others.)* Look here, I'll show it to you.

NARRATOR: He takes the sushi tub,
Opens it, *(turning it upside down)*
And out tumbles
Three kamme in silver.

YAZAEMON: What! This is money! What's going on here?

---

16. That is, all of the Buddha worlds in the universe.

## Scene 3: The Sushi Shop

NARRATOR: He stands there dumbfounded.
The wounded Gonta gazes at his father.

GONTA: You were in a terrible situation, father. I'm so rotten to the core that you had no one to discuss matters with. You had the wrong idea. You were in danger for taking that young man's head and handing it over to the Kamakura men just as it was, forelock and all.[17] Would a samurai like Kajiwara come here with an armed force without knowing that you'd given Koremori the name Yasuke and made him look like a young townsman? The fact that he didn't say anything about it shows just how clever he was. That money there that I stole, I was going to give it to Koremori and his wife for their traveling expenses. Thinking that the heavier sushi tub had the money in it, I took the wrong one, and when I opened it, there was a severed head inside. I was astonished, for it was precisely the head you had put there in the first place. But luckily I was able to shave the top of the head and place it back in the tub.

YAZAEMON: You're still just as wicked. Why did you tie up Lady Naishi and her son and hand them over to the Kamakura authorities?

GONTA *(slowly, painfully)*: Those two who appeared here, . . . they were . . . my wife and . . . my son.

YAZAEMON: Then . . . then, where are Koremori and his wife, and their son?

GONTA: Oh, I'll show them to you.

NARRATOR: He draws from his sleeve
A toy whistle, and blows it.
*(Laboriously, Gonta blows the whistle several times.)*

---

17. That is, with the hair on the top of the head still in place and pulled back, together with the sidelocks, into a kind of long chignon, which is then waxed and curved back over the top of the head. The townsman hairstyle, affected as a disguise by Yasuke/Koremori in this scene, involves shaving the top of the head, the waxed chignon being formed by pulling back only the remaining sidelocks, which are then led forward across the shaven pate.

At the sound, in rushes Lord Koremori.
With him comes Lady Naishi,
Dressed in the clothes
Of a tea serving maid
And leading her son by the hand.
*(They enter from SR. Naishi and Rokudai are, respectively, dressed in the clothes of Kosen and Zenta.)*
KOREMORI: To you, Yazaemon, and to your wife and Gonta, we offer our than- . . . Oh, Gonta's been wounded!?
OSATO *(to Koremori and his family)*: You're all right?
NARRATOR: She is stunned to see them,
But in an instant
All her joy vanishes.
Gonta's mother clings to her son in grief.
MOTHER *(weeping)*: If you possessed such an upright character as this, why did you behave so that you were condemned and shunned by everyone? If everything had been as it should be, surely your father would never have so rashly inflicted this wound on you. How cruelly things have turned out!
NARRATOR: She sobs convulsively
And cries out her lament.
Gonta speaks.
GONTA *(in pain)*: No need to mourn . . . no need. If everything had been as father had planned, Kajiwara would never have gone off thinking that head was genuine. If he'd still had some doubt, would he have spared father's life as a reward to me? And if I'd merely said thank you for that, he'd have thought at once to investigate everything more fully. Because I bickered with him about the reward, he became careless. Calamity, goes the proverb, after three years becomes good fortune. When you severed all ties with me because of my wickedness, I just naturally became taken up with gambling. Today, when I cheated this lady here out of twenty ryō, I looked into her baggage and saw a picture of a lofty person due great reverence. It was a portrait drawn from life of the very face of Yasuke. I couldn't understand, and so on a ploy

of begging money from mother, I got into the house and concealed myself. I heard all about the difficulties that had plagued Lord Koremori. If I don't change my evil ways this time, I thought to myself, then there probably will never come a time when I can get back into father's good graces. I made a complete change behind this mask of evil. I had a head to substitute for that of Koremori, but there was no one to take the place of Naishi and young Rokudai. I was at a loss what to do, when my wife Kosen came in with our boy. She said to me, "You've been disowned by your father. And then there's such a thing as loyalty to a former master. Why are you so distraught? Use me and Zenta," she said, "as a means to get around the problem." Then my son said to me, "Send mother together with me." I tried and I tried to tie them up with a rope, but . . . I just couldn't do it. I'd tie a knot, and it would just slip loose. By what karma should so cantankerous a person as I have such an upstanding son? And then I wept. I tied them up, and then I wept more. When I had their hands tied behind them, I wept tears of blood, unable to bear my heart of a demon, my black and wicked heart. And when my sweet, my pitiful wife also cried out in grief, I was in such agony I could have coughed up blood.

(*Throughout Gonta's long monologue, his words are frequently interrupted by gasps of pain and fits of weeping as he reveals his tragic dilemma.*)

NARRATOR: Thus he speaks,
Bearing up under the strain.

YAZAEMON (*weeping bitterly*): I didn't understand, Gonta, I didn't understand! If you had such agonizing grief, why didn't you tell us? In all this wide world, I have only one daughter-in-law, only one little grandchild. When children were playing together in a group, and I would think to ask them if there was a child around with a rather sinister look about him like his father, I'd say, "Hey children, is Gonta's little boy here?" The youngsters would ask me, "What Gonta are you talking about? What's his other name?" I just couldn't bring myself to tell them that he's called Good-For-Nothing Gonta. Since the boy's the child of such a wastrel, I'd think that the children would all treat him as an outcast, and then I'd detest Gonta all the more for that. If only you'd reformed half a year ago as you have now! Isn't that so, Mother?

MOTHER: Oh, Father, we could have known our daughter-in-law and our grandchild. But now it's too late.

YAZAEMON: That's the very thing I regret . . . but it's too late.

NARRATOR: Choked with tears
And trembling with emotion,
He crumples to the floor.
Throughout the telling,
Naishi has wept in sadness,
And Lord Koremori is overcome,
As heavy hangs his heart.

KOREMORI: You may grieve, Yazaemon, but destiny ordains that we meet only to part, that we die having never met. The severed head you brought was that of Shume no Kokingo, a retainer of long standing to me who was accompanying Naishi. If he fulfilled his loyalties only slightly in life, his faithful service has proved so much greater in death. Here too, how strange are the workings of fate.

YAZAEMON: But then, if that is so, everything that has happened has been the doing of that armed force from Kamakura.

KOREMORI: What you say is true. It is the inhumanity that has spread abroad under the power of that General of the Right Guards Yoritomo.[18] How it infuriates me that I cannot do away with him with a stroke of my sword!

NARRATOR: Wrath mingles with his tears.

YAZAEMON: Ah, how right you are.

NARRATOR: Yazaemon picks up the cloak
Left by Kajiwara.

YAZAEMON: This cloak here, he said it used to be Yoritomo's,

---

18. One of several honorary titles Yoritomo held.

and he left it to serve as a reward. Even if I tore it to tiny shreds they could not number all the members of your clan who died. But, as an offering gesture to them, let us each tear it once. Here, my lord.

NARRATOR: He hands the cloak to Koremori.

KOREMORI *(eying the cloak)*: Wait, did he say this was Yoritomo's cloak? Then we will follow the example of Yu Jang of China's ancient Chin Dynasty, and by tearing this cloak we will dispel the rancor of my clan.[19]

NARRATOR: He grasps his short sword,
Then takes the cloak and lifts it up.
On the back he sees what seems
To be the last lines of two poems.

KOREMORI *(reading the poem)*:

"Do you yearn for that which lies within?"
"Indeed, I yearn for that which lies within."

I wonder why these two lines are written side by side. There was a poem sent to the poetess Komachi that runs like this:

Though the cloud-pent realm
Where once you dwelled
Has altered not since long ago;
The jeweled hangings once you knew—
Do you yearn for that which lies within?

And everyone knows of her answering verse.[20] Strange that these poems should be given such importance here. But,

---

19. Yu Jang was a minister in the Chin state in the fifth and sixth century B.C. When his master was slain by viscount Hsiang of the Chao state, Yu Jang vowed revenge. He made several attempts upon the viscount, but was discovered each time. On the last attempt he asked that the viscount allow him to ease his conscience by merely piercing the viscount's coat with his sword. The viscount generously assented. After Yu Jang had run his dagger through the coat, he stabbed himself and died. See Giles, *A Chinese Biographical Dictionary,* 957–58.

20. The poem comes from the Nō play *Ōmu Komachi* (The Parroting Komachi), in which a messenger brings a poem to the famed and once beautiful Ono no Komachi (ninth century) from the retired Emperor Yōzei. The poem alludes to her earlier life at court (whose members were called "dwellers above the

Kajiwara is a warrior who has a rather special interest in poetry. The line "Do you yearn for that which lies within?" must be linked to the idea "Indeed, I yearn for that which lies within," and he must mean within the seams of this cloak.

NARRATOR: He cuts and loosens
The thread about the neck,
And lo! what tumbles out before him:
A cassock and a stole
For a Buddhist priest.
Even a rosary lies concealed within.

KOREMORI: What can this be?

YAZAEMON: Why on earth . . . ?

NARRATOR: Both men are amazed;
Then Lord Koremori speaks.

KOREMORI: Ah, that must be it. Long ago at the time of the Hōgen and the Heiji disturbances, my father Shigemori and the nun Ike no Zenni arranged between themselves that Yoritomo, then sentenced to death, be exiled instead to Itō.[21] As payment of that debt of gratitude, Yoritomo now spares Koremori's life and tells him to enter the priesthood. Thus that parroting poem bespeaks a debt repaid.[22] Ah, now I see: though he is my enemy, Yoritomo is a splendid general. More than "that which lies within the jeweled hangings," something gracious and elegant lies within Yoritomo's heart.[23]

---

clouds"). Komachi replies with the same poem, changing only a single syllable of the original, thus altering the final line from "Do you yearn for that which lies within?" to "Indeed, I yearn for that which lies within." See Nomura, *Yōkyoku shū*, 1:352–57.

21. In the Hōgen insurrection (1156) and the Heiji insurrection (1159–60) the Genji clan was defeated by the Heike, leading to two decades of Heike preeminence. During the latter disturbance it was the nun Ike no Zenni's plea to clan leader Taira Shigemori (Koremori's father) that led him to spare Yoritomo's life and exile him to the town of Itō (in present-day Shizuoka prefecture). Ike no Zenni was the widow of Heike leader Taira no Tadamori (1095–1153).

22. This is a play on similar sounding words: *ōmugaeshi*, replying by parroting the original speaker's words; and *ongaeshi*, the repayment of a debt of gratitude.

23. Yet another play upon the words of Komachi's poem quoted earlier.

NARRATOR: He takes up the cloak.
KOREMORI *(raising the cloak to his forehead in respect):* In truth, I owe much to my father Shigemori.
NARRATOR: Fitting indeed it is that he
Should show reverence to this robe.
All those around him are now consumed
By tears of joy. The wounded Gonta
Crawls forth and edges close.
GONTA: I just wasn't smart enough. I thought I had tricked Kajiwara, but he knew everything. As I think about it, up till now I'm the one who's done all the cheating. How wretched that this has finally led to being cheated myself . . . cheated out of my own life.
NARRATOR: In this last lament
Comes the ending of his days.
KOREMORI: By denying the Buddha up till now, merely paying lip service to his teachings, I have not escaped the painful cycles of birth, death and rebirth. Now is the time to break away from that. *(He picks up his short sword.)*
NARRATOR: With a single stroke
He cuts off his topknot of hair.[24]
Naishi, Rokudai, and Osato
Rush forward and cling to him.
OSATO: I will become a nun and accompany you. Please, let me be in your service.
NARRATOR: They entreat him, but Koremori
Rejects their pleas
And brushes all aside.
KOREMORI: Naishi, you are to take Rokudai to Takao and seek protection for him from the priest Mongaku.[25] And Osato, it is important that you take your brother's place and be a filial child to your parents.

---

24. The symbolic gesture of receiving the tonsure and entering the Buddhist priesthood.
25. Takao is now part of the city of Kyoto. Mongaku (died in the early thirteenth century) was a priest of the Shingon sect, an impetuous man with a fundamentalist religious bent. Exiled after an affront to the Emperor Goshira-

**NARRATOR:** As he starts to go, Yazaemon speaks up.

**YAZAEMON:** Accompanying Lady Naishi is a task this old man will undertake.

**NARRATOR:** As each prepares for a journey,
Yazaemon's wife attends her dying son.

**MOTHER:** Oh Father, how cold-hearted you are. Your son is near death. Look upon him one last time.

**NARRATOR:** Yazaemon comes to a halt and weeps.

**YAZAEMON** *(overwrought):* In this life I have killed my own flesh and blood son. How can I look upon him a final time? If I see him dead before me, how can I walk a single step? When I could do nothing while breath was in him, what can I do to help him now? And you, the only person I can rely on, you hold me back. You ask too much.

**NARRATOR:** As the father speaks,
He bursts into tears;
And weeping even more,
The mother and her daughter.
How wretched, how piteous,
Thinks Koremori, as about his neck
He places the simple stole
And takes in hand the Buddhist robe.
As a parting gift
He bears a holy scripture
Telling of the highest Buddha wisdom
To cast aside delusion
And open wide the enlightened way.
Now the departure from the gateway:
Naishi and Rokudai to Takao,
Koremori bound for Takano[26]—

---

kawa, he came into contact with Yoritomo, also in exile, and urged him to rebel against Heike rule. Later in his life, Mongaku was repeatedly banished to remote islands, eventually dying in exile. For the *Heike monogatari* account of Mongaku, see *The Tale of the Heike,* 178–84.

26. Another reading for the characters of Mount Kōya, used here in keeping with the metric rhythm of the lines.

## Scene 3: The Sushi Shop

A wife and husband now
Must go their separate ways;
A parent and a child
Must say their last goodbye.
*(Gonta tries to bring his hands together in prayer, but they miss each other. Unable to bear it, Yazaemon runs to him. Osato and her mother lift Gonta's crumpled body up as a farewell to his father.)*
   The farewell to a dying son,
   Face next to face—
   Never shall their yearning
   For each other end.
*(Koremori at SL and Naishi at SR both offer their prayers for Gonta.)*
   And remaining still in Yoshino,
   Along the road to Yamato,
   This celebrated sushi shop
   Of Koremori-Yasuke.
   In this village of flowers,
   Where cherry blossoms flourish still,
   It manifests itself in all its fame.
*(The clappers close the act as Koremori at SL faces forward in grief, Yazaemon at SR tearfully takes the hands of Naishi and Rokudai, and within the room Osato and her mother cling sorrowfully to the body of the dead Gonta.)*

# *Act Four*

## SCENE I
## MICHIYUKI: THE JOURNEY WITH THE DRUM

*(This is a dance scene, with at least three narrators and as many as five samisen accompanists. Throughout the scene, one narrator delivers Shizuka's lines, another delivers Tadanobu's. At other times all three narrators sing narrative lines as a chorus. As the narration begins, the set is concealed by a curtain with broad vertical stripes of red and white. At the point indicated in the text this curtain is dropped and pulled offstage, revealing a vista of the deep green Yoshino mountains, interlaced with clouds of blossoming pink cherries. At both SR and SL clusters of cherry trees stand in bloom, those at SR on a low hill. Across the top of the proscenium hang strands of festive cherry blossoms. At center stage in the near foreground is a single tall cherry tree, the stump of another tree downstage of it. Just behind the tree is a stage flat, a low hill painted in*

horizontal bands of white shading to sky blue, representing the mists that weave through the mountains).[1]

NARRATOR: Love and loyalty:
    Which is the heavier burden?
    Considered, weighed upon a scale,
    One cannot say.
    To Tadanobu, a warrior
    Steadfast and true of heart,
    His master Yoshitsune
    Has entrusted one he loves,
    The gentle Lady Shizuka.
    Behind them forlornly lies
    The Capital through which they've moved
    In silence and in stealth.
    Now they start their journey,
    Happy to be dressed
    In plain and simple garb.
    The gossip brings them news
    That Yoshitsune, tossed by waves,
    And drifting without course,
    Has arrived at Naniwazu[2]
    And made his destination Yoshino.
    They take this clue
    As counsel for their route
    And make for the Yamato Road
    To follow after.

*(The red and white striped curtain falls, revealing the set. Shizuka stands at center. She wears a bright red gown decorated with embroidered pink cherry blossoms and flowing lines of mist in silver. She carries a thin cane and a black lacquered wicker hat with crimson cords. Slung across her back is a small bundle (the drum) wrapped in a lavender cloth. She and Tadanobu are traveling together, but she is alone on stage. In the long passage that follows, Shizuka dances.)*

    1. Since this scene is frequently staged as an independent unit, there are variations to the set.
    2. Part of the modern city of Osaka.

## Scene 1: Michiyuki. The Journey with the Drum

The country lanes are unfamiliar,
Thickly grown with weeds
And difficult to follow.
Shizuka makes her way
Amid young grasses
Growing left and right,
While pheasants foraging for food
Cry *hororoken, hororotsu*.[3]
"You birds long for your young,"
Thinks Shizuka, "And we who stray
Upon the road of love,
Ah, discontent are we
With what the world has dealt us.
How we envy you."
On wings spread wide
Like well starched *hakama*,[4]
The first geese of the autumn fly above.
A mated pair, how joyous they seem;
A better fate for them
Than that of humans.
The brushwood points the way
To the Uga no Mitama Shrine,[5]
Glimpsed sacred, shining through the mists.
At Mika Moor,
Where the river Izumi

---

3. Japanese onomatopoeia for the cry of a pheasant.
4. Skirtlike trousers, part of formal dress of the Tokugawa period.
5. Commonly known as Inari, Uga no Mitama is the Shinto female deity of cereals, especially rice. Her messenger is the fox, a creature endowed in folklore with magical powers, particularly the power of transforming itself into other forms, including human. The ubiquitous Inari shrines are readily identified by their bright red *torii* gateways, often in great numbers at a single shrine, and the stone foxes that usually stand as guardians at the gates.

Rises and flows forth,[6]
Shizuka holds close the keepsake drum
With its leather drumheads,
And in her mind repeats the reverie:
"How cherished is my lord,
And dear, so dear, this keepsake drum."[7]
Her thoughts are like the sweet exchange
Of lovers in their chamber.
"Oh to be embraced by him,
Just as this drum is swathed in silk"—
With such thoughts to give her hope,
She leans upon her staff;
But forlorn her lonely heart
As she moves along the narrow road.
As far as she can see,
The boughs of trees are starting into bloom.
In the village of Utahime[8]
The village men all sing aloud
The Plum Branch Song:[9]

> My wife's in bliss,
> She's making eyes at me,
> Putting out our pillows
> In the daytime—

---

6. An allusion to a poem by Fujiwara no Kanesuke in the collection *Shin kokin waka shū* (comp. 1205):

> When, I wonder, did I meet her
> That for her I should yearn so?
> Here along the river Izumi
> That rises and flows forth
> In Mika Moor?

See Hisamatsu Sen'ichi, Yamazaki Toshio, and Gotō Shigeo, eds., *Shin kokin waka shū*, 218.
 7. A play on the words *kawa* (leather/skin), referring to the leathers on the drum, and *kawaii* (beloved/cherished).
 8. Now part of the city of Nara.
 9. The song is probably of folk origin.

### Scene 1: Michiyuki: The Journey with the Drum

>What a silly woman!
>A silly woman she!

To such a funny tune the young men sing,
So like a flock of crows
That even rustics raised from birth
In cottages with roofs of straw
Are set to rounds of laughter.
In spring the kicking ball's kicked up
To counts of "one" and "two."
And if one listens carefully,
One hears the eastern wind of spring join in,
Melting last year's ice,
Like the happy *manzai* songs
That wish one endless youth.
Just so prays Shizuka:
For her lord a bounteous life.
What winsome charm she has,
Such promise for the future.
"If indeed my lord's in Yamato,
I'll hurry to his hiding place.
With this Hatsune Drum," she thinks,
"I wish my lord a long and fulsome life.
Ah, would that to the present
I could bring the past of long ago,
Like the first sweet song
Of the valley nightingale."

*(From the off-stage musicians, concealed from the audience in an enclosure at SR, there are sounds suggesting the call of the nightingale.)*

>"And to entice the bird to follow me
>I'll play this Hatsune Drum,
>This Drum of Hatsune."

*(She strikes the drum. There is an ominous roll of drums, and a white fox emerges at SR. It romps along the front edge of the stage, comes close to Shizuka, who is oblivious to its presence. The fox, apparently*

*drawn to the drum, then goes to the low hill at SR and moves behind it. In a matter of seconds, the hinged upper half of the stage flat on which the hill is painted drops forward, revealing Tadanobu dressed in a black robe edged in red. On his back is a cloth-wrapped bundle containing the suit of armor given him earlier by Yoshitsune.)*

>Now tardy Tadanobu comes,
>Dressed in traveling garb,
>Bearing tightly tied upon his back
>A bundle bound in cloth.
>Cheerfully he comes along,
>Through roads across the meadows,
>Along the paths between the paddy fields,
>All composure in his simple dress.
>To keep from standing out,
>He's put some distance
>Between himself and Shizuka,
>But he's misguessed the speed
>With which the lady walked.

TADANOBU: You must have been anxious about me. Luckily, there's no one here to see us.

NARRATOR: Tadanobu takes out the armor
>Received from his master—
>Along with the bestowal of his name—
>And humbly now he bows before it,
>As though it were his lord himself.

*(Tadanobu sets the armor up on the tree stump in front of the center cherry tree.)*

>To represent his august face,
>Atop the armor Shizuka sets the drum.

*(Shizuka places the drum on top of the armor; both she and Tadanobu bow before it. During the following narration, the two dance, Shizuka adroitly using her fan to mime actions to the words. At one point, with her back to Tadanobu, she throws and he catches the fan—a virtuoso display of puppet manipulation.)*

>>My sleeve is like the stones offshore,
>>That even in the ebbing tide

### Scene 1: Michiyuki: The Journey with the Drum

During the michiyuki journey through the Yoshino mountains, a magical fox appears in response to Shizuka's beating of the drum. (Act 4, scene 1)

>Remain to all unseen:
>Though my love is unaware,
>My sleeve is never dry.[10]

In secret to the west country
Has Yoshitsune gone,
Across the waters
Churned by wave and wind,
Until his boat was blown ashore
Into Sumiyoshi Bay.[11]
From there, according to the news,
He has traveled on to Yoshino.
"Let us go there now," they say,
And each retrieves the keepsake

10. A poem from the collection known as *Hyakunin isshu*, thought to have been compiled in the thirteenth century by the noted poet Fujiwara no Teika. The play text quotes only a portion of the poem, but I have rendered it in full.
11. Sumiyoshi is in the southern part of the modern city of Osaka.

Tadanobu (*on the left*) and Shizuka dance during their journey through the Yoshino mountains in the michiyuki. (Act 4, scene 1)

Given by their lord.[12]
Geese and swallows: which of these
Possess the greatest charm?
More dear, we feel, are swallows,
Who spend the spring with us
And raise their little ones.
Yet even if it be the geese,
Who turn their backs
Upon the blossoms of the spring,
Still do they bring us tidings,[13]
And thus we have a bond with them.

---

12. The following twelve lines are not in Tsurumi, *Takeda Izumo shū*, the most complete text of the play. They have been drawn from the text in Yūda, *Bunraku jōruri shū*, 211.

13. An allusion to a story in the Chinese official history of the former Han dynasty (202 B.C.–A.D. 8), the *Han Shu* by Pan Ku. The story is of Su Wu (died 60 B.C.), the Han emperor's envoy to the barbarian Hsiung-nu on China's northwestern frontier. The Hsiung-nu detained Su Wu and tried several times

## Scene 1: Michiyuki: The Journey with the Drum

"Oh yes, oh yes, such fun it is
As voices sing the rhythm out."[14]

"Surely," Tadanobu thinks,
"This gift of armor from my lord
Betokens the loyal service
Rendered by my brother Tsuginobu."[15]
*(The following approximately twenty lines are delivered in the chanting style of the Nō theater.)*
His mind can see it now.
That scene at Dannoura.[16]
*(As Tadanobu recalls and recounts the story of the battle, he pulls down the top of his black robe, revealing beneath it a red under-robe dyed with the white Genji-guruma pattern—a large carriage wheel, the axle centering on his neck. Throughout the following narration he mimes the story in dance.)*
In the water the soldiers' ships
Flying the Heike flags of red!
On the land the Genji troops
With their banners of white!
"See what a pompous sight!"

---

without success to win him to their side, eventually sending him north to tend sheep. Years later, the Chinese emperor asked for Su Wu's return, but his captors claimed that he was dead. The emperor, however, had shot a goose to whose leg was tied a message from Su Wu. After nineteen years in captivity, Su Wu was restored to his homeland. See Burton Watson, tr., *Courtier and Commoner in Ancient China: Selections from the History of the Former Han Dynasty* by Pan Ku, 34–45; also Giles, *A Chinese Biographical Dictionary,* 684–85. The story is also recounted, with slight variations, in *The Tale of the Heike,* 94–95.

14. Apparently a fragment of a folk song.
15. The long passage from this point and ending with the line "In the lines of battle" is not found in Tsurumi. *Takeda Izumo shū*; it has been incorporated from the text in Yūda, *Bunraku jōruri shū,* 211–12.
16. The following lines derive largely from the Nō play *Kagekiyo.* See the translation by Arthur Waley in *The Nō Plays of Japan,* 132–33. Dannoura was the scene of the final and decisive battle between the Heike and the Genji. The battle that Tadanobu describes, however, is the one at Yashima, which took place about a month prior to the clash at Dannoura.

Cries a Heike warrior,
And up he hoists his lance,
Flashing in the setting sun.
To the other side he shouts,
And loudly he proclaims his name:
"I am a samurai of the Heike,
By name, Akushichibyōe Kagekiyo!"
As fiercely he strides forth, strides forth,
The lesser soldiers on the Genji side
Move back, like blossoms
Scattered pell-mell in a gale.
"Have all of you lost your pride?"
Shouts out a Genji general.
"Here I am, Miyonoya no Shirō!"
He says, and to the water's edge
He springs out smartly to attack.
Sideways with their swords they slash,
And dance their lances about.
But evenly the sides are matched,
As amid the sounds of waves
They trade blows with each other.
Then Miyonoya's long sword
Snaps off at its hilt,
And back he retreats
Like a receding tide.
"Ah," shouts Kagekiyo,
"Will you, like the geese that wing away,
Turn your back upon
The flowers of the fray?"
Beneath his arm
He tucks his lance and short sword,
And seizes tight the neck strap
Of Miyonoya's helmet.
Back pulls Kagekiyo,
Reeling, staggering.

### Scene 1: Michiyuki: The Journey with the Drum

The other way heaves Miyonoya,
Tottering, faltering.
Then with a snap the strap
Of Miyonoya's helmet gives way,
And both men fall back
And down upon their buttocks.
"How strong," shouts one,
"The arm of Kagekiyo!"
"Oh no," comes the reply, "how stout
The shaft of Miyonoya's neck!"
"Ha ha ha ha ha," laughs Miyonoya.
"Ho ho ho ho ho," bellows Kagekiyo in return.
But after this exchange of mirth,
Many were their fierce encounters
In the lines of battle.
"In the fight at Yashima," thinks Tadanobu,
"My brother Tsuginobu stood
And blocked the way of my master's horse
As he started for the thick of battle.
Oh, then I heard there was
Among the Heike troops
A mighty archer, great of fame—
Noritsune, Lord of Noto.
Hardly had he shouted out his name
Than with a whir he loosed a shaft.
The arrow's point—oh, bitter the memory:
The instant that it drove
Into my brother's breast,
Head above his heels he pitched.
A warrior who dies a tragic death
Leaves behind a name
As a faithful subject,
A retainer ever true.
I but think upon it, and my sleeve
Is never dry of tears,

As ever moist the well pipes of Tsutsui."[17]
"Someday," thinks Shizuka,
"My lord will know distress no more;
His life will be as long
As the threadlike willow limbs
At Yagyū[18] in the springtime,
And we will be forever joined
As trees of different trunks
May share a common bough.
How ever can such bonds decay away?"
Though they try to hurry on,
Lending each the other's strength,
Their progress seems so slow,
As they cross the Ashihara Pass,
Move through the villages of Gō,
Put behind them Tsuchida and Mutsuda.[19]
Soon, blown along the meadow lanes
By the zephyrs of spring,
Misjudging vistas filled with cherry blooms
For congeries of clouds,
They reach the village at the base
Of beautiful Mount Yoshino.

17. This is a pun on *tsutsui,* a circular well, and the place Tsutsui, now the city Kōriyama, just southwest of the city of Nara.
18. A town just east of Tsutsui.
19. All the places mentioned are in modern Nara prefecture, in the vicinity of the Yoshino Mountains.

SCENE 2
# THE ZAŌ HALL

*(Large rocky outcrops slant down toward the stage from SR and SL. Tall cherry trees in bloom stand at SL and upstage center. Beyond, somewhat to SR and situated on a rocky rise, is a building with a thatch roof, stone steps leading up to its main room. This is the Zaō Hall. The area in front of the building constitutes its courtyard where local farmers are busy sweeping.)* [1]

NARRATOR: The cherries of Mount Yoshino
 Would soften even the scowl
 Of the angry visaged Buddha Zaō,
 A full sixteen *shaku* tall.[2]

---

1. This scene is now rarely, if ever, performed. The only source I have been able to find of what may perhaps be the set is in *Gidayū nenpyō: Meiji-hen*, 461 (second drawing from the top, center column). The scene is not included in any of the texts that provide staging information, so it is impossible to know details of stage action.

2. Approximately 4.85 meters, or nearly 15 feet.

The eaves of the houses are buried in the mist,
And surpassing all in loveliness,
Is the Zaō Hall.[3]
Not yet are the cherries in bloom,
And every branch and twig looks bare
Beneath the sky of early spring.[4]
Knowing that the priests
Of all the temples on Mount Yoshino
Are soon to start their new year council,
The farmers under the temple's sway
Dance attendance on their betters
And sweep the precincts clean.
More fearful are they
Of the chastening priests
Than the Buddha they should respect.
Shizuka, "Quiet Gentle One," she's called,
But the name belies the haste
With which she comes along the road,
Tadanobu watching over her with care,
As they seek to follow Yoshitsune.
At length his trail has led them here,
And though the time is mid-Third Month,
How beautiful this view of Yoshino
As far as eyes can see.
Among themselves the farmers talk.

FARMER #1: My, what a beautiful lady from the Capital. But it's still a bit early to be here for flower-viewing.

FARMER #2: What do you mean, flower-viewing? A man and a woman traveling together: why, she's probably gotten pregnant and there was nothing to do but elope. You reckon that's the case?

---

3. On Zaō Hall, see act 3, scene 1, "The Pasania Tree," note 2.

4. There may be an inconsistency here, the previous scene having been one in which the cherry trees were in full bloom. However, a visitor to Mount Yoshino suggests that altitude affects the timing of the blossoms: those lower down were in full bloom, while those higher up were still only in bud. Zaō Hall may be some distance up the mountain.

## Scene 2· The Zaō Hall

SHIZUKA: Oh no, that's not it at all. We've come on business with His Reverence Kawatsura.[5] Which way should we go from here?

NARRATOR: Without hearing more,
The farmers quickly understand.

FARMER #1: Eh, I see, I see. You've come to go into service as a concubine. Well, in that case you're in luck. His Reverence Kawatsura is the head of all the priests on this mountain. He does whatever he wants anywhere in Yoshino. What's more, he has a wife and eats all the fish and fowl he likes.[6] He may seem a degenerate priest, but he's allowed to be married and he holds a high rank; so, please ma'm, you just accommodate him—and good luck to you.

SHIZUKA *(archly):* I can see you're a person of fine judgment. And is there perhaps an important guest staying with His Reverence?

FARMER #1: Oh, I wouldn't know about such things. But it's surely lively there. I hear the koto and samisen playing every day. You go up this road here. In this direction is the Shrine of the Nursemaid God.[7] Women aren't allowed to go there. This side of it there's a path, and you'll see His Reverence's house on the left. It's the place with the big gate.

SHIZUKA: Yes, yes, thank you very much.

NARRATOR: Impatiently, they make their way
Quickly up the path together.

---

5. Kawatsura is referred to throughout the play by the title of Hōgen, the middle of three rankings of priests, the rank of Hokkyō being the lowest. It is interesting that the playwrights have made him a friend and supporter of Yoshitsune in the play. In the *Gikeiki*, he is the leader of a rabble of warrior priests attacking Yoshitsune and his party. See McCullough, *Yoshitsune,* 180ff.

6. Marriage and eating living things were normally forbidden to members of the Buddhist clergy. Perhaps by virtue of his rank such a diet is permitted Kawatsura.

7. The formal name of the shrine is the Mikumari Shrine, which the local dialect changes to Mikomori (Honored Nursemaid).

SCENE 3
THE CONFERENCE AT
THE ZAŌ HALL[1]

*(A building stretches about half the way across the stage from SL, its principal room open to the audience, its entryway to SR. The SR portion of the set shows a somewhat more distant view of two mountains sloping down to a valley between them. The mountain at far SL is Mount Se; the other mountain is Mount Imo. Each mountain is green with pine trees and other vegetation. On each mountain, and downstage of it, stands a more prominent pine tree. The forestage is the courtyard.)*

NARRATOR: At the early meeting bell,
   In comes Yamashina Hokkyōbō,[2]

   1. I have been unable to discover a description of the set for this scene; I have presumed something along the lines given here.
   2. A henchman of Yokawa no Kakuhan, one of Yoshitsune's enemies in Yoshino. In the *Gikeiki* he appears as Yamashina no Hōgen. See McCullough, *Yoshitsune,* 187ff.

### Scene 3: The Conference at the Zaō Hall

So ruthless and bold a prelate
That he has a shorter name:
Wild Hokkyō he is called.
Coming hard upon his heels,
A priest who bears the name of Demon,
A rascal not at all unlike his name:
Umemoto, the Demon Sadobō.
And with them comes the doctor priest,
Kaerizaka no Yakuibō.[3]
Though all are proper priests,
Great swords are strapped to their waists,
They wear the wide-hemmed *hakama*,[4]
And each is eager to be first
To show his witless face
At the council for today.
The rustic farmers all turn tail
And crawl abjectly off.
Demon Sadobō glares about him.

SADOBŌ: Still haven't finished sweeping? I gave you an order some time ago. Lazy sluggards, the lot of you! Wait till it's time for the land tax!

NARRATOR: How he scolds them.
"Yessir, yessir, yessir," say the farmers.
Catching the hint, each and every one
Turns with a will to the sweeping.
They sweep upwind, so dust and dirt
Cover the cassocks and stoles of the priests.

SADOBŌ: You abominations! What do you think you're doing?

NARRATOR: No holding him back
When it comes to abuse.

FARMER: We're sweeping, sir.

---

3. Another of Kakuhan's followers. His name, Yakuibō, indicates that he is a doctor or pharmacist. In the *Gikeiki* he is called Yakui no Kami, Kaerisaka no Kohijiri. See McCullough, *Yoshitsune*, 350.

4. The formal skirtlike trouser, in this case with a wider than usual opening at the hem, presumably for greater freedom of movement in combat.

## ACT FOUR

NARRATOR: Themselves bedecked in dust,
  The farmers flee the scene pell-mell.
  Now in walks Kawatsura Hōgen,
  Director General of all temples
  Standing on Mount Yoshino.
  Not fond of bright display,
  His robes are of a pale green hue,
  With billowing trousers
  Bound with cords at his feet.
KAWATSURA: Ah, all of you are early.
NARRATOR: After greetings all around,
  His priests attend him
  Seated on round cushions.
  A pause, then Kawatsura Hōgen speaks.
KAWATSURA: I sent around a message that we have this early meeting. I am most happy to see you in attendance. The matter before us is as follows.
NARRATOR: He brings out a letter
  From the folds of his robe.
KAWATSURA: This letter has come to me from my brother-in-law Ibara Saemon, a retainer to our lord in Kamakura. Please listen to what it says so that the matter will be clear to you.
NARRATOR: He spreads the letter before him.
KAWATSURA (*reading the letter*): "I write to you in great urgency. Regarding Kurō Hōgan Yoshitsune, his elder brother Yoritomo has been empowered by a decree of the Retired Emperor to hunt him down. Moreover, since learning of the killing of Tosabō Shōzon, of Yoshitsune's flight from the Capital, and of the latter's movement along the Yamato Road, Yoritomo, Lord of Kamakura, has been most grievously angered. You are to set forth at once and attack him, and you are to execute the issuance of warrants for him throughout the provinces. A reward will be given for his death. In the event that you give him shelter, all of the temples on Mount Yoshino will be destroyed. Given by my hand on this the thirtieth day of the First Month to Master Kawatsura Hō-

## Scene 3: The Conference at the Zaō Hall

gen." It is signed and sealed, Ibara Saemon. You hear that, all of you? This is the matter we are to discuss. That Yoshitsune, who has been blameless from the start, is traveling along the Yamato Road surely means that he is coming to this temple to ask us for help. When he comes, shall we hide him as he will request, or is it your view that we should attack him? When each of you has considered this in his heart, you are to discuss the matter with me candidly.

NARRATOR: Hardly has he heard these words
Than Wild Hokkyō speaks up.

HOKKYŌ: What you have said is all quite well. However, there is no need to query us in council. You, as head of all of the temples on this mountain, should take care of the matter. If your reverence's intention in this issue is stated unequivocally, no one is going to oppose it; all will be of the same mind. First, then, tell us what you think we should do.

KAWATSURA: Ah, I have my own views. But if I tell you first what I think, then if that does not match your own views you will be unlikely to speak in opposition. Should that occur, it could lead us to make blunders. I will tell you later of my own opinion, but first each of you must say frankly what you think.

NARRATOR: Reserve yet hangs about them,
And for a spell they fail to answer.
Then Kaerizaka Yakuibō abruptly speaks out.

YAKUIBŌ: First, then, this humble monk's opinion. We might hide Yoshitsune here two or three, up to twenty or thirty, years, and the food to sustain him alone might be small enough. But that hog Benkei—why, with him the food simply goes in one end and out the other! I just can't imagine what it would take to feed him! If we say that we won't hide Yoshitsune, why that outrageous rascal just might use one of his seven weapons, such as his saw, and cut his way into our storehouse. Rather than be robbed of so much, maybe we should feed him tea and rice gruel made up by calculating the share contributed by each temple.

NARRATOR: Though His Reverence finds this speech
   Amusing and curious . . .
KAWATSURA: Hmmm, what you say may be important. Now, you other two.
NARRATOR: At once, one of them speaks up.
HOKKYŌ: Come now, we don't need to calculate anything in this matter. It's the duty of men of the cloth such as us to give aid to people. If an army comes from Kamakura to attack us because we've given shelter to the blameless Yoshitsune, we should put aside our robes of tolerance and don the armor of a demon queller; we should mount a counter-attack and kill our attackers. We'll chase every one of them back to Kamakura, and we'll let Yoshitsune explain his innocence. Then we'll line up those who have falsely accused Yoshitsune and cut them down one by one. And if that isn't possible, we'll attack Yoritomo, a man who can't distinguish right from wrong. Then Lord Yoshitsune will take control of the country. That's my opinion on the matter. I should like to hear His Reverence's views.
KAWATSURA: No, I'll not speak yet. Thanks to the kindness of Brother Hokkyō, we have of late had a visiting priest with us: the Zen master Yokawa no Kakuhan.[5] He has not yet joined us here, but I must hear his opinion also. It is late, and I've waited long for him to come.
NARRATOR: A moment later,
   Slowly along the mountain path
   Comes the priest whose name
   Is known to all: Yokawa no Kakuhan.
   The sleeves of his robe are tied with cord
   And rolled back up his arm;
   A great sword three and a half feet long
   Hangs ready at his side.

   5. In the *Gikeiki*, Yokawa no Kakuhan is a monk of extraordinary stature and strength who battles and is eventually killed by Yoshitsune's retainer Satō Tadanobu. See McCullough, *Yoshitsune*, 183–86.

## Scene 3: The Conference at the Zaō Hall

He takes his place at the lowest seat,
But such is his height and priestly stature,
He seems far more impressive.

*(Kakuhan enters from SR.)*

KAWATSURA: Ah, Master Kakuhan. We've been looking forward to your arrival. Please, come closer.

NARRATOR: As he beckons him to draw near,
His Reverence rises gently.

KAWATSURA: Look, Kakuhan, see over there the two mountains shrouded in the mist. Those are the Imose Mountains,[6] a famous setting for poems about bringing people together. They are divided by the Yoshino River: to the west beyond the river is Mount Imo, and on this the eastern side is Mount Se. *Imo* means younger sister, or younger brother. Mount Se, the elder brother mountain, of course represents Yoritomo. Thus, the friendship of the older and younger brothers—Yoritomo and Yoshitsune—is breached by the Yoshino River. Though they are but mountains, such poems as this have been written about them:

> Let us accept it.
> Love's course can but remind us
> Of the Yoshino,
> The river falling between
> Husband Mountain and Wife Hill.[7]

---

6. Located in modern Nara prefecture, the two mountains stand on either side of the Yoshino river and have long been sung in poetry as mountains representing girl (Mount Imo) and boy (Mount Se) lovers. Kawatsura has them symbolize Yoritomo (Mount Se) and his younger brother Yoshitsune (Mount Imo).

7. An anonymous poem (no. 828) in the *Kokin waka shū*. See Saeda Umetomo, ed., *Kokin waka shū*, 264. The translation here is by McCullough, *Kokin Wakashū: The First Imperial Anthology of Japanese Poetry*, 180. Mounts Imo and Se were often likened to lovers or to husband and wife, as well as to the sibling relationship that Kawatsura uses. As McCullough explains in her note to the poem, it means that one should be resigned to the impermanence of any relationship between a man and a woman.

Even such as we of the cloth who have cast aside all things mundane, are we not to respond to a call for aid? Or do we cut down the supplicant with a well tempered blade? I would hear your brief response. Please speak.

NARRATOR: Kakuhan needs no time for reflection.
 He quickly stands and gives a nod,
 Then takes a bow and arrow
 Offered as a votive gift at Zaō Hall.
 He strings the bow.

KAKUHAN: See, Master Kawatsura, my concise response. The two trees you see before you standing on each mountain. They are the objects of my aim. Observe.

NARRATOR: He mates the arrow to the bowstring;
 Unhesitatingly, with a whir he lets it fly.
 Now there the white fletched arrow stands,
 Thrust deep in the tree upon Mount Se.
 His Reverence observes it sharply.

KAWATSURA: You've drawn your bow against Mount Se that has been likened to Yoritomo. This must mean that you oppose Yoritomo and are Yoshitsune's ally. Hmmm, I see.

NARRATOR: He rolls up the letter he had read
 And puts it into the breast fold of his robe.

KAWATSURA: Yamashina Hokkyō, Yakuibō, this is the same position you take, is that not so?

NARRATOR: Both chime in together.

BOTH: We stand with Yoshitsune!

KAWATSURA: Hmmm. In that case, I will now make clear where I stand.

NARRATOR: The selfsame bow and arrow
 He takes into his hand
 And stretches taut the bow.
 What will be his target,
 To which tree will the arrow fly?
 As all look on, he sends it winging
 To Mount Imo, the younger brother peak
 That stands for Yoshitsune.

## Scene 3: The Conference at the Zaō Hall

THREE PRIESTS: Yaa, then Your Reverence stands with Yoritomo! You draw your bow against Yoshitsune!

KAWATSURA: Just so. Rather than join forces with a fugitive, I follow the tenor of the times. It is my responsibility to see that every temple on this mountain is not destroyed.

KAKUHAN: Are you quite sure of your position?

KAWATSURA: Why do you ask, Kakuhan? If Yoshitsune seeks aid here, go ahead and give him refuge. I will certainly seek him out, and you will see that I shall kill him. When that time comes, we will be on opposite sides. I've wasted my time consulting with these ignorant priests. This concludes today's council. I bid you all good day.

NARRATOR: But strange his attitude,
As with these parting words,
And not waiting for his palanquin,
He sets out for his quarters.
Behind him Wild Sadobō
Stands with mouth agape.

SADOBŌ: Hey, just what is this? What does he mean? We were of one accord; we must have misunderstood him. Kakuhan, what do you think?

NARRATOR: Yamashina and the rest
All turn to Kakuhan,
Who bursts out into laughter.

KAKUHAN: All of you have so little understanding, you don't know what His Reverence really thinks. If you considered his words carefully, you'd know that deep within his heart he is already giving refuge to Yoshitsune. He was able to perceive that my support for Yoshitsune was false. If we wait too long, His Reverence may try to help Yoshitsune escape. We shall fix our plan for tonight at the stroke of eight.[8] We'll attack Yoshitsune in the dark and kill him; and, incidentally, we shall be the recipients of a reward from the Lord of Kamakura, Yoritomo. Now, come and hear Kakuhan's strategy for this night attack.

---

8. 2 A.M. by Western reckoning

NARRATOR: On a rotting root beneath a giant tree
He sits down heavily.
KAKUHAN: At various times during my religious disciplines I have committed to memory Sun Tzu's book of strategy.[9] Do not err from what I now tell you. Hokkyō, you will take ten men in full armor from the Stone Lantern Crossroad[10] to Ichimonji and creep up to His Reverence's residence, where you are to ring a small bell boisterously three or four times. Sadobō will go directly behind the Nyoirinji Temple, remove the bridge at Rokujizō, wait until the enemy attempts to flee, and then stop them with a fusillade of arrows. I, Kakuhan, will set fire to the priests' quarters in Shimbō Valley, sending them up in flames, and chase Kawatsura's priests down Shōden Hill. A victory tonight is almost in our hands. Take heed, take heed!
NARRATOR: Yakuibō shakes his head.
YAKUIBŌ: That's what we think too. But what if our opponents are strong, and what if they drive back Hokkyō's force? Suppose they surge out in a full speed attack of their own, make Katte Shrine their base, and then start to beat frantically on the gate, what then?
KAKUHAN: Aha, you challenge my plan with good reason. In that case, we'll climb to the top of Scarf Waving Peak at the Kongō Zaō Hall of the Hachiōji Temple and shoot straight down upon them. If we shoot our arrows at them for a while, they won't be able to withstand the attack and will retreat.
HOKKYŌ: Oh, the cherries still won't be in bloom, but they'll move behind the trunks and under the branches of the trees.

---

9. Sun Tzu (also known as Sun Wu) was a sixth-century B.C. Chinese who wrote a famous treatise on the strategy of warfare.
10. This and the several other places mentioned below are identifiable locations on Mount Yoshino. This plethora of detail about the establishments and geography of Mount Yoshino seems intended to show off the playwrights' knowledge of the Yoshino locale and to appeal to the sense of local geography of contemporary audiences, most of whom would have come from the general area of Kyoto, Osaka, and Nara.

### Scene 3: The Conference at the Zaō Hall

They'll escape along the narrow road that winds among the trees to Tennōbashi Bridge and the Stupa of the Great General. And they might go to the corner tower of the castle and wait there so they can chase us and fire on us from hiding. How do we handle that?

KAKUHAN: You're a shrewd one, Hokkyō. But no matter how much the fugitives shoot at us, they won't have many arrows. We'll withdraw and then attack, attack and withdraw again. We'll make them use up all their arrows, and it won't take any time at all to kill them off. Don't be afraid. Just be silent and prepare yourselves! Let's go, all of you. During one of Emperor Temmu's battles, a heavenly maiden came to earth and performed a dance for him. That was the beginning of our protective magical rites.[11] Now, on to victory!

NARRATOR: He stamps upon the ground,
Seven steps to the left,
Seven steps to the right.
To left and right, fourteen paces all,
And he brings his dance to a close.

KAKUHAN: Now go! Advance!

NARRATOR: Rare it is to see such grit
As that of Zen priest Kakuhan,
And at a spirited pace
He hurries full tilt away.

---

11. Temmu (reigned 673–86) was Japan's fortieth emperor. He was named heir to his brother Tenchi, but to escape his enemies he shaved his head and retired to Mount Yoshino. Later, in a battle with Tenchi's son (who had succeeded his father on the throne), it is said that a heavenly maiden appeared to Temmu on Scarf Waving Peak and performed a dance, after which Temmu's army went on to victory. The magical rites refer to ancient practices, involving a kind of dance, performed to ward off calamity when one left home See Tsurumi, *Takeda Izumo shū*, 260, n. 57.

SCENE 4

# THE MANSION OF KAWATSURA HŌGEN

*(The stage is dominated by the interior of a palatial building running from SL approximately three-quarters of the way toward SR. At SL is a smaller room enclosed by shōji panels. The main room, open toward the audience, is devoid of furnishings and has at its rear three wide bamboo blinds, edged in crimson and with crimson ribboning down the center. In front of the rooms is a low balustrade, lacquered in black and with gold fittings. At both the center of the open room and at its SR end are short stairways, each with a continuation of the balustrade down the steps. The room is raised off the ground by wooden supports in tan. Across the top of both rooms is a series of panels bordered in black lacquered wood, each panel decorated with three rosettes of cherry leaves and blossoms. Downstage of the room is the courtyard. At SR, outside the room is a tall bamboo fence woven in a herringbone pattern enclosing the compound. Across the top of the*

## Scene 4: The Mansion of Kawatsura Hōgen

*fence may be seen flowering cherry trees. The top of the proscenium is decorated with hangings of pink cherry blossoms. As the narration begins, there is no one on stage. At the point noted below, the bamboo blinds roll up to reveal a wide arched doorway hung with an embroidered curtain made up of vertical bands of cloth varying in colors and patterns. The walls on either side of the doorway continue the rosette patterns of cherry leaves and blossoms.)*

NARRATOR:

    If there be no song
    Of the nightingale
    In mountain hamlets,
    Where snow has yet to melt away,
    How to know that spring has come?[1]

Spring indeed has come,
But for Kurō Hōgan Yoshitsune
No spring of reconciliation does it bring,
As in an inner chamber
Of Kawatsura's residence
He is consoled by melodies
Of koto and samisen.[2]
Even these are tuned
To quiet modes and softened
With muffled bridges for the strings—
The better from the world to lie concealed.
Like an echelon of geese rise
The bridges of the instrument;[3]
But unlike these birds

---

1. A poem by the Middle Councilor Tomotada in the collection *Shūi waka shū* (comp. ca. 996).
2. While the koto, a long 13-stringed zitherlike instrument, is of ancient origin, the samisen is one of those expected anachronisms of eighteenth-century history-based puppet dramas the play is set in the late twelfth century, but the samisen came to Japan in the late sixteenth century.
3. The tall bridges that hold up the strings on the koto may resemble in their arrangement on the instrument an echelon of geese.

That turn their back on spring,[4]
The kindness of His Reverence,
Determined to stand by his friend,
Is surely a happy augury.

*(At this point, the bamboo blinds at the back of the main room roll up, revealing the arched and curtained doorway. Kawatsura Hōgen enters slowly and pensively from SR.)*

Now returns, slowly and deliberately,
His Reverence Kawatsura,
Absent since this morning,
His countenance betraying
Some design that lies within his heart.
Asuka, his wife, comes out to meet him.

*(Asuka enters through the arched doorway.)*

ASUKA: Oh, you've returned earlier than I expected. The council today, was it about your management of all the temples on the mountain, or did it concern our guest inside, Yoshitsune?

KAWATSURA: Oh, it was about Yoshitsune, all right.

ASUKA: Hmm, and did there appear to be full agreement that everyone here also supported Yoshitsune?

KAWATSURA: Of course, the lower priests Kaerizaka no Yakuibō, Yamashina the Wild Hokkyō, and Umemoto the Demon Sadobō all did. And Yokawa no Kakuhan in particular declared himself a partisan of Yoshitsune. But since I knew they were trying to find out my own personal feelings, I declared that I stood with Kamakura, and then I left.

ASUKA: I see. And in saying that you stood with Kamakura, you were also trying to fathom what your priests were really thinking, is that right?

KAWATSURA: Oh no, I've had a change of heart today. Yoshitsune and I are now on opposite sides.

ASUKA: What? You're going to turn Yoshitsune over to . . .

KAWATSURA: I intend to turn Yoshitsune over to Yoritomo. If you don't understand, just look at this.

---

4. An echo of lines in the opening scene of this act, "The Journey With the Drum."

### Scene 4: The Mansion of Kawatsura Hōgen

NARRATOR: From the breast fold of his robe
He flings the letter down.
His wife takes it up
And reads it to the end.
ASUKA: According to this letter, the people in Kamakura know that Lord Yoshitsune is hiding on this mountain.
KAWATSURA: You're quite right, it does. Heaven has no mouth, but speaks through the hearts of men, says the proverb. Unless there is somebody who revealed his presence here to Kamakura, why would my brother-in-law Ibara Saemon send such a letter? Now that Yoshitsune has been betrayed and they know that he's here, he cannot escape. Therefore, rather than let someone else get the credit for the deed, I have decided that he will die by my hand.
ASUKA: What! Are you serious?
KAWATSURA: I am.
ASUKA: You really mean that you intend to kill Lord Yoshitsune?
KAWATSURA: Stop nagging me!
NARRATOR: Carefully in her heart
She weighs the matter.
Then swiftly she draws her husband's sword.
Seeing that his wife would kill herself,
He snatches away the blade.
KAWATSURA: What are you doing? Why kill yourself?
NARRATOR: He watches her face intently.
ASUKA: You're being unreasonable, my lord. Why have you kept me out of this? However many letters offering a reward might come, a thousand, ten thousand, it's not like you to change your mind once you have made a promise. Because this letter came to you, you suspect me, the younger sister of Yoritomo's loyal retainer Ibara Saemon. You thought that I had informed my brother about Lord Yoshitsune's hiding place. I'll not waste time protesting my innocence. If you suspect me, kill me, my lord, at once.
NARRATOR: The bitter tears she sheds
Show the truth of what she speaks.

His Reverence hears her out;
Then he takes the letter
And, unhesitating, tears it into shreds.

KAWATSURA: Don't throw your life away for a falsehood. In doubting my own wife I must appear to you irresolute, but I am completely loyal to Lord Yoshitsune. This letter is not genuine; I was using it to probe the hearts of my priests. Now, I have torn it up, and you may rest easy. Give up any thoughts of your own destruction, my wife.

NARRATOR: As he explains himself,
Her bitterness disappears
Like the snow in spring.
Lord Yoshitsune emerges
From the inner room.

*(Yoshitsune enters from the shōji paneled room at SL.)*

YOSHITSUNE: Ah, Your Reverence, you've returned. I would like to speak with you. *(Asuka bows and withdraws through the arched doorway.)* You have never forgotten our friendship on Mount Kurama.[5] It is impossible to express in words how grateful I am for all your kindnesses. As we discussed the matter earlier, I am aware of the details of your council today with the other priests.

NARRATOR: At his words, Kawatsura
Bows his head in thanks.

KAWATSURA: I have instructions from our mentor Tōkōbō[6] on Mount Kurama that you are a most special person. You know my determination to support you fully. Since you've sent Musashibō off to your ally Hidehira[7] in the far north,

---

5. In the play, Kawatsura has the role of Yoshitsune's ally. In the *Gikeiki*, however, he is a bumptious and hostile monk who leads a rabble of monks against Yoshitsune. See McCullough, *Yoshitsune*, 180–89.

6. Tōkōbō was the priest who was Yoshitsune's scholarly mentor on Mount Kurama to the north of Kyoto when Yoshitsune was a youth. See McCullough, *Yoshitsune*, 71–76.

7. Fujiwara no Hidehira (died 1187), the lord of the northeastern province of Rikuoku (now Iwate and Aomori prefectures, the northernmost on the main island of Honshu) protected Yoshitsune as a youth and gave him shelter later when he was escaping from Yoritomo's agents. Yoshitsune eventually died in Hidehira's domain.

### Scene 4: The Mansion of Kawatsura Hōgen

and your retainers are few in number, count me as one of them, like Kamei and Suruga.

NARRATOR: As he speaks, a servant comes in. *(From SR.)*

SERVANT: Satō Shirōbei Tadanobu is here seeking his master Yoshitsune's whereabouts. Shall I show him in?

YOSHITSUNE: Ah, I see that he is safe. Send him in; I will see him.

NARRATOR: As his command is passed on,
Kawatsura and his wife
Withdraw to the neighbor room.
*(Kawatsura and Asuka leave through the arched doorway.)*
Led in by a servant,
Shirōbei Tadanobu enters.
*(Tadanobu enters from SR. He carries his sword in his left hand, and he wears formal long trousers that trail along the floor behind him.)*
He comes into the room
Where Yoshitsune waits,
And for a while he pauses,
Gazing on his master's visage.
Then without a word he bows,
Tears of anguish streaming down his face.
His general is most pleased to see him.

YOSHITSUNE: Since parting with you, the Lord of Kamakura has pursued me relentlessly from one place to another. When I had nowhere else to go, I was given shelter by His Reverence Kawatsura, a disciple of Tōkōbō. I face a cold and compassionless spring, but for a while I have kept body and soul together. That you are still well since I bestowed my own name upon you shows that my luck has not yet run out. Ah, that augurs well for the future. I am most pleased. And how is Shizuka since I placed her in your care?

NARRATOR: At his lord's inquiry,
Tadanobu listens, seeming puzzled.

TADANOBU: Your question surprises me, my lord. After the Heike clan was defeated at the battle of Yashima, and my lord proclaimed himself victorious in unifying the country, I received news that my mother was ill. When you heard of this you graciously granted me leave, and I returned to my home in the north in the Third Month of last year.[8] Shortly thereafter, my mother passed away. In the midst of the forty-nine-day mourning period that followed, my battle wound began to throb with pain, developing into the illness known as tetanus. I had given up any hope of recovery when I learned of the rift that had developed between you and your brother and of your flight from the Horikawa Mansion. This so grieved and angered me that my illness grew worse. I was filled with such bitterness that I thought of killing myself, but I prayed that at least once more I might be able to pay my respects to my lord face to face. My prayers were answered, and I recovered. During that first long journey after getting well, I heard that your own secret travels had brought you safely to this residence. And so, I have just now arrived here. I have not the slightest recollection of what my lord says—that he bestowed his name upon me or that he placed Lady Shizuka in my care. *(He bows.)*

NARRATOR: Hardly has he spoken
Than the quick-tempered general
Addresses him sharply.

YOSHITSUNE: See here, don't feign ignorance, Tadanobu! When I set out from the Horikawa Mansion, you arrived from your home province just in the nick of time. You rescued Shizuka from a difficult situation, so I gave you a suit of my own armor, and I bestowed upon you the name Kurō Yoshitsune. *(Showing growing anger.)* After I entrusted Shizuka to you and we parted, I suppose you abandoned me as a fugitive and handed Shizuka over to Kamakura. And have you come here to seek out Yoshitsune's hiding place? Just now returned from your home province—what a double dealing bald-faced lie! I have gone through some difficult times, but I haven't grown weak minded! You go too far to think you can dupe me. Disloyal, two-faced villain! I'll have you seized and bound! Kamei! Suruga!

---

8. The third month of the lunar calendar of 1186.

### Scene 4: The Mansion of Kawatsura Hōgen

NARRATOR: At his angry summons
　The doughty warriors dash out, *(from SL)*
　Tuck the hems of their robes
　Into their sashes and stand
　On Tadanobu's right and left,
　Ready to draw their blades.

KAMEI: We've all heard your story. All right, hands behind you, Shirōbei.

SURAGA: Now, give us a full confession. Where is Lady Shizuka? Or shall we kick you and tie you up?

KAMEI: Or shall we torture it out of you? What'll it be?

BOTH: What'll it be?!

NARRATOR: They crowd around him
　Pressing for an answer.
　Tadanobu throws before him
　His swords, both long and short.[9]

TADANOBU: Wait, both of you! Do nothing rash.

KAMEI: Wait, eh? Well, do you have an explanation? If so, let's hear it. Come on, let's hear it!

NARRATOR: Then, at the peak of Tadanobu's predicament...

GATEKEEPER *(enters from the fence at SR)*: My lord, Shirōbei Tadanobu has arrived. He says he is escorting Lady Shizuka.

NARRATOR: At the gateman's words
　All present are stunned!

YOSHITSUNE: What? Tadanobu has come again? I cannot understand this.

NARRATOR: Aroused by what he hears,
　The present Tadanobu stands.

TADANOBU: Whoever it is who falsely assumes my name, he's an imposter and a villain! I'll tie him up and bring him before the general here, and that will clear my name of suspicion. *(He picks up his sword.)*

NARRATOR: He starts to dash off, but...

KAMEI: You stay right where you are! Don't move till the inves-

---

9. A gesture to show that he is unarmed and presents no threat.

## ACT FOUR

tigation is over. *(He pushes Tadanobu back, and together with Suruga he holds out his arms to block Tadanobu's movement.)*

NARRATOR: . . . and Kamei no Rokurō blocks his way.

YOSHITSUNE: No, wait Rokurō. Tadanobu is here, and yet another Tadanobu comes escorting Shizuka. There must be something at the bottom of all this. Bring him in at once.

KAMEI: As you wish, my lord.

NARRATOR: Kamei leaves for the neighboring room. *(Exits SR.)*
  Apprehensive, Tadanobu is taciturn,
  Casting eyes about his surroundings.
  Now, Shizuka walks impatiently
  Through Kawatsura's inner hall,
  Restless her desire
  In the months since parting
  To meet her lord, to see his face.
*(Shizuka enters hurriedly from SR, still carrying across her back the bundle wrapped in lavender cloth.)*

SHIZUKA: Oh, is it you, my lord? How I've missed you!
*(She runs to Yoshitsune, who is seated in the center of the open room.)*

NARRATOR: Heedless of the eyes of those around her,
  She clings to her lord,
  All her pent up love and yearning
  Showing in her tears.

YOSHITSUNE: Ah, I can well understand the lamentations of a woman's heart. As I told you when we parted, I must rely on the compassion of others, and so I could not cling to my own personal desires regarding you. That is why I had to treat you cold-heartedly. Tadanobu was accompanying you. Where is he?

SHIZUKA: Why, he was with me till just now in the next room. Hasn't he come in yet?

NARRATOR: She looks around.

SHIZUKA *(seeing Tadanobu seated at center SR, she points at him)*: Oh, there he is. *(To Tadanobu:)* My, you got here quickly, didn't you. *(Teasing.)* I would have met our lord together with you, Tadanobu, but you just slipped on ahead and got

### Scene 4: The Mansion of Kawatsura Hōgen

here first. Did you think you were advancing on a battlefield? You do like to do things your own way, don't you.

NARRATOR: Tadanobu's suspicions
Are not allayed, but multiply
At this bantering complaint.

TADANOBU: My lord made the same sort of inquiry, about which I have no recollection. I have only just now returned from the province of Dewa.[10] Since I was given leave last year, this is the first time I have seen you.

SHIZUKA *(coquettishly)*: Oh, how you chatter away, making sport of me.

TADANOBU: I make no sport. I am quite serious.

SHIZUKA: There you go, still trying to take me in, and with a straight face too! *(She leans over the balustrade and regards Tadanobu.)*

NARRATOR: Amid this coquetry
Kamei no Rokurō returns. *(Kamei runs in from SR.)*

KAMEI: My lord, I went to bring in the Tadanobu whom we thought had accompanied Lady Shizuka here, but he isn't in the next room. I have inquired at the entryway, the main house, and at several other places, but nobody knows anything about him.

NARRATOR: Yoshitsune is puzzled.

YOSHITSUNE: See here, Shizuka, this person here *(pointing at Tadanobu)* says he has just returned from his home province and is not the Tadanobu to whom I entrusted you. The suspicious one, whom we cannot seem to find but who accompanied you here—might he not be an imposter who resembles Tadanobu? Has this occurred to you?

NARRATOR: As he speaks, Shizuka
Looks intently at Tadanobu.

SHIZUKA: Hmmm, now that you mention it, somehow his under-robe and other parts of his dress seem different. *(Tadanobu stands and spreads out the broad sleeves of his robe for her to*

---

10. The large northern province stretching along the coast of the Japan Sea, encompassed today by Yamagata and Akita prefectures.

*see.)* Oh, wait a moment. Can it be that? Yes, it must be! *(She slaps her knee as Tadanobu resumes his seat.)* I just remembered something. The Hatsune Drum you gave me as a keepsake when we parted. *(She picks up the cloth wrapped bundle she was carrying when she entered and hugs it to herself.)* Here, as you see, I'm never parted from it. When I strike it, Tadanobu is always there to attend me. At Yawata and Yamazaki and at Ogura Village[11] and other places, he'd be nowhere to be seen. Whenever he was absent and when in my longing for you I would strike the drum to console myself, he would always come back to me. The way he was so strongly drawn to the drum's notes, he was like a person intoxicated. When I stopped sounding the drum, he would just stand there looking unconcerned, but he did seem so attached to the drum. I'd strike it the first time, and he'd stop and be sunk in thought. At the second and the third and fourth beat—my how he seemed to change! At the fifth beat he would rise up strangely; and at the sixth beat it was frightening how he would just stand there. I didn't strike the drum any more than that. When I heard that my lord was here, I was so impatient to hurry on that sometimes I would stray away from Tadanobu. Then I'd think of the drum, and if I'd strike it—how strange it was!—he seemed to appear before me as though out of nowhere. In my simple woman's heart I'd wonder if my eyes were playing tricks on me. I wondered what would happen once we got here.

YOSHITSUNE: Hmmm, he comes back to you when you strike the drum, you say. That very fact will make our investigation easier. Shizuka, there's something I wish you to do. You must use this drum and question this Tadanobu who escorted you here. If there is anything suspicious, make use of this sword.

NARRATOR: He reaches out and lays a sword before her.

YOSHITSUNE: I myself may not strike this drum, but you are free to play it. As I listen to its wondrous notes, I shall retire

---

11. All places in the vicinity of Kyoto.

## Scene 4: The Mansion of Kawatsura Hōgen

and let the sound of the drum refresh me. Quickly now, beat the drum.

NARRATOR: These his parting words,
As to the inner room he goes,
While Kamei and Suruga
Lead Tadanobu away.

*(Yoshitsune enters the shōji paneled room at SL. Kamei and Suruga lead Tadanobu out downstage at SL, leaving Shizuka alone in the open room. She then withdraws through the curtains of the arched doorway. At this point there is usually a change of narrator and his samisen accompanist.)*

SCENE 5

THE FOX

• •

*(The scene remains the same, with only the traditional change of narrator and accompanist.)*

NARRATOR: Unlike the Sonohara broom
   tree [1]—
Apparent from afar
But vanishing upon approach—
Surely the man she saw was there,
Though who he is remains in doubt.
Soft are Shizuka's steps

1. A reference to a poem by Sakanoue Korenori (tenth century) in the *Shin kokin waka shū*, that refers to a legendary broom tree (*hahakigi*) on the plain of Sonohara on the border between old Shinano and Mino provinces (modern Nagano and Gifu prefectures, respectively). Like a mirage, from a distance the tree appears to exist, but when one approaches nearer it disappears. The poem also appears in *The Tale of Genji*, providing the title to the second chapter. See Edward G. Seidensticker's translation of *The Tale of Genji*, 48.

## Scene 5: The Fox

As she now moves forth
To carry out her questioning.[2]
*(Shizuka enters slowly through the curtains of the arched doorway, bringing with her the drum resting on a small stand.)*
Low she is in spirit,
But she takes the drum to hand,
As her lord has bid her,
Grasping it by the crimson cord
That twines about it
And modulates its tone.
She squeezes tight the cord
And to her shoulder lifts the drum.
Graceful are the movements of her hand
As she sounds its notes;
Clear and fresh the beats ring out.
*(Shizuka first goes through the motions of preparing the drum, wiping the drumheads, breathing on them to warm them prior to playing. With her left hand she lifts the drum to her right shoulder, hesitatingly strikes it with her right hand, then moves quickly to SR and looks around: She repeats this action of striking the drum and looking around several times.)*
Shizuka listens with her heart
To the wondrous notes,
Unmatched in all the world.
Such must have been the sound,
She thinks, of that drum of old
That hung in the Thunder Gate
In China's city of K'uai-chi.
Its notes were carried leagues
That numbered in the hundreds,
To be heard in the capital of Loyang.[3]

---

2. These opening lines do not appear in the standard editions of the text, including Tsurumi, *Takeda Izumo shū*. They were spoken, however, in the performance I saw in Tokyo's National Theater in 1981.

3. The sound of the bell was said to be audible in Loyang, some 1,000 kilometers to the north. Elaboration on the story in the work *Ruri tengu* says that

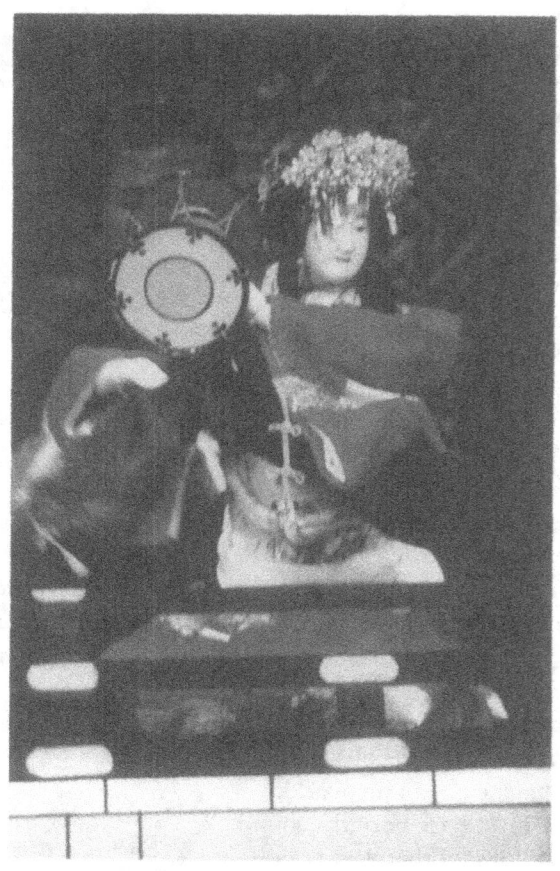

NARRATOR: She squeezes tight the cord
And to her shoulder lifts the drum.
Graceful are the movements of her hand
As she sounds its notes.
*(Shizuka plays the drum to summon Tadanobu.)*
(Act 4, scene 5)

## Scene 5: The Fox

Now, as though beckoned onward
By the breezes of spring,
Sato Tadanobu comes and bows before her,
Rapture for the drumbeat clear upon his face.

*(To the roll of drums and flute music, as Shizuka continues to beat the drum, a white fox bursts through the paneling facing the audience above the room enclosed by shōji. It descends to the floor, runs about the courtyard and dashes off to disappear behind the bamboo fencing at SR. In a rapid change, the fox puppet is replaced with that of Tadanobu. The puppet handler's costume is also quickly changed: strategic threads are pulled from the costume allowing the upper part to fold down, the inner lining of the top half now matching the under kimono and forming a new costume. Tadanobu is now dressed in formal attire, with long trousers sweeping the floor behind him, similar to the dress of the Tadanobu who has just left the stage. He ascends the stairway on the SR side of the open room, draws near the drum, and bows.)*

Shizuka watches him there
But does not cease her drumming.
Tadanobu yields himself
To rapt enchantment with the sound,
As Shizuka studies him more closely.
Now she stays her hand,
Perceiving in him one who's to be doubted.
She feigns a careless air.

*(She puts the drum on a small wooden stand before her and slowly takes up the sword.)*

SHIZUKA: You are late, Tadanobu. My lord Yoshitsune has waited impatiently to see you. Come now, let us go inside.

*(She stands up, hiding the sword behind her back. Tadanobu is hesitant to rise.)*

---

the phenomenon was due to a white crane whose spirit flew into the drum and then flew away when the people from Loyang came to take the drum. See Yūda, *Bunraku jōruri shū*, 386, n. 58.

To the roll of drums and music of the flute, a fox breaks through the upper paneling of the room where Shizuka beats the Hatsune Drum. Then, as depicted here, the puppet fox and its manipulator are lowered by a stage suspension device that simulates magical flight. (Act 4, scene 5)

NARRATOR: Though Tadanobu nods assent,
  He is slow to rise
  And remains with eyes cast down.
  Making sure he's off his guard,
  Shizuka slashes with her sword.
  Nimbly, Tadanobu leaps and jumps aside.
TADANOBU: What is this? What are you doing?
NARRATOR: Thus challenged, Shizuka
  Gives an affected laugh.
SHIZUKA: Ho ho ho ho ho ho ho. I see you are surprised. To please you, I am but practicing my dance, which you've not seen for some time—the dance that relates the tale of the battle of Yashima.[4]
NARRATOR: She quickens the tempo of the drum and sings:
  "Thus did the Genji and the Heike clash:
  As the Heike boats approached the shore,
  To the beaches moved the Genji troops.
  The Heike ships rowed ever closer in,
  And both sides sounded gongs and drums of war."
  Again, as Shizuka gazes on,
  Tadanobu yields in childlike rapture
  To the notes of the drum.
*(She returns the drum to its stand and again picks up the sword.)*
SHIZUKA: Tadanobu! You'll not escape me!
NARRATOR: Again she slashes at him,
  But Tadanobu dodges
  From the path of the blade,
  Seizing his chance as he brushes past
  To take a grip upon its hilt.
TADANOBU: What offense am I guilty of that you should try to strike me unawares? I do not understand.
NARRATOR: He wrests the sword from her hand
  And casts the weapon aside.

---

4. A reminder of the act 4 travel scene ("The Journey With the Drum") when Shizuka and Tadanobu re-enacted the Yashima battle where Tadanobu's brother Tsuginobu died while protecting Yoshitsune from the arrows of Noritsune.

TADANOBU: What offense am I guilty of that you should try to strike me unawares? I do not understand. (Act 4, scene 5)

SHIZUKA: False Tadanobu! Reveal yourself! *(She beats him about the head with the drum.)* I, Shizuka, have been commanded to question you. If you will not talk, here's how I will make you speak.
NARRATOR: She snatches up the drum
And flicks her hand across its head.
Tadanobu, roused by the tapping
Of the woman's silken hand,
Bows down abjectly.
"Yes, yes, I will," he says,
As Shizuka strikes the drum
To wring confession from him.
SHIZUKA: Well then! Reveal yourself!
*(She throws the drum aside and again picks up the sword, brandishing it at Tadanobu. He leaps back toward SR and moves to the cover of the flats that run across the front of the stage as the ominous roll of drums commences again. In another quick change, he rises up from*

*the flats now clad in the black robe with its gold embroidered designs that he wore earlier when he and Shizuka were traveling in the Yoshino Mountains—"The Journey With the Drum." He leaps back into the open room and bows before Shizuka.)*

NARRATOR: Yet silent he remains,
   Not a word escapes him,
   As he stays prostrate before her.
   At length he lifts his head,
   And picks up the Drum of Hatsune.
   With deference, with deep reverence,
   He lifts it to his head and bows,
   Then back again he places it
   Before the Lady Shizuka.
   He rises with composure, descends
   Into the garden's broad expanse,
   And there with heavy heart
   He bends his wretched body low to bow.

*(Since Tadanobu now confesses that he is in fact a fox, he is so designated from this point.)*

FOX: Until this day, I had managed to hide so that people did not know of me. But now that trouble has arisen and suspicion has attached to the true Tadanobu who has returned from his home province, I am obliged to reveal myself. The story has its beginning in that Hatsune Drum. It was in the reign of Emperor Kammu that within the palace prayers were offered up for rain.[5] Two foxes, one female and one male, which had lived for a thousand years and had acquired magical powers, were hunted down in this very province of Yamato, and their living skins were used to make that drum. Sacred dances were then offered as solace to the god of rain. The sound of drums was originally thought to be like the sound of waves, and the fox is regarded as a creature of the Yin forces, so the prayers and drumbeats brought water and the rain fell. At this, all the people and the farmers raised

---

5. See act 1, scene 1, "The Imperial Palace," note 8.

their voices in joy for the first time. And so the Emperor gave to the drum the name of Hatsune—First Voice. That drum is made from the skins of my parents; I am the child of that drum.

NARRATOR: At his story, Shizuka feels
Her hair stands up in fright.
Then she calms her racing heart.

SHIZUKA: Hmm. If this drum is made from your parents and you are a child of the drum, then you must be a fox!

*(Again the ominous drums roll and another quick change of costume is effected by the pulling of special threads in the costume of both the puppet and its operator. The fox's black robe in his guise as Tadanobu is removed to reveal beneath it a white gown, edged in red and with red fox fire designs (kitsunebi) dotting its surface. The puppet handler, in some performances, is similarly dressed.)*

FOX[6]: Yes, that is true. When my parents were captured and killed for those prayers for rain, I was yet a young fox and understood nothing about parents and children, or about sorrow. I have grown up now. I can transform myself into other forms, and I have lived long enough to acquire many magical powers, but not for a single day have I taken care of my parents. If I do not repay to them the love they showed by bringing me into this world, then I am no better than such lowly creatures as pigs and wolves. I am, thus, the most lowly of all the 64,000 foxes in my family, scorned as nothing but a wild fox of the fields, with no hope of realizing my desire to rise in position among my kind.[7] When a child is

---

6. This long monologue of the fox, as well as the one that precedes it, is a minutely choreographed presentation as the magical fox relates his story. The narrator delivers the fox's lines in a high pitched voice and somewhat staccato manner, and the fox's quick movements are animal-like, with leaps and crouches punctuating his story. His hands (a special puppet hand is used) are held with fingers tucked in toward the palm and the wrist bent sharply downward to suggest paws. Notations of the movements have been omitted here so as not to interrupt the flow of the fox's monologue, considered a highlight of the play. For details of stage movement, see the production notes in Yūda, *Bunraku jōruri shū*, 221ff (bottom of page, marked by triangles).

7. Even among foxes, it seems, there were hierarchies, the lowest being the

## Scene 5: The Fox

The fox, now transformed from his guise as Tadanobu, mimes the action as he tells his story. His costume is decorated with representations of the magical will-o'-the-wisp flames (kitsunebi) associated with the fox; special hands are used, the fingers bent downward to suggest a fox's paws. (Act 4, scene 5)

unfilial to his parents, human beings call him a mere brute, say he's a worthless fox. Yet the young dove shows deference to its parent by perching on a lower branch, and the crow brings food to its parent in return for its own upbringing. All these are filial acts. If this is true even among birds, then

---

"wild fox of the fields." It is not clear why the figure 64,000 is used, except to suggest a very large number.

how much more must it be so for a fox who can speak the language of men and knows their feelings! How can it be, then, that even the most stupid of beasts would fail to know about filial love? But . . . my parents are gone. My only hope to be a faithful child lies in that drum. Through the lofty nobility my parents achieved over a millennium, their spirits now lodge in those skins. And since their very essence has entered into the drum, the instrument is, in short, my mother and my father. I felt it would be my highest act of filial duty to accompany and protect them. And yet—oh the wretchedness of it all!—the drum has been kept within the imperial palace, and I have been afraid to approach it because of the countless gods that stand guard at night. I lost all hope; it must be, I thought, that I had done some wrong to a human being in a previous life. The sutra that speaks of cause and effect says that one who harms another will be reborn a fox.[8] Ah, how the bitterness grows within me. Each day three times and thrice at night it pains me through and through; my tears are those of blood. The fox fires that appear as drifting will-'o-the-wisp flames are blazes that scorch at my breast. But even one such as I may be blessed by heaven, though I may bear a heavy burden of guilt from a former life. For, as fortune would have it, the Hatsune Drum passed into Lord Yoshitsune's hands. It emerged from the imperial palace, and I was no longer afraid to go near it. How happy, how overjoyed I was! It has been thanks to Lord Yoshitsune that from that day I have been in attendance on the drum. At the grove in front of the Inari Shrine, I thought that if Tadanobu should happen to appear I might be able to repay my gratitude to Lord Yoshitsune by consoling you in your grief. And so I became that Tadanobu. And as a reward for saving you, Lady Shizuka, from danger—though it was more than a mere beast deserved—I received the honored name

---

8. This may be a reference to the Buddhist sutra *Gōhō sabetsu kyō*, which does not refer to foxes in particular but says simply that such wrongdoers will be reborn as beasts. See Yūda, *Bunraku jōruri shū*, 223, n. 20.

Genkurō Yoshitsune, a descendant of Emperor Seiwa. It is a blessing that fills me with awe. For this reason too, I wish to do all I can to fulfill my duty to my parents. They are first in my thoughts, and my heart's desire has been fulfilled. To have been granted the honored name of the general is the same to me as having the good karma to be reborn as a human being instead of a beast. Thus, my parents are yet all the more dear to me. Out of longing for your lord, you, Lady Shizuka, play upon this drum, from which I cannot be separated for even a moment. The notes do not seem unusual to you, but to my ears they are the voices of my parents calling me to them, and that is why I have been summoned to come back to the drum so many times. The sounds you just played were the words of my father and my mother. They tell me that for their sakes I have made Tadanobu's master doubt him, that for a while I have brought trouble to that loyal servant. This is wrong, they say, and they tell me to make haste and go back whence I came. There is nothing now for me to do but to return to my home in the fields. In your compassion, Lady Shizuka, I beg you convey to General Yoshitsune my humble apology for having deceived him.

NARRATOR: Up from the courtyard he leaps
And faces toward the drum,
The drum that is to him
Both a father and a mother.
His words are couched in reverence,
His voice so filled with tears.
More loving is this fond farewell
Than one by human voices spoken.

FOX: Father, mother, I will do as you say. And now I take my leave. But how this farewell grieves me. *(Weeps.)* When I was first separated from my parents, and I knew nothing of what had happened, I wept throughout the night. And as each day passed, I lived with the desire to be, however briefly, at their side and to repay them for the kindness of raising me. The days and months of longing have now been four hundred years.[9] When I think how they were killed in order that there might be prayers for rain, what rancor do I feel toward the shining sun! They say that raindrops falling from a cloudless sky betokens the marriage of foxes. But no, they are my tears. Though I have rejoiced that my desire to be near my parents has been fulfilled, I think of my own fox-wife, grown dear to me over the years, and of the fox-children born to us. And though my cruel heart has been drawn to them and their comfortless misery I know not how many times, yet I have left them abandoned in the wilderness, not knowing if they have starved, or frozen to death, or have been taken by hunters. Do they long for me as I have longed for my parents? My mind so tormented by anxiety for my family shows how ensnared I am by the unseverable bonds of our karma, by the chains of my loving devotion to them. Since I abandoned my beloved wife and children—oh, how it crushed my heart to do so!—and came to be near the drum last spring, barely a full year has passed. What shall I do now that I have been told to leave? Shall I simply sigh and go away? If I fail to obey my parents, it will be an unfilial act, and all of my devotion will have gone for nothing. What evil did I do in a former life that I must go back to my home so filled with sorrow? At least I have a memory that will be known to later generations: the name Genkurō bestowed upon me by General Yoshitsune. Yet, how am I to bear this sorrow? Lady Shizuka, please pity me, please understand my heart.

NARRATOR: He weeps, he pleads, and cringes in his heart;
Down he sinks, wailing out his grief.
In the province of Yamato, wretched indeed
Is the legend of Genkurō the Fox.
Shizuka, true to her woman's heart,
Is not without compassion.

---

9. As Yūda (*Bunraku jōruri shū*, 224, n.6) notes, from the time of Emperor Kammu's prayers for rain in 786 to the time of the play's setting, 1186, is four hundred years.

## Scene 5: The Fox

Seeing his eyes cloud over,
Filled with earnest tears,
She turns toward the inner room.
*(She moves toward the SL room and bows before it.)*
SHIZUKA: My lord, are you there?
NARRATOR: She has but spoken when the shōji part.
*(Yoshitsune emerges from the SL room and seats himself on a cushion.)*
YOSHITSUNE: I have heard it all. So, you are not a human being at all, are you? I, Yoshitsune, have never known what it is to be a fox, but now I feel great pity for you.
NARRATOR: The fox, at Yoshitsune's words,
Lowers its head and bows
Over and over, kneeling down
In reverence to the noble general.
He slowly rises from his place,
And gazes, gazes back
Longingly at the drum.
He neither leaves nor disappears,
But the onlookers' eyes are clouded,
And like the mists of spring . . .
He is gone.
Yoshitsune's heart is much aggrieved.
*(The fox moves slowly to SR, with many backward glances at the drum. As the drums roll to suggest his wizardry, a flat painted as a cloudy mist is lowered at SR, and behind this the fox disappears.)*
YOSHITSUNE: Call him back. Strike the drum. Perhaps he'll come back to its notes. Quickly, the drum, the drum!
NARRATOR: Shizuka lifts the drum again
And strikes it. Yet, strangely,
No sound comes forth.
SHIZUKA: What's this?
NARRATOR: She grasps the drum anew,
But though she beats upon it,
The drum is silent.
SHIZUKA: Oh, the spirits of his parents that remain with the drum are saddened by this separation from their child, and

that must be why the sound has ceased. Can even those who are not human long so for a child?

NARRATOR: She is heartsick at the thought.

YOSHITSUNE: Ah, how I am struck by the constancy of affection in all living creatures. I was never filial for a day toward my dead father Yoshitomo, cut down by Osada Tadamune,[10] and I grew up hiding on Mount Kurama hoping I might serve my brother Yoritomo. How bitter it is that my fortunes in the battles of Yashima and Dannoura in the western sea and all my loyal services have become my very enemy. Here I have been abandoned by the brother whom I have looked on as a parent. Genkurō, to whom I gave my name, is affected by some evil from a former life. It is the same with me; what unbroken attachments, and in what sort of previous existence, can have visited upon me such a karma as this?

NARRATOR: To Yoshitsune's tears of pity for the fox
Shizuka now joins her own.
In the courtyard, Genkurō the Fox,
Still unseen to their eyes,
Considers the lot that fate has dealt him
Yet cannot bear to liken it
To Yoshitsune's misfortunes.
Loudly he wails his lament;
And with his cry,
The enfolding mist of spring
Vanishes away,
And there he stands revealed.
Yoshitsune rises, picks up the drum.

YOSHITSUNE: Ah, there you are, Genkurō. Hear me. For a long time you have watched over Shizuka while she was in your care. I cannot find the words to thank you. This drum I have

---

10. During the Heiji insurrection of 1159–60, Tadamune (dates unknown) and another warrior treacherously attacked and killed Yoshitomo as he was fleeing to the northeast.

received from the imperial court, precious though it is to me, I give it to you.

NARRATOR: He holds out the drum.

FOX: What? *(He leaps up, advances to the center stairway.)* You say you will give me the drum? Oh, thank you, thank you, thank you! *(He receives the drum on its stand from Yoshitsune, then withdraws into the courtyard somewhat to SR and bows.)* This drum—my parents for whom I've longed so dearly—why, I'll not be shy about it and refuse. I will accept it! And, in gratitude for your profound kindness, I shall henceforth stay close to you and protect you to the fullest whenever you are in danger. How wonderfully happy I am! *(Straightens up, as a thought comes to him.)* Oh, I almost forgot. I've been so engrossed in relating my own life to you that I failed to tell you something. All of the evil monks of the temple plan to raid this mansion tonight, when of course they hope to attack you at close quarters. But, by my magical powers to transform myself, I will trick the lot of them and draw them in here. Then I'll split them all right down the middle and slice them up sideways. *(He mimes the action energetically.)* When they try to attack you in a bunch, I'll come in at them from all directions like the legs of a spider, and I'll slash them up and down and sideways, and slantwise right and slantwise left! *(Still miming vigorously.)* If they strike high and sideways at me, I'll duck and let the blow pass by; if they swing their swords at my legs, I'll fly into the air. With my nimble magic I will do with them as I please, then turn them over to you for final dispatch! Be sure you are on your guard!

NARRATOR: With that, he takes the drum and bows.

And then, as though borne off on wings,

He vanishes without a trace.

*(Production practices vary at this point. In earlier productions, the fox disappeared by exiting over a hedge at SR. Nowadays, the puppet performance often imitates the extremely popular Kabuki practice of flying through the air. The puppet operator, having previously been*

*fitted with a body harness, is lifted off the stage into the air as he holds and operates the fox puppet and is drawn off high into the SR wings, seeming to leave "as though borne off on wings."*)
    Listening to all of this,
    Tadanobu is amazed.
    Along with Kamei and Suruga
    He approaches his lord.

TADANOBU: So eloquent an expression of fidelity by a living creature has cleared away both my general's and my own suspicions. Nothing could bring me greater joy.

NARRATOR: Hardly has he finished
    Than in comes Kawatsura Hōgen.

KAWATSURA: Confucius said that he never discussed prodigies, feats of strength, disorders of nature, or spirits,[11] but this Genkurō says that the priests of the temple are coming to attack you tonight. This coincides exactly with what I secretly overheard a little while ago. What do you think about our taking matters into our own hands and sallying forth to attack our enemies?

NARRATOR: Tadanobu answers.

TADANOBU: I have an excellent plan. Though you gave your name to the fox, you would originally have bestowed it upon me. If I take my lord's place and the attackers kill me, then the whole matter will be finished. I beg you most strongly to grant me leave to carry out this scheme.

NARRATOR: To his urgent plea
    His general replies.

YOSHITSUNE: There are matters that I must consider, so for the moment do not go. If you would deceive these priests and die calling yourself by my name, then I too will die. There is no need for you to be killed.

NARRATOR: With these warm and gracious words,
    To Tadanobu he hands
    The sword thrust in his sash.

---

11. From the Confucian *Analects*. My translation is adapted slightly from that of Arthur Waley, translator, *The Analects of Confucius*, 127.

He summons Shizuka to his side,
And together they withdraw.
*(Yoshitsune, Shizuka, and Tadanobu enter the center curtained doorway.)*

Hardly a moment passes, when,
Unescorted, in barges Wild Hokkyō
Boasting and brandishing his sword.[12]

*(He enters from SR.)*

HOKKYŌ *(speaking to Kawatsura)*: Ah Lord Hōgen, I am most gratified at your swift appearance. Hearing that you had arrested Yoshitsune, I have come at once to congratulate you.

NARRATOR: As he speaks, all present exchange glances.
"Surely," thinks Lord Hōgen,
"In gratitude for the drum,
The fox has tricked this lout
And sent him to us."
He nods in silence to himself.

KAWATSURA: To be sure, to be sure. He is tied up within. Come and see him.

NARRATOR: He starts to leave,
Giving to Kamei a wink.
A shout, and with his strong right arm
Kamei grabs the priest.
Quickly, with a thud,
He slams him to the floor,
Holding him down
And trampling him under foot.
Swiftly he binds his captive with a rope,
Hauls him into the air,
And prances off to show him to his lord.
Now surely it is clear
That all is the clever scheme
Of that Genkurō who is not Yoshitsune.

12. Though the text says "sword," in production Hokkyō usually carries a long halberd.

## ACT FOUR

Next to enter: Demon Sadobō, *(also from SR)*
Looking belligerently about,
As though he'll handle anyone.
Unaware he is bewitched
By the unseen Genkurō,
He thrusts out his white-robed sleeve
And glares about,
Peering into every nook and cranny.

SADOBŌ: See here, Lord Hōgen, one of us came just now to congratulate you on the capture of Yoshitsune. He hasn't come back, and I thought everything would be handled quickly. Now, where is the prisoner?

NARRATOR: A look of triumph on his face,
He moves along the corridor,
Only to be kicked backwards
And lose his footing on the floor.
Then the nimble Suruga
Gives him a taste of his footwork.
Before he can vent his chagrin,
Like his partner, off he's dragged within.
Now comes number three—
The doctor priest, Yakuibō,
Glum and sullen faced
As he enters the room.

YAKUIBŌ *(he moves in as though pushed from behind)*: Such a hurry, such a blasted hurry! I'm going! Now, wait! My robe will get torn if you drag me like that! What a rude attendant you are!

NARRATOR: Bewitched by Genkurō,
All his protests go for naught,
For within him move
The workings of the fox.

KAWATSURA: Ah, I have been waiting for you, Yakuibō. Please, this way.

NARRATOR: He motions the place with a nod.

## Scene 5: The Fox

    Then, with a wrenching grip
    He twists the prelate's arm.
YAKUIBŌ: Oh! Ouch! Hey, what're you doing?
KAWATSURA: This!
NARRATOR: And up upon his shoulder
    He hoists the heavy priest.
KAWATSURA: I, Kawatsura Hōgen, will prepare a homemade feast made up of you alone. I'm just waiting for Lord Yoshitsune's bill of fare to cut you up to order.
NARRATOR: Laughing, he goes within.
    Now comes one unmatched in pluck,
    Yet unaware of these events,
    Pounding on the ground
    The ferrule of his great bare bladed lance.
    Beneath his robe is armor,
    Its segments linked by chains
    And overlapping like a prawn's shell.
    Cowl-like about his head is wound
    The long stole of a priest.
    The one who enters now with swaying gait,
    No ordinary man—
    Yokawa no Kakuhan.
    In the courtyard, he draws himself full height,
    And calls out as he walks . . .
KAKUHAN: Master Kawatsura, where are you? Some traveling priests have come here. Are they inside? Quickly, I would speak with you. *(Entering, like the others, from SR, he stops, surveys his surroundings and turns toward SR.)*
NARRATOR: From the shōji behind him
    A voice calls out.
VOICE: You, general of the Heike, Lord of Noto, Noritsune! Wait!
NARRATOR: Unthinking, he looks back sharply.
KAKUHAN: Hmmm. A voice, but there is no one there. It could hardly have been calling me. But it did give me a start, and

some embarrassment, this calling out of a name I do not know. Ha ha ha ha ha. There's no one there, no reason to become rattled.

NARRATOR: He mutters to himself
As he is about to go.

VOICE: Ah, cowardly Noritsune, Lord of Noto! Long have I waited for you, I, Kurō Hōgan Yoshitsune.

NARRATOR: Suddenly the shōji are flung open.
*(Yoshitsune emerges from the SR room.)*
Noritsune turns, hoping to confront his foe.
With the long handle of his lance
Tucked beneath his arm,
His face is that of one about to charge.
Fearless before such a countenance,
Yoshitsune smiles.

YOSHITSUNE: You may try to disguise the red banner of the Heike beneath those priestly robes, but you cannot hide it. You, Noritsune, famed as a swimmer, pretended to drown yourself off the waters of Yashima.[13] You dived to the bottom then later surfaced. I have long known that you were alive; your face is unmistakable. Don't deny it!

NARRATOR: He speaks in elegant phrases.

KAKUHAN: What insolence! Whether I be Noritsune or anyone else, are you such a sycophant that you think appearing here without armor to do battle with Kakuhan will gain you his mercy? I'm obliged, Kurō Yoshitsune, to learn that you hold your life so dear.

NARRATOR: He laughs in derision.

YOSHITSUNE: You seem to have a high opinion of yourself. I may not equal you with the bow, but your sword is no match for mine. If you wish to attack Yoshitsune with a Heike blade no longer blessed by providence, go ahead and try, Lord of Noto!

---

13. Noritsune actually died in the last great battle between the Genji and Heike clans at Dannoura.

## Scene 5: The Fox

NARRATOR: Hardly has he spoken
    Than Noritsune with his lance
    Makes a sweep across the dais.
    But on his short sword
    Yoshitsune catches the stroke
    With a clanging parry.
    A lunge at Yoshitsune's body
    With the lance's ferrule
    Is taken neatly, kicked aside.
    Then, finding no opening to his foe,
    And in contrast with his own defiance,
    Yoshitsune withdraws
*(Yoshitsune moves back into the SL room.)*
NORITSUNE: You'll not escape! I will not let you!
NARRATOR: He kicks away the shōji
    Barring entry to the inner room
    And charges in. But what is this?
    There, ensconced upon a regal seat,
    And lovely in his youth,
    Sits the Emperor Antoku.
NORITSUNE: Oh! How mean and shameful of me! My liege, how do you come to be here?
NARRATOR: Humbly posing his query,
    His breast is in a tumult.
    In an exalted voice, the Emperor speaks.
ANTOKU: I had heard that your nurse and all of our clan had drowned in the sea, but that was not so for Noritsune, was it?
NORITSUNE: You are right, my lord.
NARRATOR: In response to the Emperor,
    Noritsune snatches away the cowl
    Hiding his jet black hair.[14]
    Arranging the sleeves of his armor,
    He bows.

---

14. Proof that he is not a true priest, whose head would be shaved.

NORITSUNE: It was Sanuki no Rokurō, the son of my wet nurse, who shouted out that he was Lord of Noto, Noritsune. Then, clasping on either side Aki no Tarō and his brother, he leaped into the sea and died. I, Noritsune, came up on a beach that no one knew about. With the help of that shaman of a priest, Yamashina Hokkyō, I disguised myself as Kakuhan. Now I have burst into this room seeking to take vengeance on Yoshitsune, only to find your gracious Majesty here. Have you been taken prisoner, my lord? I beg Your Majesty to tell me what has happened.

NARRATOR: Even the youthful monarch
Is blinded by his tears.

ANTOKU: As you know, Noritsune, I escaped from the palace at Yashima. As I waited here for help in this disappointing world, I encountered Yoshitsune, and I found compassion in a warrior of the Genji. Tomomori, feeling himself disgraced, pleaded with Yoshitsune on my behalf and then cast himself into the sea. My coming here after that and our meeting today have all been arranged by Yoshitsune. I was born the master of Japan, but I must have given offense to the Heavenly Goddess of the Sun, for I have been a torment to the people of the country that I rule over. In this narrow land and in my present straits, I yearn for my mother. And she must long, as she did in the Capital, to see the white snows of Mount Fuji, the spring blossoms of Yoshino. But she is in the village of Ohara.[15] For one like myself, who longs so for his mother, what meaning can there be in either the cherry blossoms or Yoshino? Have pity, Noritsune, for so wretched a fate as mine. *(He weeps.)*

NARRATOR: And with this, down he sinks in tears.
How wretched is he, what loss he has known.

NORITSUNE: Ah, we have failed you, we have failed you, Tomomori and I! What splendid plans, what ingenious strata-

---

15. Following the Heike defeat, Antoku's mother, Kenreimon'in, became a nun and went to spent the remainder of her days in the Jakkōin, a temple located in the village of Ohara a little to the north of Kyoto.

gems we had, and all have been found out by Yoshitsune! How could our fortunes on the battlefield have all gone so awry? Ah, but there was no help for it; how bitter it all is now.

NARRATOR: In humiliation, he gnashes his teeth
Till it seems the blood would flow.
So tightly clenched his fists,
The nails seem to grow
Right through his palms.
So heavy his grief, his eyelids feel
Pressed beneath a ponderous weight.
He cannot bear the strain.
Suddenly, his clamped shut eyes
Now open wide.

NORITSUNE: Ah, I have misunderstood. When I sought to grapple with Yoshitsune at the battle of Yashima, he leaped across eight vessels, retreating toward his own boats in order to seek out what lay at the bottom of our strategy. That was not cowardice, was it? And now, fleeing from me to these inner compartments: he knew of my plan and had me come before your imperial countenance. Surely, that was a warrior's mercy. I see, I've been saved on this occasion. But I shall come again to do battle with him another time. Until then, Your Majesty, please come with me to my hiding place. I shall make the wide world yours to rule once again, and I will bring you to you mother. Come, I shall stand attendance on you.

NARRATOR: He sweeps the Emperor into his arms,
His right hand gripping his long lance.

NORITSUNE: Though this floating world is a cheerless place, know that you will yet have your reign.

NARRATOR: Thus he addresses his sovereign.
As he is about to leave,
Sharp voices cry out,
And then comes the sound
Of three blades at their work.

NARRATOR: He sweeps the Emperor into his arms,
 His right hand gripping his long lance.
(*Kakuhan holds the young Emperor in his arms.*)   (Act 4, scene 5)

---

Quickly he pulls his lance beside him.
Hardly has he made a backward glance,
When in dash Kamei and Suruga
And Kawatsura Hōgen, *(all from SR)*
Each with bloody swords
And severed heads in their hands.
(*During this narration, Yoshitsune withdraws through the curtained archway.*)
KAWATSURA: You behave like a coward, Lord of Noto. See how we've slain your followers one by one! For shame, Noritsune,

## Scene 5: The Fox

to flee with the Emperor as a hostage. The gate has been shut, you cannot escape. Now then, do you fight, or do you surrender? Make your choice!

NARRATOR: In a chorus they fling down the challenge,
But no sooner have the words been spoken
Than angrily Noritsune glares back.

NORITSUNE: How dare you wag your jaws with words of surrender, or compare me with that rabble of priests! Why, I could take each one of your heads off with me, but why should I waste time on you? I am thankful that Yoshitsune placed the Emperor in my care. But you quite amaze me, running away with no thanks to me for not killing you. If I didn't think it would defile my attendance on His Majesty, I'd slaughter the lot of you, you miserable thugs! Stand back and give three bows in respect!

ALL THREE: Such insolent defiance, such effrontery! Let's take him on and put an end to his boasting.

NARRATOR: Arms spread, the trio surrounds him,
And closes in, kicking sand about.
Noritsune draws himself up tall,
Towering above, his eyes turned down upon them,
Standing like a fleet-footed god.
As they glare at one another,
The Emperor, in his fear,
Looks like one for whom
The thread of life might soon be cut.
Yoshitsune shouts out.

*(Yoshitsune re-enters through the curtained archway. He is now dressed in courtly robes.)*

YOSHITSUNE: Wait, all of you! Do not act rashly!

NARRATOR: There he stands in tall court hat,
Dressed in a flowing hunting cloak,
No weapons in his hands.

YOSHITSUNE: Make way for the Emperor's progress. You show want of respect if you block his passage or throw into disarray the deference of a vassal to his lord. Be still, all of you. I,

Yoshitsune, will also bid the Emperor farewell. As you see, I have prepared appropriate robes for myself. You may say that I am letting Noritsune escape by himself, but he has neither the power to fly up to heaven nor the skill to burrow into the earth. How can he hope to escape? None of you lay a hand on him. Tadanobu happens not to be here just now, but it is only fitting that I should let him strike down the enemy of his brother Tsuginobu and dispel the dead man's rancor in the hell of endless strife. You, Noritsune, live in a world constrained about you, and I too shrink away from society's eyes. We have neither castles nor shields to protect us. So let our differences be settled here on the battlefield of Yoshino, the cherry trees our battle towers.[16] Since it has been proclaimed that the Emperor drowned at sea, and since his role within the palace has come to an end, it matters not which of us wins or loses. But nothing untoward is to happen to His Majesty.

NORITSUNE *(sneering)*: Hoo, a commendable speech, Yoshitsune. I am most pleased. Noritsune does not concern himself with trifles; my objective is not Yoshitsune alone. I shall also take the puny head of Yoritomo, who has arrogated the realm to himself, and then I will restore my Emperor's rule. When that happens, perhaps he may let Yoshitsune have a manor of his own.

YOSHITSUNE: Yaaa, your words grow tedious, Noritsune. Never mind the designs you have on me. But I will not let pass your animosity to my brother Yoritomo!

NARRATOR: On his sword the general claps his hand,
　But swiftly it appears
　That Genkurō the fox—
　Who borrowed Tadanobu's form,
　And who is thankful for the name
　Bestowed by Yoshitsune—
　Has swept into the depths

---

16. This line accounts for part of the play's subtitle.

Of Yoshitsune's heart to soothe his ire.
The unconscious calming
Of Yoshitsune's mind—
All the work of his unseen guardian.

NORITSUNE: Farewell, then, Yoshitsune. I go, but I will show you my gratitude for your having spared the Emperor's life: call me Noritsune or call me Lord of Noto, we shall not fight. When next we meet, know me as Yokawa no Kakuhan; in the Yoshino mountains I will confront Tadanobu, and there we will do battle. At that time, at that time indeed, both our lives will hang in the balance.

NARRATOR[17]: "Make way, my menials,
For the imperial progress!
Assemble the escort!" shouts Kakuhan,
And once again he takes the Emperor
Up into his arms.
But Antoku is a sovereign
Who holds no sway in his realm,
And Noritsune is a vassal
Who holds no office of the land,
So only as Yokawa no Kakuhan
May he serve as an escort for his lord.
Though foes they yet remain,
Yoshitsune calls out loudly, "Clear the way!"
Majesty there is here,
And scores yet for the settling,
And the grace of a warrior's compassion.
Taking the procession's lead
Is Kawatsura Hōgen,
With Suruga as his footman
And Kamei as lower houseman.
No officers of the court, these men,
And though they hold in check
Their spoiling for a fight,

---

17. The first three lines are delivered in the slow chantlike style of the Nō theater.

Unwittingly their swords are breached
  A scant space from their sheaths,
  To show the glint of metal there within.
YOSHITSUNE *(to the Emperor):* We will be noticed at the gate, Your Majesty. So, by your leave, please excuse us from attending you further.
NARRATOR: In deep respect he bows.
  Yet both the generals
  Glare at one another
  Across the space between them
  At this parting.
  Genkurō Yoshitsune,
  Genkurō the Fox—
  Famed are these names
  In the tales told in Japan.

# Act Five

## SCENE I

## IN THE MOUNTAINS OF YOSHINO[1]

NARRATOR: Mountains mantled in white,
　Branches etched sharply
　Under a burden of snow:
　An impressive vista indeed.
　In a loud voice, Satō Tadanobu calls out.
　*(Tadanobu has for the moment assumed the identity of Yoshitsune.)*
TADANOBU: I am Minamoto no Yoshitsune, scion of Emperor Seiwa, holder of the fifth court rank and officer in the Imperial Constabulary! You followers of Yoritomo: at-

---

1. I have discovered no description of the stage set for this scene. One may presume it is a fairly simple one depicting a snow scene, perhaps with white mantled mountains in the distance and a ravine closer in. Doubtless the narration was intended to convey to the audience additional details of the setting, for it would be difficult to stage the conflict that is described.

tack me as your enemy and you show yourselves to be ruthless men who would rebel against your own master Yoritomo! Through the mysterious powers of the *tengu*,[2] I will kick the lot of you dead and leave you as river flotsam on the valley floor. Resign yourselves to that!

NARRATOR: From the Kamakura soldiery,
  That hem him in to left and right
  And march as allies of those
  Who would defame Tadanobu's lord,
  Shouting voices rise.

VOICE: Your talk of master and servant is absurd! A master is a master, is he not? We'll cut you down for all to see. Come on men, charge!

NARRATOR: From all sides they set upon him,
  But he scorns their threats,
  Mowing them down on the right
  And sweeping all before him on the left.
  Faced with such a savage onslaught,
  The Kamakura host calls out "Retreat!"
  But Tadanobu grants them no escape,
  And down a steep descending path
  Pell-mell he chases after.
  Now comes the Heike general,
  Lord of Noto, Noritsune,
  Once again to meet Tadanobu.
  True to his pledge, he has a Buddhist stole
  Wound cowl-like 'round his head
  And comes as Yokawa no Kakuhan,
  So others may not find him out.
  He comes with heavy tread

---

2. The *tengu* is a kind of goblin, gnome, or troll that lives in remote or mountainous haunts. In popular legend *tengu* may have wings, claws, and beaks (or a large nose resembling a beak). They have magical powers, can fly, change their forms, and influence people's fortunes. One of the legends surrounding Yoshitsune's life is that as a youth he went by night into the mountains behind Kurama Temple (on the northern outskirts of modern Kyoto) and there was taught swordsmanship and other secret arts practiced by the *tengu*.

## Scene 1: In the Mountains of Yoshino

Upon the clean white snow,
His footing sure among
The rocks that edge the mountain.
Tadanobu now returns,
Having put his foes to rout.
The long awaited adversary,
The foe who's promised this encounter,
Waits there for him.
While the Kamakura men are still in flight,
These adversaries shout their names,
Advancing on each other for a fight.
Then they smile and wait.
A brave general, a loyal warrior,
Square off and each to the other beckons.

TADANOBU: I am Shirōbei Tadanobu, younger brother of Satō Saburōbei Tsuginobu. In the Third Month of last year, on the beach at Yashima, my brother stood as shield against the arrows aimed at his master Yoshitsune and his mount, and for his loyal devotion he was shot down by an arrow—yours. Now Noritsune, general of the Heike and Lord of Noto, you will feel my sword of vengeance!

NORITSUNE: Ah, what a modest one you are, Tadanobu. Having named me as the enemy of your brother, you intend to cut me down. But too bad for you, Tadanobu: it is I, protector of the Emperor and one who will return the country to his rule, I, Noritsune, who will kill *you!* You may make your amends to your brother in hell! Then, Zen priest Yokawa no Kakuhan will pronounce your funeral oration.

NARRATOR[3]: Standing with his halberd for a staff,
And leaning far, far back,
Kakuhan puffs his chest
And bellows out a laugh.
Their war of words complete,

---

3. The fight that is described in the following lines parallels that depicted in the *Gikeiki*. See McCullough, *Yoshitsune*, 184–86.

Tadanobu lifts his sword above his head,
Prepared to strike a blow.
Noritsune parries the blade
As Tadanobu lunges,
And they trade a ringing clash of swords.
Noritsune dodges another blow,
And with a sweep of his lance
He counters the tip of Tadanobu's steel.
But Tadanobu is undaunted.
When Noritsune slashes to the right,
Tadanobu dances to the left;
When to the left Noritsune cuts,
Tadanobu swings his weapon to position,
And down against the ferrule
Of Noritsune's lance
Comes Tadanobu's naked blade,
Ringing with a *chin, chin* . . .
Chinese crimson is the latter's armor,
Laced with braids of red.[4]
As the contest settles to a stalemate,
For either side no sign of victory,
Noritsune presses his attack.
Up springs Tadanobu nimbly
To perch in safety on a branch
In a giant cherry tree.
Noritsune comes in hot pursuit,
Halberd at the ready,
And starts to hack obliquely at the tree.
As he shoves it with his foot,
In the middle the tree trunk cracks,
Sending Tadanobu swinging
Over to the stream's far bank,

---

4. These last two lines carry forward onomatopoetically the sound of clanging metal *karakara,* "chin chin," with *kara kurenai,* "Chinese crimson."

### Scene 1: In the Mountains of Yoshino

Leaving the trunk as a bridge.
"Perfect," thinks the dauntless Noritsune,
And starts to go across.
He makes a misstep, stops, then slips.
About to plunge to the valley floor,
He does a backward somersault, but then
Both legs become entangled in the branches.
"Now!" thinks Tadanobu, "Just one stroke."
But Noritsune, swinging his halberd
Like a waterwheel, sweeps the sword aside.
The clack of armor hip flaps,
The ring and rattle of a sword guard—
A contest truly to astound the eye!
Now the scattered Kamakura men return,
Shouting threats at Tadanobu.
Again he sends them off in disarray.
"By all that's holy! You get in my way!" he shouts.
As Tadanobu fends them off,
Noritsune finds respite and cuts
Around both feet entangled in the tree,
And then he's free.
Tadanobu dashes to pursue and slay
The Kamakura army,
Leaving his foe to fall.
In the valley Noritsune, still unfaltering,
Moves with quick and practiced steps.
He thrusts his halberd upright
On a massive rock and upward pulls himself.
Crushing into earth held cold by snow,
Climbing boulders slick with icicles,
Slipping, he finds a foothold
On a steeply growing plum tree bough.
Halfway up he stands upon an outcrop,
And there running toward him to the left
Is Satō Tadanobu, who by now
Has put the Kamakura troops to flight.

ACT FIVE

Tadanobu beckons to Noritsune;
Then, impatient with the time
It takes his foe to climb,
"No, I'll come there!" he shouts,
And from atop a lofty point,
With vigor far more agile than a bird,
He lightly leaps and flies.
Noritsune also tries to fly,
And in a twinkling he's ensnared
In the tree limbs by the cords
That bind his armor to him.
There he dangles, swaying to and fro,
Looking like a little child
At play upon a swing.
Seeing his foe thus caught,
Tadanobu is about to slash,
But Noritsune bends aside,
Turning so the bough snaps off.
Now cut free, it seems that death's at hand,
And wide he spreads his arms.
Tadanobu flings his sword aside,
Unwilling to attack an unarmed foe.
Yelling, they grapple together,
Tadanobu shoving, pugnacious
As the deity Bishamon.[5]
Nimbly they spring apart,
And with a shout, "Here goes!"
Each firmly stands his ground,
As though befriended by
The warrior goddess Marishiten.[6]
They come together in their conflict,

---

5. Bishamonten, the all-hearing deity, is one of the twelve guardians of Buddhism. He is usually depicted clad in armor in a belligerent stance.

6. Often portrayed standing on the back of a wild boar, Marishiten is a Buddhist deity who protects warriors.

## Scene 1: In the Mountains of Yoshino

Trampling down the snow.
Tadanobu's gauntlet is wrenched off,
And as he goes back to the fray
He's firmly grabbed and hurled away.
Then Noritsune pins him to the ground,
His knees on Tadanobu's arms.
Yet now—how strange!—
Another Tadanobu lunges in,
Colliding full tilt into his opponent.
He spies a gap in Noritsune's armor,
And precisely there he stabs.
Though wounded, Noritsune does not wince.
Then turning round to look,
Noritsune is surprised.

NORITSUNE: Tadanobu? What is this?

NARRATOR: He grabs the armor fitted with its cords
And lifts it up to find—
No Tadanobu! Only armor
Given him by Yoshitsune.
Amazed to find it empty,
He examines it with care.
As he ponders, from behind him
Tadanobu slashes in.
But Noritsune, fearless fighter still
And heedless of his wound, calls out.

NORITSUNE: Saa! Come and get me, Tadanobu! I'll take your head!

NARRATOR: But ere the words have left his mouth,
Swiftly in runs Yoshitsune.

YOSHITSUNE: Hear me, Noritsune! Emperor Antoku has entered the priesthood at the village of Ohara; there he will become a disciple of his mother Kenreimon'in. I congratulate you, Noritsune, you are justly famed. But the fox Genkurō, all powerful in his magical arts, has through this armor lent his strength to Tadanobu, and all your stratagems have been anticipated.

NARRATOR: Hardly has he spoken than in comes
Kawagoe Tarō Shigeyori, opportunely arrived,
And bringing with him Left General Tomokata,
Arms trussed high behind his back.
KAWAGOE: It has been a while since we met, Lord Yoshitsune. The drum that the Emperor gave you was used as a ruse by Tomokata. You need have no further fears about it. It has come to light that it was Tomokata himself who said it was the Emperor's wish that you attack and subdue Yoritomo. I come with His Majesty's command that you take what measures you see fit in the matter.
NARRATOR: Hearing this, Noritsune springs up.
NORITSUNE: And I have heard that the imperial order to subjugate the Heike also came from the machinations of Tomokata. Killing that blackguard would be an apology to all of my clan.
NARRATOR: As swiftly as he speaks,
He cuts off Tomokata's head.
NORITSUNE: Now, Yoshitsune! Come and take Noritsune's head!
YOSHITSUNE: No. Noritsune, Lord of Noto, drowned in the waters off Yashima. It is the head of Yokawa no Kakuhan, and I leave that to Tadanobu.
NARRATOR: As he says the words,
Tadanobu swings his sword,
And as an offering to his brother's soul
He cuts his brother's enemy down.
And now, in this imperial age,
One will travel far to the north,
While another makes his journey to Ohara.[7]
Annihilated now the Heike clan,
And within the four seas,
All is peace, the people all secure.

---

7. Namely, that Yoshitsune will continue his flight from Yoritomo, heading for the domain of Fujiwara no Hidehira in the north, while the Emperor Antoku will travel to take up a Buddhist life with his mother at the Jakkōin temple in the village of Ohara near Kyoto.

*Scene 1: In the Mountains of Yoshino*

It is a time when grains in the fields
Shall be full in their abundance,
And this land rich in rice ears,
This land called Akitsukuni—
The Land of the Dragonflies of Autumn—[8]
Shall know no equal.


Playwrights:  Takeda Izumo
              Miyoshi Shōraku
              Namiki Senryū

Fourth year of Enkyō (1747), eleventh month, sixteenth day.

---

8. This is an amalgam of possible translations of the word *Akitsukuni* suggested by Donald Philippi in his translation of the *Kojiki*; see the entry *Aki-du-sima* on p. 452.

# BIBLIOGRAPHY

Adachi, Barbara. *Backstage at Bunraku*. Tokyo: Kōdansha International, 1985.
Adachi, Barbara. *The Voices and Hands of Bunraku*. Tokyo: Kōdansha International, 1977.
Araki, James. *The Ballad Drama of Medieval Japan*. Berkeley: University of California Press, 1964.
Aston, W. G., tr. *Nihongi*. In *Transactions and Proceedings of the Japan Society*. Supp. 1, vol. 1. London, 1896.
Brandon, James R., tr. *Kabuki: Five Classic Plays*. Cambridge: Harvard University Press, 1975.
Brandon, James R., ed. *Chūshingura: Studies in Kabuki and the Puppet Theatre*. Honolulu: University of Hawaii Press, 1982.
Brandon, James R., William P. Malm, and Donald H. Shively. *Studies in Kabuki: Its Acting, Music, and Historical Context*. Honolulu: University of Hawaii Press, 1979.
Bunraku Kyōkai, ed. *Bunraku no ningyō*. Tokyo: Fujin Gahōsha, 1976.

Dore, R. P. *Education in Tokugawa Japan.* Berkeley: University of California Press, 1965.
Dunn, C. J. *Early Japanese Puppet Drama.* London: Luzac, 1966.
Gerstle, C. Andrew. *Circles of Fantasy: Convention in the Plays of Chikamatsu.* Cambridge: Harvard University Press, 1986.
Gerstle, C. Andrew, Kiyoshi Inobe, and William P. Malm. *Theater As Music: The Bunraku Play "Mt. Imo and Mt. Se: An Exemplary Tale of Womanly Virtue."* Ann Arbor: University of Michigan, 1990.
Gidayū Nenpyō Hensan-kai, ed. *Gidayū nenpyō (Meiji hen).* Osaka: Gidayū Nenpyō Kankō-kai, 1956.
Giles, Herbert A. *A Chinese Biographical Dictionary.* Taipei: Literature House, 1962.
Hara Michio. "'Jitsu wa' no sakugeki hō—*Yoshitsune senbon zakura* no baai," Part I. *Bungaku* (August 1978), 116–27.
Hara Michio. "'Jitsu wa' no sakugeki hō—*Yoshitsune senbon zakura* no baai," Part II. *Bungaku* (October 1978), 65–81.
Hibbett, Howard. *The Floating World in Japanese Fiction.* London: Oxford University Press, 1959.
Higuchi Yoshichiyo, ed. *Kessaku jōruri shū, Vol. 2: Ryūsei jidai. Hyōshaku Edo bungaku sōsho.* Tokyo: Dai Nihon Yūbenkai Kōdansha, 1935.
Hisamatsu Sen'ichi, Yamazaki Toshio, and Gotō Shigeo, eds. *Shin kokin waka shū. Nihon koten bungaku taikei,* vol. 28. Tokyo: Iwanami Shoten, 1958.
Ihara Toshirō, comp. *Kabuki nenpyō.* 8 vols. Tokyo: Iwanami Shoten, 1956–1963.
Iwanami Shoten, ed. *Nihon koten bungaku daijiten.* 6 vols. Tokyo: Iwanami Shoten, 1985.
Jones, Stanleigh H., Jr. "*Miracle at Yaguchi Ferry:* A Japanese Puppet Play and Its Metamorphosis to Kabuki." *Harvard Journal of Asiatic Studies* (1978), 38(1):171–224.
Jones, Stanleigh H., Jr. "The Richness of *The Love Suicides at Sonezaki.*" In Patricia Pringle, ed., *An Interpretative Guide to Bunraku,* 17–22. University of Hawaii at Manoa, Honolulu: Community Service Division of the College of Continuing Education and Community Service, March 1992.
Jones, Stanleigh H., Jr., tr. *Sugawara and the Secrets of Calligraphy.* New York: Columbia University Press, 1985.

Kawatake Shigetoshi. *Nihon engeki zenshi*. Tokyo: Iwanami Shoten, 1959.
Kawatake Shigetoshi, ed. *Jōruri kenkyū bunken shūsei*. Part 2. Tokyo: Hokkō Shobō, 1944.
Keene, Donald. *Bunraku: The Art of the Japanese Puppet Theatre*. Tokyo: Kōdansha International, 1965.
Keene, Donald. *World Within Walls: Japanese Literature of the Pre-Modern Era, 1600–1867*. New York: Holt, Rinehart and Winston, 1976.
Keene, Donald, tr. *The Battles of Coxinga*. London: Taylor's Foreign Press, 1951.
Keene, Donald, tr. *Chūshingura, The Treasury of Loyal Retainers*. New York: Columbia University Press, 1971.
Klopfenstein, Eduard. "Gesaku: Co-Authorship in Classical Jōruri of the 18th Century." In Ian Nish and Charles Dunn, eds., *European Studies on Japan*, 283–89. Tenterden, Kent: 1979.
Klopfenstein, Eduard, tr. *Tausend Kirschbaume Yoshitsune, Ein klassisches Stuck des japanischen Theatres der Edo-Zeit*. Bern: Peter Lang, 1982.
Kuroki Kanzō. *Chikamatsu igo*. Tokyo: Daitō Shuppansha, 1942.
Legge, James, tr. *The Chinese Classics, Part 1*. New York: John B. Alden, 1883.
McCullough, Helen Craig, tr. *Kokin Wakashū: The First Imperial Anthology of Japanese Poetry*. Stanford: Stanford University Press, 1985.
McCullough, Helen Craig, tr. *The Tale of the Heike*. Stanford: Stanford University Press, 1988.
McCullough, Helen Craig, tr. *Yoshitsune: A Fifteenth-Century Japanese Chronicle*. Stanford: Stanford University Press, 1966.
Miner, Earl. *An Introduction to Japanese Court Poetry*. Stanford: Stanford University Press, 1968.
Mori Shū. "Ningyō jōruri no tenkai to taisei." Vol. 7: *Jōruri*, 37–56. In Geinō-shi Kenkyū-kai, ed., *Nihon no koten geinō*. Tokyo: Heibonsha, 1970.
Morris, Ivan. *The Nobility of Failure*. New York: New American Library, 1976.
Murasaki Shikibu. *The Tale of Genji*. Tr. by Edward G. Seidensticker. New York: Knopf, 1977.
Nippon Gakujutsu Shinkōkai, ed. *Japanese Noh Drama*. Tokyo: Nippon Gakujutsu Shinkōkai, 1955.

Nomura Hachirō, ed. *Yōkyoku shū*. 2 vols. in the series *Yūhōdō bunko*. Tokyo: Yūhōdō Shoten, 1926.
Ōgi Shinzō et al., eds. *Edo Tōkyō gaku jiten*. Tokyo: Sanscidō, 1988.
Ōnishi Shigetaka and Yoshinaga Takao, eds. *Bunraku*. Tokyo: Kōdansha, 1959.
Philippi, Donald L., tr. *Kojiki*. Princeton: Princeton University Press, 1969.
Sacki Umetomo, ed. *Kokin waka shū*. Vol. 8 in the series *Nihon koten bungaku taikei*. Tokyo: Iwnami Shoten, 1958.
Satō Hirosuke and Hirata Kōji, eds. *Sekai jimmei jiten: Nihon hen*. Tokyo: Tōkyōdō, 1987.
Seidensticker, Edward G. *Tokyo Rising: The City Since the Great Earthquake*. New York: Knopf, 1990.
Toita Yasuji, ed. *Meisaku Kabuki zenshū*. vol. 2. Tokyo: Tokyo Sōgen Shinsha, 1968.
Tsukamoto Tetsuzō, ed. *Yōkyoku shū*. Vol. 2 in the series *Yūhōdō bunko*. Tokyo: Yūhōdō Shoten, 1926.
Tsurumi Makoto, ed. *Takeda Izumo shū*. In the series *Nihon koten zensho*. Tokyo: Asahi Shinbunsha, 1956.
Uchiyama Mikiko. "Bunraku no sakushatachi—Chikamatsu, Izumo, Sōsuke." *Koten geinō shiriizu #1, Bungaku kanshō monogurafu*, 48–62. Osaka: Kokuritsu Bunraku Gekijō, 1985.
Uchiyama Mikiko. "Jōruri no gikyoku sakuhō." In Geinōshi Kenkyūkai, ed., *Jōruri: katari to ayatsuri*, 191–221. *Nihon no koten geinō*, vol. 7. Tokyo: Heibonsha, 1970.
Uchiyama Mikiko. "Sugawara denju tenarai kagami nado no gassakusha mondai." *Engeki-gaku* (March 1984), no. 25, pp. 134–50.
Waley, Arthur. *The Life and Times of Po Chu-i*. London: Allen & Unwin, 1949.
Waley, Arthur, tr. *The Analects of Confucius*. London: Allen & Unwin, 1938.
Waley, Arthur, tr. *The Nō Plays of Japan*. New York: Grove Press, 1953.
Waseda Daigaku Engeki Hakubutsukan, ed. *Engeki hyakka daijiten*. 6 vols. Tokyo: Heibonsha, 1960.
Watson, Burton, tr. *Basic Writings of Mo Tzu, Hsun Tzu, and Han Fei Tzu*. New York: Columbia University Press, 1967.
Watson, Burton, tr. *Courtier and Commoner in Ancient China: Selec-*

tions from the History of the Former Han Dynasty by Pan Ku. New York: Columbia University Press, 1974.

Yoshida Minosuke. *Zukin kabutte gojūnen*. Kyoto: Tankōsha, 1991.

Yūda Yoshio, ed. *Bunraku jōruri shū*. Nihon koten bungaku taikei, Vol. 99. Tokyo: Iwanami Shoten, 1965.

## TRANSLATIONS FROM THE ASIAN CLASSICS

| | |
|---|---|
| *Major Plays of Chikamatsu*, tr. Donald Keene | 1961 |
| *Four Major Plays of Chikamatsu*, tr. Donald Keene. Paperback ed. only. 1961; rev. ed. | 1997 |
| *Records of the Grand Historian of China, translated from the Shih chi of Ssu-ma Ch'ien*, tr. Burton Watson, 2 vols. | 1961 |
| *Instructions for Practical Living and Other Neo-Confucian Writings by Wang Yang-ming*, tr. Wing-tsit Chan | 1963 |
| *Hsün Tzu: Basic Writings*, tr. Burton Watson, paperback ed. only. 1963; rev. ed. | 1996 |
| *Chuang Tzu: Basic Writings*, tr. Burton Watson, paperback ed. only. 1964; rev. ed. | 1996 |
| *The Mahābhārata*, tr. Chakravarthi V. Narasimhan. Also in paperback ed. 1965; rev. ed. | 1997 |
| *The Manyōshū*, Nippon Gakujutsu Shinkōkai edition | 1965 |
| *Su Tung-p'o: Selections from a Sung Dynasty Poet*, tr. Burton Watson. Also in paperback ed. | 1965 |
| *Bhartrihari: Poems*, tr. Barbara Stoler Miller. Also in paperback ed. | 1967 |
| *Basic Writings of Mo Tzu, Hsün Tzu, and Han Fei Tzu*, tr. Burton Watson. Also in separate paperback eds. | 1967 |
| *The Awakening of Faith, Attributed to Aśvaghosha*, tr. Yoshito S. Hakeda. Also in paperback ed. | 1967 |
| *Reflections on Things at Hand: The Neo-Confucian Anthology*, comp. Chu Hsi and Lü Tsu-ch'ien, tr. Wing-tsit Chan | 1967 |
| *The Platform Sutra of the Sixth Patriarch*, tr. Philip B. Yampolsky. Also in paperback ed. | 1967 |
| *Essays in Idleness: The Tsurezuregusa of Kenkō*, tr. Donald Keene. Also in paperback ed. | 1967 |
| *The Pillow Book of Sei Shōnagon*, tr. Ivan Morris, 2 vols. | 1967 |
| *Two Plays of Ancient India: The Little Clay Cart and the Minister's Seal*, tr. J. A. B. van Buitenen | 1968 |
| *The Complete Works of Chuang Tzu*, tr. Burton Watson | 1968 |
| *The Romance of the Western Chamber (Hsi Hsiang chi)*, tr. S. I. Hsiung. Also in paperback ed. | 1968 |
| *The Manyōshū*, Nippon Gakujutsu Shinkōkai edition. Paperback ed. only. | 1969 |

*Records of the Historian: Chapters from the Shih chi of Ssu-ma Ch'ien*, tr. Burton Watson. Paperback ed. only.　1969
*Cold Mountain: 100 Poems by the T'ang Poet Han-shan*, tr. Burton Watson. Also in paperback ed.　1970
*Twenty Plays of the Nō Theatre*, ed. Donald Keene. Also in paperback ed.　1970
*Chūshingura: The Treasury of Loyal Retainers*, tr. Donald Keene. Also in paperback ed. 1971; rev. ed.　1997
*The Zen Master Hakuin: Selected Writings*, tr. Philip B. Yampolsky　1971
*Chinese Rhyme-Prose: Poems in the Fu Form from the Han and Six Dynasties Periods*, tr. Burton Watson. Also in paperback ed.　1971
*Kūkai: Major Works*, tr. Yoshito S. Hakeda. Also in paperback ed.　1972
*The Old Man Who Does as He Pleases: Selections from the Poetry and Prose of Lu Yu*, tr. Burton Watson　1973
*The Lion's Roar of Queen Śrīmālā*, tr. Alex and Hideko Wayman　1974
*Courtier and Commoner in Ancient China: Selections from the History of the Former Han by Pan Ku*, tr. Burton Watson. Also in paperback ed.　1974
*Japanese Literature in Chinese*, vol. 1: *Poetry and Prose in Chinese by Japanese Writers of the Early Period*, tr. Burton Watson　1975
*Japanese Literature in Chinese*, vol. 2: *Poetry and Prose in Chinese by Japanese Writers of the Later Period*, tr. Burton Watson　1976
*Love Song of the Dark Lord: Jayadeva's Gītagovinda*, tr. Barbara Stoler Miller. Also in paperback ed. Cloth ed. includes critical text of the Sanskrit. 1977; rev. ed.　1997
*Ryōkan: Zen Monk-Poet of Japan*, tr. Burton Watson　1977
*Calming the Mind and Discerning the Real: From the Lam rim chen mo of Tson-kha-pa*, tr. Alex Wayman　1978
*The Hermit and the Love-Thief: Sanskrit Poems of Bhartrihari and Bilhaṇa*, tr. Barbara Stoler Miller　1978
*The Lute: Kao Ming's P'i-p'a chi*, tr. Jean Mulligan. Also in paperback ed.　1980

| | |
|---|---|
| *A Chronicle of Gods and Sovereigns: Jinnō Shōtōki of Kitabatake Chikafusa*, tr. H. Paul Varley | 1980 |
| *Among the Flowers: The Hua-chien chi*, tr. Lois Fusek | 1982 |
| *Grass Hill: Poems and Prose by the Japanese Monk Gensei*, tr. Burton Watson | 1983 |
| *Doctors, Diviners, and Magicians of Ancient China: Biographies of Fang-shih*, tr. Kenneth J. DeWoskin. Also in paperback ed. | 1983 |
| *Theater of Memory: The Plays of Kālidāsa*, ed. Barbara Stoler Miller. Also in paperback ed. | 1984 |
| *The Columbia Book of Chinese Poetry: From Early Times to the Thirteenth Century*, ed. and tr. Burton Watson. Also in paperback ed. | 1984 |
| *Poems of Love and War: From the Eight Anthologies and the Ten Long Poems of Classical Tamil*, tr. A. K. Ramanujan. Also in paperback ed. | 1985 |
| *The Bhagavad Gita: Krishna's Counsel in Time of War*, tr. Barbara Stoler Miller | 1986 |
| *The Columbia Book of Later Chinese Poetry*, ed. and tr. Jonathan Chaves. Also in paperback ed. | 1986 |
| *The Tso Chuan: Selections from China's Oldest Narrative History*, tr. Burton Watson | 1989 |
| *Waiting for the Wind: Thirty-six Poets of Japan's Late Medieval Age*, tr. Steven Carter | 1989 |
| *Selected Writings of Nichiren*, ed. Philip B. Yampolsky | 1990 |
| *Saigyō, Poems of a Mountain Home*, tr. Burton Watson | 1990 |
| *The Book of Lieh Tzu: A Classic of the Tao*, tr. A. C. Graham. Morningside ed. | 1990 |
| *The Tale of an Anklet: An Epic of South India—The Cilappatikāram of Iḷaṅkō Aṭikaḷ*, tr. R. Parthasarathy | 1993 |
| *Waiting for the Dawn: A Plan for the Prince*, tr. with introduction by Wm. Theodore de Bary | 1993 |
| *The Lotus Sutra*, tr. Burton Watson. Also in paperback ed. | 1993 |
| *The Classic of Changes: A New Translation of the I Ching as Interpreted by Wang Bi*, tr. Richard John Lynn | 1994 |
| *Beyond Spring: Tz'u Poems of the Sung Dynasty*, tr. Julie Landau | 1994 |

| | |
|---|---|
| *The Columbia Anthology of Traditional Chinese Literature*, ed. Victor H. Mair | 1994 |
| *Scenes for Mandarins: The Elite Theater of the Ming*, tr. Cyril Birch | 1995 |
| *Letters of Nichiren*, ed. Philip B. Yampolsky; tr. Burton Watson et al. | 1996 |
| *Unforgotten Dreams: Poems by the Zen Monk Shōtetsu*, tr. Steven D. Carter | 1997 |
| *The Vimalakirti Sutra*, tr. Burton Watson | 1997 |
| *Japanese and Chinese Poems to Sing: The* Wakan rōei shū, tr. J. Thomas Rimer and Jonathan Chaves | 1997 |
| *Breeze Through Bamboo: Kanshi of Ema Saikō*, tr. Hiroaki Sato | 1998 |
| *A Tower for the Summer Heat*, by Li Yu, tr. Patrick Hanan | 1998 |
| *Traditional Japanese Theater: An Anthology of Plays*, by Karen Brazell | 1998 |
| *The Original Analects: Sayings of Confucius and His Successors (0479–0249)*, by E. Bruce Brooks and A. Taeko Brooks | 1998 |
| *The Classic of the Way and Virtue: A New Translation of the Tao-te ching of Laozi as Interpreted by Wang Bi*, tr. Richard John Lynn | 1999 |
| *The Four Hundred Songs of War and Wisdom: An Anthology of Poems from Classical Tamil, The Puṟanāṉūṟu*, ed. and tr. George L. Hart and Hank Heifetz | 1999 |
| *Original Tao:* Inward Training (Nei-yeh) *and the Foundations of Taoist Mysticism*, by Harold D. Roth | 1999 |
| *Po Chü-i: Selected Poems*, tr. Burton Watson | 2000 |
| *Lao Tzu's* Tao Te Ching: *A Translation of the Startling New Documents Found at Guodian*, by Robert G. Henricks | 2000 |
| *The Shorter Columbia Anthology of Traditional Chinese Literature*, ed. Victor H. Mair | 2000 |
| *Mistress and Maid (Jiaohongji)*, by Meng Chengshun, tr. Cyril Birch | 2001 |
| *Chikamatsu: Five Late Plays*, tr. and ed. C. Andrew Gerstle | 2001 |
| *The Essential Lotus: Selections from the* Lotus Sutra, tr. Burton Watson | 2002 |
| *Early Modern Japanese Literature: An Anthology, 1600–1900*, ed. Haruo Shirane 2002; abridged | 2008 |

*The Columbia Anthology of Traditional Korean Poetry*, ed.
   Peter H. Lee   2002
*The Sound of the Kiss, or The Story That Must Never Be Told:
   Pingali Suranna's Kalapurnodayamu*, tr. Vecheru
   Narayana Rao and David Shulman   2003
*The Selected Poems of Du Fu*, tr. Burton Watson   2003
*Far Beyond the Field: Haiku by Japanese Women*, tr. Makoto
   Ueda   2003
*Just Living: Poems and Prose by the Japanese Monk Tonna*,
   ed. and tr. Steven D. Carter   2003
*Han Feizi: Basic Writings*, tr. Burton Watson   2003
*Mozi: Basic Writings*, tr. Burton Watson   2003
*Xunzi: Basic Writings*, tr. Burton Watson   2003
*Zhuangzi: Basic Writings*, tr. Burton Watson   2003
*The Awakening of Faith, Attributed to Aśvaghosha*,
   tr. Yoshito S. Hakeda, introduction by Ryuichi Abe   2005
*The Tales of the Heike*, tr. Burton Watson, ed. Haruo
   Shirane   2006
*Tales of Moonlight and Rain*, by Ueda Akinari, tr. with
   introduction by Anthony H. Chambers   2007
*Traditional Japanese Literature: An Anthology, Beginnings
   to 1600*, ed. Haruo Shirane   2007
*The Philosophy of Qi*, by Kaibara Ekken, tr. Mary Evelyn
   Tucker   2007
*The Analects of Confucius*, tr. Burton Watson   2007
*The Art of War: Sun Zi's Military Methods*, tr. Victor
   Mair   2007
*One Hundred Poets, One Poem Each: A Translation of the
   Ogura Hyakunin Isshu*, tr. Peter McMillan   2008
*Zeami: Performance Notes*, tr. Tom Hare   2008
*Zongmi on Chan*, tr. Jeffrey Lyle Broughton   2009
*Scripture of the Lotus Blossom of the Fine Dharma*, rev. ed., tr.
   Leon Hurvitz, preface and introduction by Stephen R.
   Teiser   2009
*Mencius*, tr. Irene Bloom, ed. with an introduction by
   Philip J. Ivanhoe   2009
*Clouds Thick, Whereabouts Unknown: Poems by Zen Monks
   of China*, Charles Egan   2010

| | |
|---|---|
| *The Mozi: A Complete Translation*, tr. Ian Johnston | 2010 |
| *The Huainanzi: A Guide to the Theory and Practice of Government in Early Han China*, by Liu An, tr. and ed. John S. Major, Sarah A. Queen, Andrew Seth Meyer, and Harold D. Roth, with Michael Puett and Judson Murray | 2010 |
| *The Demon at Agi Bridge and Other Japanese Tales*, tr. Burton Watson, ed. with introduction by Haruo Shirane | 2011 |
| *Haiku Before Haiku: From the Renga Masters to Bashō*, tr. with introduction by Steven D. Carter | 2011 |
| *The Columbia Anthology of Chinese Folk and Popular Literature*, ed. Victor H. Mair and Mark Bender | 2011 |
| *Tamil Love Poetry: The Five Hundred Short Poems of the Aiṅkuṟunūṟu*, tr. and ed. Martha Ann Selby | 2011 |
| *The Teachings of Master Wuzhu: Zen and Religion of No-Religion*, by Wendi L. Adamek | 2011 |
| *The Essential Huainanzi*, by Liu An, tr. and ed. John S. Major, Sarah A. Queen, Andrew Seth Meyer, and Harold D. Roth | 2012 |
| *The Dao of the Military: Liu An's Art of War*, tr. Andrew Seth Meyer | 2012 |
| *Unearthing the Changes: Recently Discovered Manuscripts of the* Yi Jing (I Ching) *and Related Texts*, Edward L. Shaughnessy | 2013 |
| *Record of Miraculous Events in Japan: The* Nihon ryōiki, tr. Burton Watson | 2013 |
| *The Complete Works of Zhuangzi*, tr. Burton Watson | 2013 |
| *Lust, Commerce, and Corruption:* An Account of What I Have Seen and Heard, *by an Edo Samurai*, tr. and ed. Mark Teeuwen and Kate Wildman Nakai with Miyazaki Fumiko, Anne Walthall, and John Breen | 2014 |
| *Exemplary Women of Early China:* The Lienü zhuan *of Liu Xiang*, tr. Anne Behnke Kinney | 2014 |
| *The Columbia Anthology of Yuan Drama*, ed. C. T. Hsia, Wai-yee Li, and George Kao | 2014 |
| *The Resurrected Skeleton: From Zhuangzi to Lu Xun*, by Wilt L. Idema | 2014 |

*The* Sarashina Diary: *A Woman's Life in Eleventh-Century Japan*, by Sugawara no Takasue no Musume, tr. with introduction by Sonja Arntzen and Itō Moriyuki 2014

*The* Kojiki: *An Account of Ancient Matters*, by Ō no Yasumaro, tr. Gustav Heldt 2014

The Orphan of Zhao *and Other Yuan Plays: The Earliest Known Versions*, translated and introduced by Stephen H. West and Wilt L. Idema 2014

*Luxuriant Gems of the* Spring and Autumn, attributed to Dong Zhongshu, ed. and tr. Sarah A. Queen and John S. Major 2016

*A Book to Burn and a Book to Keep (Hidden): Selected Writings*, by Li Zhi, ed. and tr. Haun Saussy, Rivi Handler-Spitz, and Pauline Lee 2016

GPSR Authorized Representative: Easy Access System Europe, Mustamäe tee
50, 10621 Tallinn, Estonia, gpsr.requests@easproject.com

www.ingramcontent.com/pod-product-compliance
Lightning Source LLC
Chambersburg PA
CBHW071347290426
44108CB00014B/1459